New Testament Studies

II

THE SAYINGS OF JESUS

THE SECOND SOURCE OF ST. MATTHEW AND ST. LUKE

BY

ADOLF HARNACK

PROFESSOR OF CHURCH HISTORY IN THE UNIVERSITY OF BERLIN

TRANSLATED BY

THE REV. J. R. WILKINSON, M.A.

LATE SCHOLAR OF WORCESTER COLLEGE, OXFORD; RECTOR OF WINFORD

Wipf & Stock
PUBLISHERS
Eugene, Oregon

Wipf and Stock Publishers
199 West 8th Avenue, Suite 3
Eugene, Oregon 97401

The Sayings of Jesus
The Second Source of St. Matthew and St. Luke
By Harnack, Adolf
ISBN: 1-59244-566-7
Publication date 2/24/2004
Previously published by Williams and Norgate, 1908

PREFACE

In the following pages an attempt is made to determine exactly the second source of St. Matthew and St. Luke (Q) both in regard to its extent and its contents, and to estimate its value both in itself and relatively to the Gospel of St. Mark. I have been moved to complete and to publish these investigations by Wellhausen's "Introduction to the First Three Gospels" (1905). The attitude of opposition I am driven to adopt towards an important result of Wellhausen's researches, does not detract from my high appreciation of the merit of this work.

A supplementary observation which I have made may serve as an additional proof of the unity of the source Q. In St. Matthew are found about 112 words, and in St. Luke (without the Acts) about 261, which occur in these gospels and do not occur elsewhere in the New Testament. Now of these 373 words, the reconstructed text of Q given on pp. 127 ff. contains at the most 16—*i.e.* 13 (12) from St. Matthew (*βιαστής, βροχή, διχάζειν* [*ἐγκρύπτειν*], *εὐνοεῖν, ἰῶτα, νοσσίον, οἰκετεία, οἰκιακός, παρομοιάζειν, παροψίς, πλατύς, ῥαπίζειν*), and 3 from St. Luke (*ἀπομάσσεσθαι, βαλλάντιον, κόραξ*); yet it is questionable whether three of these really belong to Q. That it is thus possible to construct the fairly extensive text of Q without making a further demand than of 12 to 16 words upon the copious and distinctive vocabularies of St. Matthew and St. Luke, is a welcome additional proof of the distinct individuality of Q. On the other hand, the variety of the stylistic, rhetorical, and poetic forms in which the discourses and sayings in Q are thus seen to be cast, is no argument against its distinctive unity, but even serves to confirm our confidence in the individuality as well as in the genuineness and originality of this source.

If in the following investigation I have correctly defined the limits and have justly estimated the value of Q, I have only given fresh utterance to the long-established judgment of competent scholars, though it is to be hoped that I have established it upon a more secure foundation than that upon which it has rested hitherto. No words of mine are needed to explain what this means for our knowledge of the history of our Lord. And yet one can scarcely hope that there will be an end of wild hypotheses in regard to that history. The temptation to confine one's gaze to isolated details, and to view these as reflected in the distorting mirror of prepossession and prejudice, without deep and reverent study of tradition, is too great for us to expect that these strivings will ever cease.

I offer my hearty thanks to my friend Professor von Dobschütz for the active and kindly interest which he has devoted to this undertaking of mine while it was passing through the press.

A. H.

BERLIN, *8th December*, 1906.

CONTENTS

INTRODUCTION

The sections which are common to St. Matthew and St. Luke, excluding those which they share with St. Mark, are, as is well known, very considerable both in number and content. They amount altogether to about one-sixth of the text of St. Luke and two-elevenths of the text of St. Matthew.[1] The researches of very many scholars have led them to the unanimous conclusion that neither St. Matthew nor St. Luke have copied the one from the other, and that these sections are thus dependent upon either one or several common sources. The former alternative is generally preferred, and rightly so; and yet one does not thereby conceal from oneself the possibility that it may well have been otherwise, and that in regard to many points of detail and many passages there is still room for the hypothesis of several written sources and even of dependence upon oral tradition. In this connection a great number of other questions arise which cannot be passed by. The most important are the following:—

1. Is it not possible that after the publication of the

[1] Here of course difficulties begin at once. It is not always a simple matter to determine the limits of these sections; different opinions may be held as to the origin of the doublets which are found both in St. Matthew and St. Luke; and in regard to a few important sections, it must remain doubtful whether they are not mutually dependent upon a much earlier source, which is thus not identical with the main source.

gospel of St. Luke and St. Matthew the one was so much corrected from the other[1] that the task of settling the text of the source has been rendered very difficult?

2. Did St. Matthew and St. Luke use the same recension of Q? Or did the former use it in one form (Q^1), the latter in another (Q^2, Q^3, Q^4, &c.)?

3. If Q first existed in Aramaic, did one or both of the evangelists pay attention to this Aramaic original,[2] and occasionally make use of it?

4. Since it is *a priori* probable that neither of the two evangelists quite exhausted the contents of the source, in which of them is it best reproduced both in regard to extent and arrangement? and which of the passages that are transmitted to us by only one of our authorities belong nevertheless to the source?

5. Judging from the investigation of those sections which may be with certainty assigned to the source, are we to regard Q as a collection of sayings or a "gospel"? And is it possible that the answer to this question may afford us a principle by which we may decide whether doubtful sections belong or do not belong to the source? Or, if this question cannot be answered, is it not hopeless to attempt to determine the extent of Q?

These problems, so numerous and of such intense importance, seem to render it so difficult to answer the question: What is Q? that one can easily understand a person of sceptical mind refusing to concern

[1] Compare, for instance, Blass's reconstruction of the text of St. Matthew ("Evang. sec. Matth. 1901").

[2] It is quite certain that in general both used one and the same Greek translation.

himself with it. Yet, on the other hand, such scepticism is only permissible when there is distinct proof of the hopelessness of all attempts to solve the question. But no proof of such a kind has as yet been produced. It is true that Q has been much written about and investigated by Weiss, Holtzmann, Wendt, and Wernle, and by other scholars following their lead, last of all by Wellhausen—though it is strange how much more attention has been devoted to St. Mark; but as yet no work has appeared which takes into account all the details. Such a work ought in the first place to confine itself with rigorous exclusiveness to the non-Markan passages which are common to St. Matthew and St. Luke; to subject these to a thorough investigation from the point of view of grammar, style, and literary criticism in general, and after having thus gained a firm standpoint, to see what definite results may be deduced. If such an investigation fails of its aim—that is, if it is shown that nothing connected or distinctive is evolved from the study of the passages in question—then it follows that Q vanishes as a tangible entity, indeed disappears altogether, and accordingly that the problem of the relationship between St. Matthew and St. Luke in those parts which are not covered by St. Mark is declared to be insoluble. The necessary consequence of this would be that the discourses and narratives contained in these portions of the gospels (whether in sections of greater or smaller extent) would have to be dealt with each by itself.

Up to the present, however, there has been no final settlement of the preliminary textual question—in which of the two gospels do these sections appear in their more original form? If we seek counsel among the critics we only meet with unconvincing statements, that both evangelists allowed themselves to make numerous changes and revisions of the text, while it is usually added that on the whole more trust is to be placed in St. Luke than in St. Matthew.[1] One seeks in vain for a proof of this thesis, in so far as its feeble character at all permits of one, and even the question which at once suggests itself—What are then the points of view and the principles in accordance with which St. Matthew and St. Luke have respectively corrected the source?—is propounded by scarcely a single critic. The situation here is the same as in the case of a dozen other important problems of the criticism of the gospels: men soar away into sublime discussions concerning the meaning of "the Kingdom of God," the "Son of Man," "Messiahship," &c., and occupy themselves with investigations into the "history of religion," and with problems of genuineness, in the light of "higher" criticism (as if the critic were inspired with absolute knowledge of historical matters from some secret source); while the "lower" problems, whose treatment involves real scavenger's labour in which one is almost choked with dust, are passed by on the other side. Or where this is not the case, the investigation is still never carried far enough; it breaks off prematurely, and the critic rests satisfied with work only half done. Hence the wretched plight

[1] Wernle forms an exception. This scholar has shown that apart from some instances of severe revision the text appears in a more trustworthy form in St. Matthew. His work on Q is quite excellent but not detailed enough.

in which the criticism of the gospels finds itself in these days, and indeed has always found itself[1]—with the exception of the work of a few critics, and apart from the Markan problem, which has been treated with scientific thoroughness.

But even in the case of the Markan problem much important work remains to be accomplished by the

[1] This wretched state of affairs is apparent above all in the case of those who are compelled to take their knowledge of the criticism of the New Testament at second-hand, or have condemned themselves to this unassuming intellectual position. They are like reeds swaying with the blasts of the most extreme and mutually exclusive hypotheses, and find everything in this connection which is offered them "very worthy of consideration." To-day they are ready to believe that there was no such person as Jesus, while yesterday they regarded Him as a neurotic visionary, shown to be such with convincing force by His own words, if only these are rightly interpreted, which words by the way have been excellently transmitted by tradition. To-morrow He has become for them an Essene, as may be proved likewise from His own words; and yet the day before yesterday none of these words were His own; and perhaps on the very same day it was accounted correct to regard Him as belonging to some Greek sect of esoteric Gnostics—a sect which still remains to be discovered, and which with its symbols and sacraments represented a religion of a chaotic and retrograde character, nay, exercised a beneficial influence upon the development of culture. Or rather, He was an anarchist monk like Tolstoi; or, still better, a genuine Buddhist, who had, however, come under the influence of ideas originating in ancient Babylon, Persia, Egypt, and Greece; or, better still, He was the eponymous hero of the mildly revolutionary and moderately radical fourth estate in the capital of the Roman world. It is evident, forsooth, that he *may possibly* have been all of these things, and may be assumed to have been one of them. If therefore one only keeps hold of all these reins, naturally with a loose hand, one is shielded from the reproach of not being up to date, and this is more important by far than the knowledge of the facts themselves, which indeed do not so much concern us, seeing that in this twentieth century we must of course wean ourselves from a contemptible dependence upon history in matters of religion.

"lower" criticism, and remarkably little is to be found in our books on the question of the relationship of Q to St. Mark. "The problem of the literary relationship between Q and St. Mark must at least be propounded and needs thorough investigation. It is indeed most extraordinary, to use only a mild expression, that such an investigation up to the present has never been set on foot" (Wellhausen, "Einleitung in die drei ersten Evangelien," s. 73). The last remark is scarcely correct; several scholars have occupied themselves with the problem. But Wellhausen's astonishment is nevertheless quite justifiable. If the criticism of the gospels had been carried on methodically, so that each scholar stood as it were upon the shoulders of his predecessor, this cardinal problem would necessarily have been thoroughly discussed long ago, the whole material for discussion would have been set in order, and the definite and final conclusion would have been drawn. Instead of this everything is still enveloped in a cloud of uncertainty, and amid the dearth of preliminary studies of a connected and scientific character, we can easily understand how it has come to pass that Wellhausen has produced a solution of the problem which has this merit, that by its very paradox it has summoned theologians to descend from the airy heights of their critical speculations and to gird themselves for strenuous labour as hewers in the mines of knowledge.

In the following treatise I begin by ascertaining the relatively original text of the sections which are exclusively common to St. Matthew and St. Luke, and by deducing at the same time the points of view and the principles according to which each of the two evangelists has worked—that is, has edited the hypothetical common source. Before coming to a conclusion as to the most approximately original text of St. Matthew and St. Mark, I have thoroughly worked through the texts adopted by Blass, Wellhausen, and others, together with the editions of older scholars. I have convinced myself anew of a fact that I had already learned at the time of my studies on the text of the Acts—namely, that Blass has assigned far too great weight to the testimony of the important Codex D with its satellites, as well as to the isolated readings of other authorities (Chrysostom !). In my opinion, even Wellhausen goes too far in this direction. Neither can I recognise that the text of St. Luke has had the subsequent influence upon the text of St. Matthew which Blass supposes; indeed, as compared with him, I keep much more closely to the text of Westcott and Hort.

As is well known, the sections of St. Matthew and St. Luke which concern us are of such a character that a very considerable portion of them occurs in practically verbal similarity in the two gospels, while another (very small) portion shows variations which are so great as to compel us to doubt whether it is even possible to accept in their case the hypothesis of a common immediate source (*vide* p. v). In between lies the great mass of the remaining sections, which show more or less numerous and important variants. The first group has the great advantage in that from it we are enabled to draw conclusions of the highest probability. I have therefore divided the material into three parts, and I shall first consider those sections in which the differences between St. Matthew and St. Luke are comparatively very slight. Equipped with the results of this investigation, I shall proceed to the examination of the second group, in which the differences are more numerous. I shall then, only after the fashion of an appendix, deal with those sections in which the difference is so great that one must seriously doubt whether they belong to Q. They include only one saying and two parables.

CHAPTER I

THE ANALYSIS AND THE TEXTUAL INVESTIGATION OF THE NON-MARKAN SECTIONS COMMON TO ST. MATTHEW AND ST. LUKE (Q).

I

St. Matthew	St. Luke
St. Matt. iii. 7^b: Γεννή-	=St. Luke iii. 7^b, 8, 9, 17.
ματα ἐχιδνῶν, τίς ὑπέδειξεν	
ὑμῖν φυγεῖν ἀπὸ τῆς	
μελλούσης ὀργῆς; (8)	
ποιήσατε οὖν καρπὸν ἄξιον	καρποὺς ἀξίους
τῆς μετανοίας· (9) καὶ μὴ	μὴ
δόξητε λέγειν ἐν ἑαυτοῖς·	ἄρξησθε ἐν ἑαυτοῖς pro-
πατέρα ἔχομεν τὸν Ἀβ-	bably wanting
ραάμ· λέγω γὰρ ὑμῖν ὅτι	
δύναται ὁ θεὸς ἐκ τῶν λίθων	[δυνατὸς ?]
τούτων ἐγεῖραι τέκνα τῷ	
Ἀβραάμ. (10) ἤδη δὲ ἡ	δὲ καὶ
ἀξίνη πρὸς τὴν ῥίζαν τῶν	
δένδρων κεῖται· πᾶν οὖν	
δένδρον μὴ ποιοῦν καρπὸν	
καλὸν[1] ἐκκόπτεται καὶ εἰς	
πῦρ βάλλεται. . . . (12)	

[1] Wellhausen omits καλόν, because it is wanting in Syr. Sin., and because the contrast lies between "fruitful and unfruitful." But Syr. Sin. by itself is too weak an authority. St. Luke has the word, and logic ought not to have the casting vote. Besides καλόν could easily fall out of the text after καρπόν.

οὗ τὸ πτύον ἐν τῇ χειρὶ αὐτοῦ, καὶ διακαθαριεῖ τὴν ἅλωνα αὐτοῦ καὶ συνάξει τὸν σῖτον αὐτοῦ εἰς τὴν ἀποθήκην, τὸ δὲ ἄχυρον κατακαύσει πυρὶ ἀσβέστῳ.	αὐτοῦ (τοῦ) διακαθᾶραι καὶ συναγαγεῖν (?) αὐτοῦ pr. perhaps wanting, αὐτοῦ sec. certain. ἀποθήκην (αὐτοῦ)

Verse 11 (=Luke iii. 16) stands also in St. Mark; there and in Q it had essentially the same form; in Q it ran as follows:—

ἐγὼ μὲν ὑμᾶς βαπτίζω ἐν ὕδατι εἰς μετάνοιαν· ὁ δὲ ὀπίσω μου ἐρχόμενος ἰσχυρότερός μού ἐστιν, οὗ οὐκ εἰμὶ ἱκανὸς τὰ ὑποδήματα βαστάσαι· αὐτὸς ὑμᾶς βαπτίσει ἐν πνεύματι ἁγίῳ καὶ πυρί.	ὕδατι βαπτίζω ὑμᾶς (without ἐν and εἰς μετάν.), as in St. Mark. The remaining variants in St. Luke are likewise due to the influence of the Markan text. ἁγίῳ is very doubtful.

The few variants are easily explained; almost always St. Luke appears as the evangelist who has altered the original text. He has substituted the plural καρπούς for the not very logical singular; he has replaced μὴ δόξητε by μὴ ἄρξησθε (a favourite phrase of his);[1] he has improved the construction by the infinitive (διακαθᾶραι),[2] and instead of the more pregnant ex-

[1] Yet this is not quite certain. J. H. Moulton ("A Grammar of N. T. Greek," 1906, p. 15) thinks, on the contrary, that ἄρξησθε is more original, because it is a Semitic idiom (so also Dalman and Wernle); but it is frequently found in St. Luke even where he is independent of Q, and seems to have been used by him purposely (in imitation).

[2] It is questionable whether St. Luke wrote συναγαγεῖν, or συνάξει with St. Matthew; the authorities are evenly balanced on this point. At all events, συνάξει stood in Q.

pression, "his wheat into the barn," he has inserted the smoother phrase, "the wheat into his barn." *Καί* in verse 10 is added by St. Luke to give more flexibility to the construction, as in the case of St. Matt. xxiv. 28, and elsewhere. The style is also improved by the placing of *ὕδατι* (without *ἐν*) at the beginning. Probably the reading *δυνατός* is original in St. Luke, but it was substituted for the reading of the source by the evangelist himself. In St. Matthew and St. Mark it is never used of a person; see, however, St. Luke i. 49; xiv. 31; xxiv. 19, and four passages in the Acts.—St. Luke perhaps wrote: *καὶ τὸν μὲν σῖτον συνάξει εἰς ἀποθήκην.* We cannot be certain that *εἰς μετάνοιαν* belonged to Q; yet it is very probable that it stood in the source, for its absence in St. Luke is not decisive, seeing that St. Luke follows the text of St. Mark; and seeing, moreover, that *μετάνοια* does not occur in St. Matthew except in this section from Q, it is not probable that that evangelist added it of his own initiative. (On the other hand, in other passages *μετάνοια* is purposely added by St. Luke; here however it could the more easily fall out of the text, seeing that it has no corresponding antithesis in the following clause.) The end of the verse as it stood in Q can no longer be restored with certainty. In St. Mark the text ran *ἐν πνεύματι ἁγίῳ*; in St. Matthew, *ἐν πνεύματι ἁγίῳ καὶ πυρί*; in St. Luke, *ἐν πνεύματι καὶ πυρί* (in both cases Syr. Sin. gives the words in the reverse order). It is therefore most probable that Q read *ἐν πυρί*, for this phrase only is covered by the succeeding clauses which do not develop *ἐν πνεύματι ἁγίῳ*.

St. Matt. vi. 21: ὅπου	=St. Luke xii. 34; xi.
γάρ [ἐστιν] ὁ θησαυρός	34, 35; xvi. 13; xii. 22–
σου, ἐκεῖ [ἔσται] καὶ ἡ	31. For *σου* both times
καρδία σου. (22) ὁ λύχνος	*ὑμῶν*. Probably *σου* after
τοῦ σώματός ἐστιν ὁ ὀφ-	*ὀφθαλμός* pr.
θαλμός. ἐὰν οὖν ᾖ ὁ ὀφ-	ὅταν ὁ . . . ἁπλοῦς ᾖ
θαλμός σου ἁπλοῦς, ὅλον	καὶ ὅλον
τὸ σῶμά σου φωτεινὸν	
ἔσται· (23) ἐὰν δὲ ὁ	ἐστιν ἐπὰν
ὀφθαλμός σου πονηρὸς ᾖ,	ὁ ὀφθαλμός σου om.
ὅλον τὸ σῶμά σου σκοτει-	καὶ τὸ σῶμά σου (om. ὅλ.)
νὸν ἔσται. εἰ οὖν τὸ φῶς	ἔσται om. σκόπει οὖν
τὸ ἐν σοὶ σκότος ἐστίν, τὸ	μὴ τὸ φῶς τὸ σκότος
σκότος πόσον! (24) οὐδεὶς	πόσον om. οὐδεὶς οἰκέτης
δύναται δυσὶ κυρίοις δου-	
λεύειν· ἢ γὰρ τὸν ἕνα	
μισήσει καὶ τὸν ἕτερον	
ἀγαπήσει, ἢ ἑνὸς ἀνθέξεται	
καὶ τοῦ ἑτέρου κατα-	
φρονήσει· οὐ δύνασθε θεῷ	
δουλεύειν καὶ μαμωνᾷ.	
(25) διὰ τοῦτο λέγω ὑμῖν, μὴ	
μεριμνᾶτε τῇ ψυχῇ ὑμῶν	ὑμῶν om.
τί φάγητε, μηδὲ τῷ σώματι	
ὑμῶν τί ἐνδύσησθε· οὐχὶ	ὑμῶν om.
ἡ ψυχὴ πλεῖόν ἐστιν τῆς	ἡ γὰρ ψυχὴ
τροφῆς καὶ τὸ σῶμα τοῦ	
ἐνδύματος; (26) ἐμβλέ-	κατα-
ψατε εἰς τὰ πετεινὰ τοῦ	νοήσατε τοὺς κόρακας
οὐρανοῦ, ὅτι οὐ σπείρου-	without τοῦ οὐρανοῦ οὔτε
σιν οὐδὲ θηρίζουσιν οὐδὲ	οὔτε οἷς οὐκ
συνάγουσιν εἰς ἀποθήκας,	ἔστιν ταμεῖον οὐδὲ ἀποθήκη

καὶ ὁ πατὴρ ὑμῶν ὁ οὐράνιος	καὶ ὁ θεὸς (om. ὑ. ὁ. οὐρ.)
τρέφει αὐτά· οὐχ ὑμεῖς	αὐτούς· πόσῳ μᾶλλον
μᾶλλον διαφέρετε αὐτῶν ;	ὑμ. διαφ. τῶν πετεινῶν ;
(27) τίς δὲ ἐξ ὑμῶν μεριμ-	
νῶν δύναται προσθεῖναι ἐπὶ	
τὴν ἡλικίαν αὐτοῦ πῆχυν	
ἕνα ; (28) καὶ περὶ ἐνδύ-	ἕνα om. In place of verse
ματος τί μεριμνᾶτε ; κατα-	28 : εἰ οὖν οὐδὲ ἐλάχιστον
μάθετε τὰ κρίνα τοῦ ἀγροῦ	δύνασθε, τί περὶ τῶν λοι-
πῶς αὐξάνουσιν· οὐ κοπιῶσιν	πῶν μεριμνᾶτε ; κατανοή-
οὐδὲ νήθουσιν· (29) λέγω δὲ	σατε τὲ κρίνα, πῶς οὔτε
ὑμῖν ὅτι οὐδὲ Σολομὼν ἐν	νήθει οὔτε ὑφαίνει·
πάσῃ τῇ δόξῃ αὐτοῦ περιε-	ὅτι om.
βάλετο ὡς ἓν τούτων.	
(30) εἰ δὲ τὸν χόρτον τοῦ	ἐν ἀγρῷ τὸν χόρ-
ἀγροῦ σήμερον ὄντα καὶ	τον ὄντα σήμερον
αὔριον εἰς κλίβανον βαλλό-	
μενον ὁ θεὸς οὕτως ἀμφιέν-	
νυσιν, οὐ πολλῷ μᾶλλον	πόσῳ for οὐ πολλ.
ὑμᾶς, ὀλιγόπιστοι ; (31)	καὶ ὑμεῖς μὴ
μὴ οὖν μεριμνήσητε λέ-	ζητεῖτε τί φάγητε καὶ τί
γοντες· τί φάγωμεν ; ἢ τί	πίητε, καὶ μὴ μετεωρίζεσθε
πίωμεν ; ἢ τί περιβαλώ-	(for verse 31)
μεθα ; (32) πάντα γὰρ	ταῦτα γὰρ (πάντα)
ταῦτα τὰ ἔθνη ἐπιζητοῦσιν·	τ. ἔθνη τοῦ κόσμου
οἶδεν γὰρ ὁ πατὴρ ὑμῶν ὁ	ὑμ. δὲ ὁ. πατ. οἶδεν
οὐράνιος ὅτι χρῄζετε τού-	(without ὁ οὐρ.)
των ἁπάντων. (33) ζητεῖτε	ἁπάντων om. πλὴν ζητ.
δὲ πρῶτον τὴν βασιλείαν	τ. βασ. αὐτοῦ (without πρῶ-
καὶ τὴν δικαιοσύνην αὐτοῦ,	τον and κ. τ. δικαιοσ.)
καὶ ταῦτα πάντα προσ-	πάντα om.
τεθήσεται ὑμῖν.	

The variants in St. Luke, in so far as they are of a stylistic character, appear throughout as secondary readings (corrections in style). This is especially clear in the case of σκόπει (σκοπεῖν is wanting in the gospels but occurs several times in St. Paul), also in the three instances where St. Luke removes the rhetorical question for the sake of smoothness (a correction which, as we shall see, he makes in other places), also in the pedantic addition of οἰκέτης (wanting in the gospels but occurring in Acts x. 7; Rom. xiv. 1; 1 Pet. ii. 18), in κατανοήσατε (constantly used by St. Luke) twice substituted for ἐμβλέψασθε εἰς and for the unusual word καταμάθετε, in πόσῳ prefixed to μᾶλλον, in πόσῳ for οὐ πολλῷ, in the καὶ which is added, as so often, in verses 22, 23, in οἷς οὐκ ἔστιν ταμ. οὐδὲ ἀποθήκη (improvement in style), in the feeble moral reflection εἰ οὖν οὐδὲ ἐλάχιστον δύνασθε (τὸ ἐλάχιστον is in the New Testament exclusively confined to St. Luke, *vide* in addition to this passage xvi. 10; xix. 17) τί περὶ τῶν λοιπῶν μεριμνᾶτε;—also the absence of ἕνα with πῆχυν is probably secondary; likewise the sentence πῶς οὔτε νήθει οὔτε ὑφαίνει, for αὐξάνουσι, appeared to be unessential; and ὑφαίνει is a stylistic improvement upon κοπιῶσιν. In St. Matthew verse 28, St. Luke has replaced "clothing" by τὰ λοιπά, while in St. Matthew verse 31, he omits it altogether; it was evidently a matter of less anxiety to him than to the native of Palestine. In the same passage he has replaced the somewhat feeble μὴ μεριμνήσητε λέγοντες by the strenuous prohibition: καὶ ὑμεῖς (one of the few cases where St. Luke has the pronoun when it is wanting in St. Matthew) μὴ ζητεῖτε, and thus leads up to the ζητεῖτε of St. Matthew verse 33 (ζητεῖν is much more frequent in St. Luke than in St. Matthew); again πλήν is inserted by him (it is found five times in St. Matthew, fifteen times in St. Luke). The phrase μὴ μετεωρίζεσθε is singular both in St. Luke and in the New Testament. No certain interpretation can be given of the phrase as found here (it occurs in Philo, Sirach, Plutarch, and the medical authors). It may mean either "be not high-minded," or "seek not after high things," or "be not covetous," or "be not driven hither and thither (by cares)." If the word stood in Q it is not without significance for determining the plane of culture of the first translator of the source; but it is much more probable that St. Luke inserted it in place of τί περιβαλώμεθα. In this case it is to be taken in the same general sense as the phrase previously inserted by him: τί περὶ τῶν λοιπῶν μεριμνᾶτε. On the other hand, the text of St. Luke is, as it seems, to be preferred where the phraseology is less biblical and liturgical than that of St. Matthew; thus where he reads τοὺς κόρακας, ὁ θεός (for ὁ πατὴρ ὑμων ὁ οὐρ.), τὰ κρίνα (without τοῦ ἀγροῦ) and ἐν ἀγρῷ τὸν χόρτον (for τ. χ. τ. ἀγρôυ), in the omission of ὁ οὐράνιος (with πατήρ), in the expression τά ἔθνη τοῦ κόσμου (τ. κόσμ. is unnecessary in the language of the Bible), in the omission of πρῶτον and τὴν δικαιοσύνην. Πρῶτον indeed is wanting in some authorities for the text of St. Matthew, and δικαιοσύνη as an element in the gospel proclamation of the synoptists is found only in St. Matthew. And yet τὰ πετεινὰ τοῦ οὐρανοῦ is perhaps to be preferred to τοὺς κόρακας, for St. Luke uses this expression also in the parable of the Mustard Seed (*vide infra*) and in ix. 58. He may have preferred to use a more specific word in this passage, because of the specific word (τὰ κρίνα) which follows. Τοῦ κόσμου may also have been added by St. Luke.

	St. Luke vi. 37, 38, 41,
St. Matt. vii. 1: Μὴ	42; xi. 9–13; vi. 31.
κρίνετε, ἵνα μὴ κριθῆτε.	καὶ οὐ stands for ἵνα.
(2) ἐν ᾧ γὰρ κρίματι	ἐν ᾧ . . . κριθήσεσθε καὶ
κρίνετε κριθήσεσθε, καὶ ἐν	wanting; the thought is
ᾧ μέτρῳ μετρεῖτε μετρη-	developed in a quite dif-
θήσεται ὑμῖν. (3) τί δὲ	ferent way. ἐν wanting.
βλέπεις τὸ κάρφος τὸ ἐν	ἀντιμετρηθήσεται
τῷ ὀφθαλμῷ τοῦ ἀδελφοῦ	
σου, τὴν δὲ ἐν τῷ σῷ	τὴν δὲ δοκ. τὴν ἐν τ.
ὀφθαλμῷ δοκὸν οὐ κατα-	ἰδίῳ ὀφθ.
νοεῖς; (4) ἢ πῶς ἐρεῖς τῷ	πῶς (without ἢ) δύνασαι
ἀδελφῷ σου· ἄφες ἐκβάλω	λέγειν ἀδελφέ, ἄφες
τὸ κάρφος ἐκ τοῦ ὀφθαλ-	τὸ κάρφος τὸ ἐν τ. ὀφθ.
μοῦ σου, καὶ ἰδοὺ ἡ δοκὸς	σου αὐτὸς τ. ἐν τ. ὀφ-
ἐν τῷ ὀφθαλμῷ σου; (5)	θαλμῷ σ. δοκὸν οὐ βλέπων;
ὑποκριτά, ἔκβαλε πρῶτον	
ἐκ τοῦ ὀφθαλμοῦ σου τὴν	τ.
δοκόν, καὶ τότε διαβλέψεις	δοκόν ἐκ τ. ὀφθ. σου
ἐκβαλεῖν τὸ κάρφος ἐκ τοῦ	τ. κάρφος τὸ ἐν
ὀφθαλμοῦ τοῦ ἀδελφοῦ	τ. ὀφθ. τ. ἀδελφ. σου
σου . . . (7) αἰτεῖτε, καὶ	ἐκβ.
δοθήσεται ὑμῖν· ζητεῖτε,	
καὶ εὑρήσετε· κρούετε καὶ	
ἀνοιγήσεται ὑμῖν. (8) πᾶς	ἀνοιχθήσεται ?
γὰρ ὁ αἰτῶν λαμβάνει, καὶ	

ὁ ζητῶν εὑρίσκει, καὶ τῷ	
κρούοντι ἀνοιγήσεται. (9)	
ἢ τίς ἐστιν ἐξ ὑμῶν ἄν-	τίνα δὲ ἐξ ὑμ. τ.
θρωπος, ὃν αἰτήσει ὁ υἱὸς	πατέρα αἰτήσει ὁ υἱὸς
αὐτοῦ ἄρτον, μὴ λίθον	ἰχθύν, μὴ ἀντὶ ἰχθύος ὄφιν
ἐπιδώσει αὐτῷ; (10) ἢ καὶ	αὐτῷ ἐπιδώσει; ἢ καὶ αἰτή-
ἰχθὺν αἰτήσει, μὴ ὄφιν	σει ᾠόν, μὴ ἐπιδώσει αὐτῷ
ἐπιδώσει αὐτῷ; (11) εἰ οὖν	σκορπίον;
ὑμεῖς πονηροὶ ὄντες οἴδατε	ὑπάρχοντες for ὄντες
[δόματα] ἀγαθὰ διδόναι	
τοῖς τέκνοις ὑμῶν, πόσῳ	
μᾶλλον ὁ πατὴρ ὑμῶν ὁ	ὑμῶν wanting. ὁ ἐξ
ἐν τοῖς οὐρανοῖς δώσει	οὐρανοῦ
ἀγαθὰ τοῖς αἰτοῦσιν αὐτόν;	πνεῦμα ἅγιον for ἀγαθά
(12) πάντα οὖν ὅσα ἐὰν	καὶ
θέλητε ἵνα ποιῶσιν ὑμῖν	καθὼς θέλετε
οἱ ἄνθρωποι, οὕτως καὶ ὑμεῖς	οὕτως καὶ ὑμεῖς om.
ποιεῖτε αὐτοῖς· οὗτος γάρ	perhaps ὁμοίως after αὐτοῖς.
ἐστιν ὁ νόμος καὶ οἱ προ-	οὗτος . . . προφῆται
φῆται.	wanting.

Here again we see at once that in matters of style Q is represented more closely by St. Matthew; this is very plain, *e.g.*, in the case of ἵνα > καὶ οὐ, of πάντα οὖν ὅσα ἐὰν > καὶ καθὼς, and of ὄντες > ὑπάρχοντες (ὑπάρχειν is a favourite word with St. Luke). Ἐν ᾧ γὰρ κρίματι κρίνετε κριθήσεσθε must be judged original; the parallelism with what follows was disturbed by St. Luke, because he inserted clauses parallel to μὴ κρίνετε (viz. καὶ μὴ καταδικάζετε καὶ οὐ μὴ καταδικασθῆτε· ἀπολύετε, καὶ ἀπολυθήσεσθε· δίδοτε, καὶ δοθήσεται ὑμῖν· μέτρον καλὸν πεπιεσμένον σεσαλευμένον ὑπερεκχυννόμενον δώσουσιν εἰς τὸν κόλπον ὑμῶν, perhaps derived from a Q which varied from the Q of St. Matthew). Ἀδελφέ is certainly interpolated by St. Luke; the vocative is wanting in St. Matthew and St. Mark—on the other hand it is very frequent in the Acts; the vocative singular occurs also in Acts xxi. 20. The Lukan variant to St. Matt. vii. 9, 10 ("egg" and "scorpion" for "loaf" and "stone," and in reverse order) is problematical. The text of St. Matthew has a more natural sound; St. Luke is perhaps influenced by a Greek proverb or he possessed another recension of Q. He manifestly improves the text by replacing ἄνθρωπος and ὁ υἱὸς αὐτοῦ by "father" and "son" (the text which Wellhausen prefers is scarcely the right one; τίς comes from St. Matthew). A serious alteration in the sense is effected by St. Luke's substitution of πνεῦμα ἅγιον for ἀγαθά, his preference for this conception is well known.

The text of St. Matthew is subject to objection in only two passages. He has replaced ὁ πατὴρ ὁ ἐξ οὐρανοῦ (*vide* St. Luke xi. 16) by his usual phrase, ὁ πατὴρ ὑμῶν ὁ ἐν τοῖς οὐρανοῖς, and in accordance with his own purpose and aim he has added to the "Golden Rule" the sentence: "For this is the Law and the Prophets."

St. Matt. viii. 19: καὶ προσελθὼν εἷς γραμματεὺς εἶπεν αὐτῷ· διδάσκαλε, ἀκολουθήσω σοι ὅπου ἐὰν ἀπέρχῃ.	St. Luke ix. 57–60. προσελθ. εἷς γραμμ. om. εἶπέν τις πρὸς αὐτόν διδάσκαλε om.
(20) καὶ λέγει αὐτῷ ὁ Ἰησοῦς· αἱ ἀλώ-	εἶπεν

πεκες φωλεοὺς ἔχουσιν καὶ τὰ πετεινὰ τοῦ οὐρανοῦ κατασκηνώσεις, ὁ δὲ υἱὸς τοῦ ἀνθρώπου οὐκ ἔχει ποῦ τὴν κεφαλὴν κλίνῃ.	
(21) ἕτερος δὲ τῶν μαθητῶν εἶπεν αὐτῷ· κύριε, ἐπίτρεψόν μοι πρῶτον ἀπελθεῖν καὶ θάψαι τὸν πατέρα μου. (22) ὁ δὲ Ἰησοῦς λέγει αὐτῷ· ἀκολούθει μοι, καὶ ἄφες τοὺς νεκροὺς θάψαι τοὺς ἑαυτῶν νεκρούς.	εἶπεν δὲ πρὸς ἕτερον· ἀκολούθει μοι. ὁ δὲ εἶπεν· κύριε om. ἀπελθόντι(-τα) without καὶ εἶπεν δὲ αὐτῷ (without ὁ Ἰ.) ἀκολ. . . . καὶ om. — add. σὺ δὲ ἀπελθὼν διάγγελλε τὴν βασιλείαν τοῦ θεοῦ post νεκρούς.

The Lukan text (corresponding to St. Matt. viii. 21–22) is certainly clearer and so far better, but it is scarcely original. As the text runs in St. Matthew, it would have absolutely compelled a thoughtful writer to begin the passage with the command of Jesus, ἀκολούθει μοι. But the εἷς γραμματεύς of St. Matthew must be omitted (St. Matthew, verse 21 of itself shows that it is a thoughtless interpolation; Blass indeed strikes it out of the text, but on insufficient grounds). We must also omit τῶν μαθητῶν, as well as the two vocatives of respect in verses 19 and 21, and ὁ Ἰησοῦς in verse 22. The historic present of St. Matthew is to be retained; St. Luke has altered it almost everywhere (also πρὸς with accusative in place of the simple dative, as well as the participle in place of the infinitive or the finite verb belong to his style).—The concluding addition in St. Luke can scarcely have stood in Q, for (1) διαγγέλλειν occurs again in the New Testament only in Acts xxi. 26 (also in Rom. ix. 17 in a quotation from the LXX); (2) the ἀκολούθει μοι which is anticipated in St. Luke required a substitute, which naturally had to be more emphatic than the simple ἀκολουθεῖν.

St. Matt. ix. 37: τότε λέγει τοῖς μαθηταῖς αὐτοῦ· ὁ μὲν θερισμὸς πολύς, οἱ δὲ ἐργάται ὀλίγοι· (38) δεήθητε οὖν τοῦ κυρίου τοῦ θερισμοῦ ὅπως ἐκβάλῃ ἐργάτας εἰς τὸν θερισμὸν αὐτοῦ.	St. Luke x. 2. ἔλεγεν δε πρὸς αὐτούς ... ἐργάτας ἐκβάλῃ

The introduction in Q ran simply: λέγει αὐτοῖς or τοῖς μαθηταῖς αὐτοῦ.—St. Matthew gives the original order ἐκβ. ἐργ.—τότε is often inserted by St. Matthew.

St. Matt. x. 10^{b}: ἄξιος γὰρ ὁ ἐργάτης τῆς τροφῆς αὐτοῦ.	St. Luke x. 7^{b}. τοῦ μισθοῦ

The labourer is worthy not only of his food, but also—so thinks St. Luke—of his hire; the original lies in St. Matthew. Seeing, however, how short the saying is, it must remain questionable whether we are justified in assigning it to the source.

St. Matt. x. 15: ἀμὴν λέγω ὑμῖν· ἀνεκτότερον ἔσται γῇ Σοδόμων καὶ Γομόρρων ἐν ἡμέρᾳ κρίσεως ἢ τῇ πόλει ἐκείνῃ.	St. Luke x. 12. ἀμὴν om. Σοδόμοις ἐν τῇ ἡμέρᾳ ἐκείνῃ ἀνεκτότερον ἔσται.

The order of the words is changed by St. Luke.—The words ἐν τ. ἡμ. ἐκ. are not quite certain either in wording or position, yet they must not be struck out, seeing that they correspond to the words of St. Matthew, while they are not interpolated from that gospel. We cannot determine whether Q had ἐν ἡμέρᾳ κρίσεως (so four times in St. Matthew, wanting in the other evangelists), or ἐν τῇ ἡμέρᾳ ἐκείνῃ (so, viz. in the sense of the Day of Judgment, twice in St. Luke, twice in St. Matthew, once in St. Mark). Perhaps the source read simply "in the Day." It is difficult to decide between γῇ Σ. κ. Γ. or simply Σοδόμοις. The former is the more probable, as γῆ = "land," never occurs in St. Luke's gospel, and in the Acts only in the speech of St. Stephen.

St. Matt. x. 16[a]: ἰδοὺ ἐγὼ ἀποστέλλω ὑμᾶς ὡς πρόβατα ἐν μέσῳ λύκων.	St. Luke x. 3. ὑπάγετε add. ante ἰδού, ἐγὼ om. ἄρνας.

ὑπάγετε is an addition of St. Luke in order to connect verse 3 with verse 2.—ἐγὼ is often struck out by St. Luke; the original word was πρόβατα (ἄρνας is more refined). For the rest, the remarks made upon St. Matt. x. 10[b] apply here also. It is questionable whether the saying belongs to Q.

St. Matthew	St. Luke
St. Matt. x. 26: οὐδὲν γάρ ἐστιν κεκαλυμμένον ὃ οὐκ ἀποκαλυφθήσεται, καὶ κρυπτὸν ὃ οὐ γνωσθήσεται.	St. Luke xii. 2. δέ for γάρ συγκεκαλυμμένον

St. Luke prefers composite words, and substitutes them for simple words.

St. Matthew	St. Luke
St. Matt. xi. 3: σὺ εἶ	St. Luke vii. 20, 22–28;
ὁ ἐρχόμενος, ἢ ἕτερον προσ-	xvi. 16. ἄλλον
δοκῶμεν; (4) καὶ ἀποκρι-	
θεὶς ὁ Ἰησοῦς εἶπεν αὐτοῖς·	ὁ Ἰησ. om.
πορευθέντες ἀπαγγείλατε	εἴπατε?
Ἰωάννῃ ἃ ἀκούετε καὶ βλέ-	ἃ εἴδετε καὶ ἠκούσατε
πετε· (5) τυφλοὶ ἀναβλέ-	
πουσιν καὶ χωλοὶ περιπα-	καὶ om.
τοῦσιν, λεπροὶ καθαρίζον-	
ται καὶ κωφοὶ ἀκούουσιν,	καὶ om.
καὶ νεκροὶ ἐγείρονται καὶ	καὶ om. καὶ om.
πτωχοὶ εὐαγγελίζονται·	
(6) καὶ μακάριός ἐστιν ὃς	
ἂν μὴ σκανδαλισθῇ ἐν ἐμοί.	
(7) τούτων δὲ πορευομένων	ἀπελθόντων δὲ τ. ἀγγε-
ἤρξατο ὁ Ἰησοῦς λέγειν	λων Ἰωάνν. ἤρξ. ὁ
τοῖς ὄχλοις περὶ Ἰωάννου·	Ἰησ. om. πρὸς. τ. ὄχλ.
τί ἐξήλθατε εἰς τὴν ἔρημον	
θεάσασθαι; κάλαμον ὑπὸ	
ἀνέμου σαλευόμενον; (8)	
ἀλλὰ τί ἐξήλθατε ἰδεῖν;	
ἄνθρωπον ἐν μαλακοῖς	ἱματίοις add.
ἠμφιεσμένον; ἰδοὺ οἱ τὰ	οἱ ἐν ἱματισμῷ ἐνδόξῳ καὶ
μαλακὰ φοροῦντες ἐν τοῖς	τρυφῇ ὑπάρχοντες [διά-

οἴκοις τῶν βασιλέων. (9)	γοντες ?] ἐν τοῖς βασιλείοις
ἀλλὰ τί ἐξήλθατε; προ-	εἰσίν. ἰδεῖν;
φήτην ἰδεῖν; ναὶ λέγω ὑμῖν,	προφήτην;
καὶ περισσότερον προφή-	
του. (10) οὗτός ἐστιν περὶ	
οὗ γέγραπται· ἰδοὺ ἐγὼ	ἐγώ om.
ἀποστέλλω τὸν ἄγγε-	
λόν μου πρὸ προσώπου	
σου, ὃς κατασκευάσει	
τὴν ὁδόν σου ἔμπροσ-	
θέν σου. (11) ἀμὴν λέγω	ἀμήν om.
ὑμῖν, οὐκ ἐγήγερται ἐν	
γεννητοῖς γυναικῶν μείζων	μείζων ἐν γενν. γυν. Ἰωαν.
Ἰωάννου τοῦ βαπτιστοῦ·	(om. τ. βαπτ.) οὐδείς ἐστιν
ὁ δὲ μικρότερος ἐν τῇ	
βασιλείᾳ τῶν οὐρανῶν μεί-	τοῦ θεοῦ
ζων αὐτοῦ ἐστιν. (12) ἀπὸ	
δὲ τῶν ἡμερῶν Ἰωάννου	vers. 12 and 13 are in re-
τοῦ βαπτιστοῦ ἕως ἄρτι	verse order; ver. 12 runs:
ἡ βασιλεία τῶν οὐρανῶν	ἀπὸ τότε ἡ βασιλεία τοῦ
βιάζεται, καὶ βιασταὶ	θεοῦ εὐαγγελίζεται, καὶ πᾶς
ἁρπάζουσιν αὐτήν. (13)	εἰς αὐτὴν βιάζεται.
πάντες γὰρ οἱ προφῆται	ὁ νόμος κ. οἱ προφ. μέχρι
καὶ ὁ νόμος ἕως Ἰωάννου	
ἐπροφήτευσαν.	ἐπροφήτευσαν om.

In the majority of cases there is no need of proof that here St. Luke's recension is everywhere secondary (for the omission of ἐγώ, *cf.* St. Matt. x. 16; of ἀμήν, *cf.* St. Matt. x. 15); accordingly St. Matthew's recension is to be preferred in the neutral cases (with the exception of ὁ Ιησοῦς occurring twice). Τὰ *μαλακὰ φοροῦντες* is an awkward expression which offended St. Luke's sense of style; *τρυφή* is a word which is wanting elsewhere in the gospels, and therefore is most probably to be ascribed to St. Luke. The present in verse 4 is changed by St. Luke into the more correct aorist. *Οὐκ ἐγήγερται* sounded to him too un-Hellenic. His *τοῦ θεοῦ* in the place of *τῶν οὐρανῶν* may alone be original. What St. Matthew (Q) reads in verses 12 and 13 was as difficult for him to understand as for us. It is certain that St. Matthew, in distinction from St. Luke, has in the main preserved the original version—note particularly *ἕως ἄρτι*,—because *εὐαγγελίζεσθαι* is a favourite word with St. Luke. Also the unusual order of *οἱ προφῆται καὶ ὁ νόμος* is original; *πᾶς εἰς αὐτὴν βιάζεται* is an attempt to explain the words of St. Matthew (Q). Are we then to suppose that St. Luke, who here everywhere shows himself to be less original than St. Matthew, is right in placing verse 13 before verse 12, and in inferring "continued unto" (in his rendering "the Law and the Prophets unto John") for "prophesied unto"? It is in his favour that his order of the sentences is more natural than that of St. Matthew. But does this decide the question?

St. Matt. xi. 16: *τίνι δὲ ὁμοιώσω τὴν γενεὰν ταύτην; ὁμοία ἐστὶν παιδίοις καθημένοις ἐν ταῖς ἀγοραῖς, ἃ προσφωνοῦντα τοῖς ἑτέροις* (17) *λέγουσιν· ηὐλήσαμεν ὑμῖν καὶ οὐκ*	St. Luke vii. 31–35; x. 13–15, 21, 22. *οὖν* (f. *δὲ*) *τοὺς ἀνθρώπους τ. γενεᾶς ταύτης καὶ τίνι εἰσὶν ὅμοιοι; ὅμοιοί εἰσιν παιδ. τοῖς ἐν ἀγορ. καθημ. καὶ προσφωνοῦσιν ἀλλήλοις λέγοντες·*

ὠρχήσασθε· ἐθρηνήσαμεν	
καὶ οὐκ ἐκόψασθε. (18)	ἐκλαύσατε
ἦλθεν γὰρ Ἰωάννης μήτε	ἐλήλυθεν Ἰωανν. [ὁ βαπ-
ἐσθίων μήτε πίνων, καὶ	τίστης] μήτε ἔσθων ἄρτον
λέγουσιν· δαιμόνιον ἔχει.	μήτε πίνων οἶνον λέ-
(19) ἦλθεν ὁ υἱὸς τοῦ ἀν-	γετε ἐλήλυθεν
θρώπου ἐσθίων καὶ πίνων,	
καὶ λέγουσιν· ἰδοὺ ἄνθρω-	λέγετε
πος φάγος καὶ οἰνοπότης,	
τελωνῶν φίλος καὶ ἁμαρ-	φίλ. τελ.
τωλῶν. καὶ ἐδικαιώθη ἡ	
σοφία ἀπὸ τῶν [ἔργων?	πάντων τῶν
τέκνων?] αὐτῆς.	τέκνων αὐτῆς.
(21) οὐαί σοι, Χορα-	
ζείν, οὐαὶ σοι, Βηθσαϊδάν·	
ὅτι εἰ ἐν Τύρῳ καὶ Σιδῶνι	
ἐγένοντο αἱ δυνάμεις αἱ	ἐγενήθησαν
γενόμεναι ἐν ὑμῖν, πάλαι	
ἂν ἐν σάκκῳ καὶ σποδῷ	
μετενόησαν. (22) πλὴν	καθήμενοι μετενόησαν
λέγω ὑμῖν, Τύρῳ καὶ Σιδῶνι	λέγω ὑμῖν om.
ἀνεκτότερον ἔσται ἐν ἡμέρᾳ	(ἐν τῇ
κρίσεως ἢ ὑμῖν. (23) καὶ	κρίσει)
σύ, Καφαρναούμ, μὴ ἕως	ἕως τοῦ
οὐρανοῦ ὑψωθήσῃ; ἕως ᾅδου	
καταβήσῃ. . . .	καταβιβασθήσῃ
(25) ἐν ἐκείνῳ τῷ καιρῷ	ἐν αὐτῇ τῇ ὥρᾳ ἠγαλ-
ἀποκριθεὶς ὁ Ἰησοῦς εἶπεν·	λιάσατο τῷ πνεύματι τῷ
ἐξομολογοῦμαί σοι, πάτερ,	ἁγίῳ καὶ εἶπεν
κύριε τοῦ οὐρανοῦ καὶ τῆς	
γῆς, ὅτι ἔκρυψας ταῦτα	ἀπέκρυψας
ἀπὸ σοφῶν καὶ συνετῶν,	

καὶ ἀπεκάλυψας αὐτὰ νηπίοις· (26) ναί, ὁ πατήρ, ὅτι οὕτως εὐδοκία ἐγένετο ἔμπροσθέν σου. (27) πάντα μοι παρεδόθη ὑπὸ τοῦ πατρός μου, καὶ οὐδεὶς ἐπιγινώσκει τὸν υἱὸν εἰ μὴ ὁ πατήρ, οὐδὲ τὸν πατέρα τις ἐπιγινώσκει εἰ μὴ ὁ υἱὸς καὶ ᾧ ἐὰν βούληται ὁ υἱὸς ἀποκαλύψαι.	γινώσκει, τίς ἐστιν ὁ υἱὸς . . . καὶ τίς ἐστιν ὁ πατὴρ εἰ μὴ (without γινώσκει)

St. Matt. xi. 16: The introduction is, as usual, more or less transformed by St. Luke. The interpolation of *οἱ ἄνθρωποι* is an improvement in style though it is somewhat pedantic, but *καὶ τίνι εἰσὶν ὅμοιοι* or rather *καὶ τίνι ἐστὶν ὁμοία*, may have come from Q. *Parallismus membrorum* is frequent in Q; St. Matthew has often destroyed it from a desire for brevity. However, in what follows we can clearly discern St. Luke's polishing hand, and that in spite of his λέγοντες. Κλαίειν is substituted by St. Luke for *κόπτεσθαι*, he is fond of the former word (used by him eleven times, by St. Matthew only twice, including a quotation from the LXX). Ἐλήλυθεν (twice) for ἦλθεν is an improvement from the historical standpoint of St. Luke, but he has thus thrown doubt upon the saying as a genuine utterance of our Lord (see Wellhausen on this passage). Ἄρτον and οἶνον are evidently interpolations, and moreover pedantic (for, as a matter of fact, "eating and drinking" signifies "eating bread and drinking wine"); likewise λέγετε in St. Luke is a natural correction for the indefinite λέγουσιν in St. Matthew.—πάντων must be regarded as belonging to the text of St. Luke, it is indeed a favourite word of his; but for this very reason we are justified in not assigning it to Q. Τέκνων is the only intelligible reading; ἔργων is a variant which gives a sense most difficult to interpret, and which besides has only found its way into a part of the authorities for the text of St. Matthew. A thoughtless scribe was probably led by ἐδικαιώθη to think of ἔργα.—ἐγενήθησαν, like the addition of καθήμενοι, is a stylistic improvement (so also the τοῦ before οὐρανοῦ).—The two words κατέβησαν and κατεβίβαζον occur in Ezek. xxxi. 16, 17; St. Luke preferred the latter form, perhaps because of its rhythmic likeness to ὑψωθήσῃ. I have given the passage, xi. 25–27 (St. Luke x. 21–22), in the form which must be adopted on the evidence of the manuscripts. But judging from the exceptionally numerous and ancient quotations of this passage, we may conclude with great probability that, on account of the importance of its subject-matter, already at a very early date it had experienced serious correction, and, moreover, (1) that both in St. Matthew and St. Luke μου was originally wanting after πατρός, (2) that the original reading in St. Luke was ἔγνω (not γινώσκει),[1] (3) that the words τὸν υἱὸν εἰ μὴ ὁ πατήρ, οὐδέ (and τις

[1] Ἔγνω is found, for instance, in quotations by Justin. "Apol." i. 63 (*bis*); "Iren." i. 20, 3 (Markosians); "Tertull. adv. Marc." ii. 27; Euseb. "Demonstr." v. 1; Euseb. "Eclog." i. 12; Euseb. "Hist. Eccl." i. 2, 2; Euseb. "Eccl. Theol." i. 12; "Dial. de recta fide," i. p. 44, ed. van de Sande; Clem. "Hom." **17**, 4; **18**. 4, 11, 13, 20.

ἐπιγινώσκει) were perhaps originally wanting in St. Matthew (the corresponding words were certainly wanting in St. Luke).—*ἐν αὐτῇ τῇ ὥρᾳ* is a specifically Lukan expression (occurring with him six times, never in St. Matthew); on the other hand, *ἐν ἐκείνῳ τῷ καιρῷ* is only found in St. Matthew (twice again), and most probably comes from Q.—*ἠγαλλιάσατο τῷ πνεύματι τ. ἁγ.* is Lukan; this does not need to be proved for *τ. πν. τ. ἁγ.*, while *ἀγαλλιᾶν* is used by him four times (gospel and Acts), and *ἀγαλλίασις* three times; it is wanting in St. Mark, and is found once in St. Matthew in the formal phrase: *χαίρετε καὶ ἀγιαλλιᾶσθε.*—*ἀπέκρυψας* is used by St. Luke for *ἔκρυψας* in accordance with his preference for compound words (*vide supra* on St. Matt. x. 26). Perhaps St. Matthew had already changed the very important aorist *ἔγνω* into the present (as if a timeless knowledge were intended), and this present was then also taken up into the text of St. Luke. *Ἐπιγινώσκειν* can scarcely be more original than *γινώσκειν.* With St. Luke's substitution of *τίς ὁ πατήρ* for *τὸν πατέρα,* compare St. Luke v. 21; vii. 49; viii. 25; ix. 9.

The text of St. Matthew is thus, apart from the present tense referred to, the more authentic. Except the omission in verse 16, the only alterations we may perhaps assign to this Evangelist are found in the solemn *λέγω ὑμῖν*, in the addition of *ἀποκριθεὶς ὁ Ἰησοῦς* to the introduction to verse 25, and in *ἡμέρα κρίσεως.* In place of the last expression the source had perhaps *ἐν τῇ κρίσει* (see St. Matt. xii. 41, 42).

St. Matt. xii. 27:	Luke xi. 19, 20, 23; xii. 10.
καὶ εἰ ἐγὼ ἐν Βεελζεβοὺλ ἐκβάλλω τὰ δαιμόνια, οἱ υἱοὶ ὑμῶν ἐν τίνι ἐκβάλλουσιν; διὰ τοῦτο αὐτοὶ κριταὶ ἔσονται ὑμῶν.	εἰ δὲ ... ὑμ. κρ. ἐσ.
(28) εἰ δὲ ἐν πνεύματι θεοῦ ἐγὼ ἐκβάλλω τὰ δαιμόνια, ἄρα ἔφθασεν ἐφ' ὑμᾶς ἡ βασιλεία τοῦ θεοῦ. . . .	δακτύλῳ (f. πνεύματι) ἐγὼ om.
(30) ὁ μὴ ὢν μετ' ἐμοῦ κατ' ἐμοῦ ἐστιν, καὶ ὁ μὴ συνάγων μετ' ἐμοῦ σκορπίζει. . . .	
(32) καὶ ὃς ἐὰν εἴπῃ λόγον κατὰ τοῦ υἱοῦ τοῦ ἀνθρώπου, ἀφεθήσεται αὐτῷ· ὃς δ' ἂν εἴπῃ κατὰ τοῦ πνεύματος τοῦ ἁγίου, οὐκ ἀφεθήσεται αὐτῷ οὔτε ἐν τούτῳ τῷ αἰῶνι οὔτε ἐν τῷ μέλλοντι.[1]	καὶ πᾶς ὃς ἐρεῖ εἰς (f. κατά) ... τῷ δὲ εἰς τ. ἁγ. πν. βλασφημήσαντι ... οὔτε . . . μέλλοντι om.

ἐγὼ is omitted by St. Luke (as in St. Matt. x. 16; xi. 10, and elsewhere), and the customary order of words is restored. The Lukan reading δακτύλῳ seems at first sight the more original, but this is scarcely so. In spite of his liking for πνεῦμα, St. Luke substitutes the Biblical expression (Exod. viii. 19;

[1] The Beelzebub pericope stood in Q as well as in St. Mark, but the text printed above is all that we can with certainty assign to Q, besides isolated words from the introduction—δαιμονιζόμενος, κωφός, λαλεῖν, οἱ ὄχλοι (perhaps also ἐξίσταντο), and ἐρημοῦται from St. Matthew verse 25 (St. Luke verse 17).

xxxi. 18; Deut. ix. 10; Ps. viii. 4); he takes no offence at certain anthropomorphic phrases which have Biblical authority—*vide* i. 51: βραχίων θεοῦ, i. 66: χεὶρ κυρίου, i. 73: ὅρκος τοῦ θεοῦ. The solemn concluding phrase of verse 32 (a verse which St. Luke has corrected in regard to style) may be an interpolation by St. Matthew.

St. Matt. xii. 38:	St. Luke xi. 16, 29, 30, 32, 31.
τότε ἀπεκρίθησαν αὐτῷ τινες τῶν γραμματέων καὶ Φαρισαίων λέγοντες· διδάσκαλε, θέλομεν ἀπὸ σοῦ σημεῖον ἰδεῖν·	ἕτεροι δὲ πειράζοντες σημεῖον ἐξ οὐρανοῦ ἐζήτουν παρ' αὐτοῦ
(39) ὁ δὲ ἀποκριθεὶς εἶπεν αὐτοῖς· γενεὰ πονηρὰ καὶ μοιχαλὶς σημεῖον ἐπιζητεῖ, καὶ σημεῖον οὐ δοθήσεται αὐτῇ εἰ μὴ τὸ σημεῖον	ἤρξατο λέγειν ἡ γενεὰ αὕτη γενεὰ πονηρά ἐστιν· σημεῖον ζητεῖ
Ἰωνᾶ τοῦ προφήτου. . . . (41) ἄνδρες Νινευεῖται ἀναστήσονται ἐν τῇ κρίσει μετὰ τῆς γενεᾶς ταύτης καὶ κατακρινοῦσιν αὐτήν, ὅτι μετενόησαν εἰς τὸ κήρυγμα Ἰωνᾶ, καὶ ἰδοὺ πλεῖον Ἰωνᾶ ὧδε.	om. τοῦ προφήτου add. καθὼς γὰρ ἐγένετο Ἰωνᾶς τοῖς Νινευείταις σημεῖον, οὕτως ἔσται καὶ ὁ υἱὸς τοῦ ἀνθρώπου τῇ γενεᾷ ταύτῃ.
(42) βασίλισσα νότου ἐγερθήσεται ἐν τῇ κρίσει μετὰ τῆς γενεᾶς ταύτης	τῶν ἀνδρῶν τ. γεν. ταύτ.
καὶ κατακρινεῖ αὐτήν, ὅτι ἦλθεν ἐκ τῶν περάτων τῆς γῆς ἀκοῦσαι τὴν σοφίαν Σολομῶνος, καὶ ἰδοὺ πλεῖον Σολομῶνος ὧδε.	αὐτούς

Either the verses 41 and 42 have been reversed in order by St. Luke, or what is more probable, verse 41 was originally wanting in the Lukan text (*vide infra*).

The introduction is transformed by both evangelists. The scribes and Pharisees, and the vocative *διδάσκαλε*, are peculiar to St. Matthew; the original introduction probably ran somewhat as follows:—(they said): *θέλομεν ἀπὸ σοῦ σημεῖον ἰδεῖν.* In St. Luke the correcting hand of the stylist is here clearly traced; likewise *ἡ γενεὰ κτλ.* is a stylistic improvement. Again, *μοιχαλίς* is elsewhere avoided by St. Luke as a vulgar word. Here also, contrary to his usual practice (see, however, St. Matt. xi. 27), he replaces the compound verb by the simple *ζητεῖ*, because he appreciates the special meaning of the compound.—The respectful affix *τοῦ προφήτου*, was most probably added by St. Matthew.—*τῶν ἀνδρῶν* is inserted by St. Luke; compare a similar insertion in St. Matt. xi. 16.

The words *καθὼς γὰρ . . . τῇ γενεᾷ ταύτῃ* in St. Luke are original (read, however, *ὥσπερ* for *καθώς*); St. Matthew has replaced them, or rather interpreted them as referring to the Descent into Hades, by verse 40: *ὥσπερ γὰρ ἦν Ἰωνᾶς ἐν τῇ κοιλίᾳ τοῦ κήτους τρεῖς ἡμέρας καὶ τρεῖς νύκτας, οὕτως ἔσται ὁ υἱὸς τοῦ ἀνθρώπου ἐν τῇ καρδίᾳ τῆς γῆς τρεῖς ἡμέρας καὶ τρεῖς νύκτας*, a clause which would never have been omitted by St. Luke if he had read it in his source. In Q the *σημεῖον* for the Ninevites lay simply in the preaching of Jonah (in disagreement with Wellhausen), that is, simply in the fact that a prophet had come to them.—The transposition of the two verses in St.

Luke can only be due to an ancient error of a scribe, unless with codex D and Blass we regard St. Matthew verse 41 = St. Luke verse 32, as an interpolation in the Lukan text. This is the more probable, in that here *τῆς γενεᾶς ταύτης* is not changed into *τῶν ἀνδρῶν τῆς γενεᾶς ταύτης*. The verse, however, certainly stood in Q. The *ἀποκριθεὶς* of verse 39 is in the style of St. Matthew.

St. Matthew	St. Luke
St. Matt. xii. 43: *ὅταν δὲ τὸ ἀκάθαρτον πνεῦμα*	St. Luke xi. 24–26. *δέ* om.
ἐξέλθῃ ἀπὸ τοῦ ἀνθρώπου, διέρχεται δι' ἀνύδρων τόπων ζητοῦν ἀνάπαυσιν, καὶ οὐχ	*μὴ*
εὑρίσκει. (44) *τότε λέγει·*	*εὑρίσκον λέγει*
εἰς τὸν οἶκόν μου ἐπιστρέψω ὅθεν ἐξῆλθον· καὶ	*ὑποστρ. εἰς τ. οἶ. μ.*
ἐλθὸν εὑρίσκει σχολάζοντα	*σχολάζοντα*
[καὶ] σεσαρωμένον καὶ κεκοσμημένον. (45) *τότε πορεύεται καὶ παραλαμβάνει*	*[καὶ]* om.
μεθ' ἑαυτοῦ ἑπτὰ πνεύματα πονηρότερα ἑαυτοῦ	*μεθ' ἑαυτοῦ* om. *ἕτερα πνεύμ. ἑαυτοῦ ἑπτά*
καὶ εἰσελθόντα κατοικεῖ ἐκεῖ, καὶ γίνεται τὰ ἔσχατα τοῦ ἀνθρώπου χείρονα τῶν πρώτων.	

Both *μὴ* and *εὑρίσκον* are improvements in style, so also the changed order of the words in verse 44[a], and the substitution of *ὑποστρέψω* for *ἐπιστρέψω* (*ὑποστρέφειν* is found in St. Luke [gospel and Acts] thirty-three times, never in St. Matthew and St.

Mark). The omission of σχολάζοντα is intelligible, not so its addition; the same is true of μεθ' ἑαυτοῦ. Ἕτερος is found in St. Mark never, in St. Matthew nine times, in St. Luke's gospel thirty-three times; it has accordingly been added here. Τότε pr. perhaps belongs to St. Matthew.

St. Matt. xiii. 16: ὑμῶν δὲ μακάριοι οἱ ὀφθαλμοὶ ὅτι βλέπουσιν, καὶ τὰ ὦτα [ὑμῶν] ὅτι ἀκούουσιν. (17) ἀμὴν γὰρ λέγω ὑμῖν, ὅτι πολλοὶ προφῆται καὶ δίκαιοι ἐπεθύμησαν ἰδεῖν ἃ βλέπετε καὶ οὐκ εἶδαν, καὶ ἀκοῦσαι ἃ ἀκούετε, καὶ οὐκ ἤκουσαν.

St. Luke x. 23, 24.
ὑμῶν δὲ om.
οἱ βλέποντες ἃ βλέπετε
καὶ τὰ . . . ἀκούουσιν om.
ἀμὴν om. λέγω γὰρ
[καιβασιλεῖς] for καὶ δίκαιοι
ἠθέλησαν
ὑμεῖς βλέπ. [καὶ ἀκ. . . . ἤκουσαν om.]

Here St. Luke begins with a stylistic correction and with a pedantic simplification of the thought. Blass, following some authorities, is right in omitting the last seven words of St. Matthew from the text of St. Luke. The "hearing" was already wanting in St. Luke's parallel to verse 16; and if the concluding sentence of verse 17 had appeared in St. Luke it should have read ὑμεῖς ἀκούετε (*cf.* the immediately preceding words of the Lukan text). Evidently St. Luke did not like it to be said that the prophets had not heard, only that they had not seen. The emphatic ὑμεῖς is strange in St. Luke, seeing that this evangelist elsewhere is accustomed rather to omit the pleonastic personal pronouns of Q; but in this passage he had omitted the ὑμῶν at the beginning, and the ὑμεῖς is not pleonastic where he places it.—ἀμήν may possibly belong to the source, but may also have been inserted by St. Matthew. Καὶ βασιλεῖς, in spite of its doubtful textual authority, must be regarded as belonging to the Lukan text; for its later addition cannot be easily explained, while it is explicable that it should have dropped out of the text. If, however, it stood in St. Luke, it stood also in Q, and the δίκαιοι of St. Matthew is a correction due to this evangelist, who has a special liking for δικαιοσύνη. Ἠθέλησαν for ἐπεθύμησαν is an obvious stylistic improvement (ἐπιθυμεῖν occurs only once elsewhere in St. Matthew). In Q, therefore, the saying ran essentially as it does in St. Matthew, with the exception of δίκαιοι (and perhaps of the ἀμήν). Note also the parallelism in St. Matthew.

St. Matt. xiii. 33:	St. Luke xiii. 20, 21.
ἄλλην παραβολὴν ἐλάλησεν αὐτοῖς· ὁμοία ἐστὶν ἡ βασιλεία τῶν οὐρανῶν ζύμῃ, ἣν λαβοῦσα γυνὴ ἐνέκρυψεν εἰς ἀλεύρου σάτα τρία, ἕως οὗ ἐζυμώθη ὅλον.	καὶ πάλιν εἶπεν· τίνι ὁμοιώσω τ. βασ. τ. θεοῦ; ὁμοία ἐστὶν ζύμῃ

Here, apart from the introduction, all is identical. The Lukan introduction seems preferable, as St. Luke elsewhere is prone to transform rhetorical questions.

Commentators rightly point out that most probably the parable of the Mustard Seed, which is found in St. Matt. xiii. 31–32 = St. Luke xiii. 18–19, side by side with the parable of the Leaven, must also be assigned to Q, although it is also found in St. Mark

(iv. 30–32). Proof:—(1) The two parables are closely allied, and it is in itself improbable that they were handed down in tradition apart from one another; (2) they occur together in St. Matthew and St. Luke; (3) the parable of the Mustard Seed has in these gospels a form which varies from that of St. Mark; (4) this form is akin to that of the parable of the Leaven.

Mark.	Matthew.	Luke.
καὶ ἔλεγεν· πῶς ὁμοιώσωμεν τὴν βασιλείαν τοῦ θεοῦ ἢ ἐν τίνι αὐτὴν παραβολῇ θῶμεν; ὡς κόκκῳ σινάπεως, ὃς ὅταν σπαρῇ ἐπὶ τῆς γῆς, μικρότερον ὂν πάντων τῶν σπερμάτων τῶν ἐπὶ τῆς γῆς, καὶ ὅταν σπαρῇ, ἀναβαίνει καὶ γίνεται μεῖζον πάντων τῶν λαχάνων, καὶ ποιεῖ κλάδους μεγάλους, ὥστε δύνασθαι ὑπὸ τὴν σκιὰν αὐτοῦ τὰ πετεινὰ τοῦ οὐρανοῦ κατασκηνοῦν.	ἄλλην παραβολὴν παρέθηκεν αὐτοῖς λέγων· ὁμοία ἐστὶν ἡ βασιλεία τῶν οὐρανῶν κόκκῳ σινάπεως, ὃν λαβὼν ἄνθρωπος ἔσπειρεν ἐν τῷ ἀγρῷ αὐτοῦ· ὃ μικρότερον μέν ἐστιν πάντων τῶν σπερμάτων, ὅταν δὲ αὐξηθῇ μεῖζον τῶν λαχάνων ἐστὶν καὶ γίνεται δένδρον, ὥστε ἐλθεῖν τὰ πετεινὰ τοῦ οὐρανοῦ καὶ κατασκηνοῦν ἐν τοῖς κλάδοις αὐτοῦ.	ἔλεγεν οὖν· τίνι ὁμοία ἐστὶν ἡ βασιλεία τοῦ θεοῦ, καὶ τίνι ὁμοιώσω αὐτήν; ὁμοία ἐστὶν κόκκῳ σινάπεως, ὃν λαβὼν ἄνθρωπος ἔβαλεν εἰς κῆπον ἑαυτοῦ, καὶ ηὔξησεν καὶ ἐγένετο εἰς δένδρον, καὶ τὰ πετεινὰ τοῦ οὐρανοῦ κατεσκήνωσεν ἐν τοῖς κλάδοις αὐτοῦ.

The text of Q accordingly ran somewhat as follows:—*ἔλεγεν· ὁμοία ἐστὶν ἡ βασιλεία τοῦ θεοῦ κόκκῳ σινάπεως, ὃν λαβὼν ἄνθρωπος ἔσπειρεν* (scarcely *ἔβαλεν*) *ἐν τῷ ἀγρῷ αὐτοῦ, καὶ ηὔξησεν καὶ γίνεται* (*εἰς*) *δένδρον καὶ τὰ πετεινὰ τοῦ οὐρανοῦ κατασκηνοῖ ἐν τοῖς κλάδοις αὐτοῦ.* It also seems to me that the introduction in St. Luke is original (*τίνι ὁμοία—αὐτήν*);

St. Matthew abbreviates. It is noteworthy that St. Luke here shows himself to be independent of St. Mark, differing in this point from St. Matthew, and also follows a simpler construction than the latter evangelist, because he has kept closely to the source. On the other hand, the *κῆπος* of St. Luke is scarcely original (St. Matt. *ἀγρός*—St. Mark *γῆ*), and the historic present of St. Matthew is to be preferred. The expression *τὰ πετεινὰ τοῦ οὐρανοῦ*, in combination with *κατασκηνοῦν*, is also found again in St. Matt. viii. 20 = St. Luke ix. 58; *τὰ πετεινὰ τ. οὐρανοῦ* again in St. Matt. vi. 26 (St. Luke has here *οἱ κόρακες*). *Κόκκος σινάπεως* also occurs again in St. Matt. xvii. 20 = St. Luke xvii. 6; likewise *αὐξάνειν*, *σπείρειν*, and the pleonastic *λαβών*, are again found elsewhere in Q.

St. Matt. xv. 14: *τυφλὸς δὲ τυφλὸν ἐὰν ὁδηγῇ, ἀμφότεροι εἰς βόθυνον πεσοῦνται.*	St. Luke vi. 39: *μήτι δύναται τυφλὸς τυφλὸν ὁδηγεῖν; οὐχὶ ἀμφότεροι εἰς βόθυνον ἐμπεσοῦνται;*

The only difference is in the form, which is more full of life in St. Luke; but is his version to be regarded as more original on that account? *Ἐάν* is very frequent in Q, and St. Luke has very often changed it. St. Luke has replaced the simple *πεσοῦνται* by the compound, as is often the case.

St. Matt. xviii. 7: *ἀνάγκη ἐλθεῖν τὰ σκάνδαλα, πλὴν οὐαὶ τῷ ἀνθρώπῳ δι' οὗ τὸ σκάνδαλον ἔρχεται.*	St. Luke xvii. 1: *ἀνένδεκτόν ἐστιν τοῦ τὰ σκ. μὴ ἐλθ.* [*οὐαὶ δὲ*] *τῷ ἀνθρώπῳ* om. *τὸ σκάνδαλον* om.

The first half of the saying is certainly most original in the version of St. Matthew (*ἀνάγκη* is found only here in this gospel, while it occurs a few times in St. Luke). Also the second half, because of the parallelism, is preferable in the form of St. Matthew. It is uncertain whether St. Luke wrote *πλὴν οὐαί* or *οὐαὶ δὲ*.

St. Matt. xxiii. 12:	St. Luke xiv. 11.
ὅστις δὲ ὑψώσει ἑαυτὸν ταπεινωθήσεται, καὶ ὅστις ταπεινώσει ἑαυτὸν ὑψωθήσεται.	*πᾶς ὁ ὑψῶν* *ὁ ταπεινῶν*

Transformation of the finite verb into the participle is frequent in St. Luke, likewise the substitution of *πᾶς* for *ὅς* and *ὅστις*.

St. Matt. xxiii. 37:	St. Luke xiii. 34, 35.
Ἱερουσαλὴμ Ἱερουσαλήμ, ἡ ἀποκτείνουσα τοὺς προφήτας καὶ λιθοβολοῦσα τοὺς ἀπεσταλμένους πρὸς αὐτήν, ποσάκις ἠθέλησα ἐπισυναγαγεῖν τὰ τέκνα σου,	*ἐπισυνάξαι*
ὃν τρόπον ὄρνις ἐπισυνάγει	*ἐπισυνάγει* om.
τὰ νοσσία [αὐτῆς] ὑπὸ τὰς πτέρυγας, καὶ οὐκ ἠθελήσατε. (38) *ἰδοὺ ἀφίεται*	*τὴν ἑαυτῆς νοσσιὰν*
ὑμῖν ὁ οἶκος ὑμῶν ἔρημος.	*ἔρημος* om.
(39) *λέγω γὰρ ὑμῖν, οὐ μή*	*γὰρ* om. [*δὲ* ?]
με ἴδητε ἀπ' ἄρτι ἕως ἂν εἴπητε· εὐλογημένος ὁ ἐρχόμενος ἐν ὀνόματι κυρίου.	*ἴδητέ με* *ἀπ' ἄρτι* om. *ἕως* [*ἂν ἥξῃ ὅτε*]

Most of the variants are without significance, and yet even here the text of St. Matthew shows itself to be the more ancient. The reading ἕως ἂν ἥξῃ (*vel* ἕως ἥξει) ὅτε is very peculiar, and little germane to the style of St. Luke. If we could accept Wellhausen's conjecture that ὅτε represents the Aramaic relative (*is cui*), and that the real subject is the Messiah, then this reading would necessarily be the more original; but the thought: "Ye will not see Me until He comes, to whom ye shall say, Blessed is He that cometh, &c.," is too amazingly circumstantial. —In reference to ἄρτι, it is to be noted that this word is found in the gospels only in St. Matthew and St. John (ἀπ' ἄρτι again in St. Matt. xxvi. 29, 64, and three times in St. John). St. Luke has omitted this vulgar and, moreover, pleonastic expression; in the parallel passage to St. Matt. xxvi. 29, he uses ἀπὸ τοῦ νῦν (a phrase which occurs again four times in the gospel and once in the Acts).—On ἀφίεται ἔρημος Wellhausen remarks: "The destruction of the city is not something in the future, it is already destroyed and *is to remain* in ruins. . . . The later commentators shut their eyes and think of all sorts of things." And again on St. Luke xiii. 34, 35: "The omission of ἔρημος is very remarkable." I cannot see why ἀφίεται ἔρημος cannot be a prophetic future; and that St. Luke omitted ἔρημος (the word, moreover, is not absolutely certain in the text of St. Matthew) because Jerusalem rose again from its ruins, is to me questionable. The saying in St. Matthew is only a reproduction of the prophecy of Jeremiah (xxii. 5): εἰς ἐρήμωσιν ἔσται ὁ οἶκος οὗτος. But the reproduction—ἀφίεται ὑμῖν ὁ οἶκος ὑμῶν ἔρημος—did not sound quite logical, for the idea of destruction has to be supplied, and also was not good Greek. St. Luke improved this version by the omission of ἔρημος. St. Matthew read: "Your temple will to your disadvantage be left in a condition of desolation"; St. Luke corrected: "Your temple will to your disadvantage be delivered up [left]." The passive ἀφίεσθαι has now the same sense as in St. Matt. xxiv. 40 f. = St. Luke xvii. 34 f., where it stands in contrast to παραλαμβάνεσθαι.—As to the question whether this saying is our Lord's, or is a quotation used by Him (or put into His mouth), *vide infra.*

St. Matt. xxiv. 43:	St. Luke xii. 39, 40, 42–46.
Ἐκεῖνο δὲ γινώσκετε, ὅτι	τοῦτο (f. ἐκεῖνο)
εἰ ᾔδει ὁ οἰκοδεσπότης	
ποίᾳ φυλακῇ ὁ κλέπτης	ὥρᾳ (f. φυλακῇ)
ἔρχεται, ἐγρηγόρησεν ἂν	ἐγρηγόρησεν αν
καὶ οὐκ ἂν εἴασεν διορυχθῆ-	καὶ om. οὐκ ἂν ἀφῆκεν
ναι τὴν οἰκίαν αὐτοῦ. (44)	τὸν οἶκον
διὰ τοῦτο καὶ ὑμεῖς γίνεσθε	διὰ τοῦτο om.
ἕτοιμοι, ὅτι ᾗ οὐ δοκεῖτε	ὥρᾳ οὐ δοκεῖτε (the whole
ὥρᾳ ὁ υἱὸς τοῦ ἀνθρώπου	ver. 44 is perhaps an inter-
ἔρχεται. (45) τίς ἄρα ἐστὶν	polation from St. Matt.)
ὁ πιστὸς δοῦλος καὶ φρό-	οἰκονόμος (f. δοῦλος)
νιμος, ὃν κατέστησεν ὁ	καταστήσει
κύριος ἐπὶ τῆς οἰκετείας	θεραπείας (f. οἰκετείας)
αὐτοῦ τοῦ δοῦναι αὐτοῖς	διδόναι αὐτοῖς om.
τὴν τροφὴν ἐν καιρῷ; (46)	ἐν καιρῷ τὸ σιτομέτριον
μακάριος ὁ δοῦλος ἐκεῖνος,	
ὃν ἐλθὼν ὁ κύριος αὐτοῦ εὑ-	
ρήσει οὕτως ποιοῦντα. (47)	ποιοῦντα οὕτως
ἀμὴν λέγω ὑμῖν ὅτι ἐπὶ	ἀληθῶς (f. ἀμήν)

πᾶσιν τοῖς ὑπάρχουσιν	
αὐτοῦ καταστήσει αὐτόν.	
(48) ἐὰν δὲ εἴπῃ ὁ κακὸς	κακὸς om.
δοῦλος ἐκεῖνος ἐν τῇ καρδίᾳ	
αὐτοῦ· (49) χρονίζει μου	ὁ κύρ.
ὁ κύριος, καὶ ἄρξηται τύπ-	μου ἔρχεσθαι (add.
τειν τοὺς συνδούλους αὐτοῦ,	post κύριος) τοὺς παῖδας
ἐσθίῃ δὲ καὶ πίνῃ μετὰ τῶν	καὶ τὰς παιδίσκας (f. τ.
μεθυόντων, (50) ἥξει ὁ	συνδούλ. αὐτ.). ἐσθίειν τε
κύριος τοῦ δούλου ἐκείνου	καὶ πίνειν καὶ μεθύσκεσθαι
ἐν ἡμέρᾳ ᾗ οὐ προσδοκᾷ	
καὶ ἐν ὥρᾳ ᾗ οὐ γινώσκει,	
(51) καὶ διχοτομήσει αὐτὸν	
καὶ τὸ μέρος αὐτοῦ μετὰ	
τῶν ὑποκριτῶν θήσει.	ἀπίστων (f. ὑποκριτῶν).

This pericope is particularly instructive in that it helps us to recognise the various motives which guided St. Luke in his correction of the text handed down to him; for almost everywhere the text of St. Matthew, when contrasted with that of St. Luke, shows itself the more original. On linguistic grounds, St. Luke replaces ἐκεῖνο by τοῦτο, δοῦναι by διδόναι (as in the Lord's Prayer), ἀμήν by ἀληθῶς (a proof, moreover, that the ἀμήν here—and thus most probably elsewhere, where it is wanting in St. Luke—stood in the source; compare also the ναί which is found in St. Luke). On the same grounds he replaces the forms ἐσθίῃ, πίνῃ, by the infinitive (at the same time transforming the descriptive phrase μετὰ των μεθυόντων); he improves the order of the words (the unnecessarily emphatic positions of μου and ἐν καιρῷ, and οὕτως in too unemphatic a position); he drops the superfluous words *ἐγρηγόρησεν ἂν καί*, *διὰ τοῦτο*, *αὐτοῖς*, and *κακός*, on the other hand he adds *ἔρχεσθαι* to *χρονίζει*, because he wishes to express the principal verb which is implied in St. Matthew. He replaces *οἰκίαν* by *οἶκος*, which is in fact the more appropriate word. He takes offence at the vulgar *οἰκετεία*, and replaces it by the classical *θεραπεία*. He changes the *δοῦλος*, who indeed even in St. Matthew is not an ordinary slave but both slave and overseer, into an *οἰκονόμος*, and accordingly the *σύνδουλοι* must also be transformed (this word is never found in St. Luke, while it occurs again four times in St. Matt. xviii. 28–33). He replaces *ὑποκριταί* by *ἄπιστοι*, a word which was more current with his readers (*ὑποκριταί* are much less frequently met with in this gospel than in St. Matthew); the colourless *τροφή* gives place to *σιτομέτριον*, certainly a technical term which moreover is not met with elsewhere—*φυλακή* to *ὥρα*, because the thief does not only come during the *φυλακή*, but at any time. Only in the case of the substitution of *ἀφῆκεν* for *εἴασεν* do I find difficulty in conjecturing St. Luke's reason for the change; *εἴασεν* is, however, certainly the original reading, for *ἐᾷν* is only found here in St. Matthew, while it often occurs in St. Luke (ten times in the gospel and Acts). Finally, St. Luke has interpolated between verses 44 and 45 of St. Matthew the words: *Εἶπεν δὲ ὁ Πέτρος· κύριε, πρὸς ἡμᾶς τὴν παραβολὴν ταύτην λέγεις ἢ καὶ πρὸς πάντας; καὶ εἶπεν ὁ κύριος.* They interrupt the connection of the passage, which shows here only a seeming hiatus, and they answer to the style and manner of St. Luke, who lays great weight upon the definite address of the discourses. Also *καταστήσει* (instead of *κατέστησεν*) is intended to be an improvement; it however stands in a certain connection with the interpolated question of St. Peter.

The verse in St. Luke corresponding to St. Matthew, verse 44, is perhaps an interpolation from St. Matthew. If so, we cannot be sure that it stood in Q.

St. Matt. xxv. 29:	St. Luke xix. 26:
τῷ ἔχοντι [παντὶ] δοθήσεται	παντὶ τ. ἐχ.
καὶ περισσευθήσεται· τοῦ δὲ μὴ ἔχοντος καὶ ὃ ἔχει	καὶ περισσ. om. ἀπὸ δὲ τοῦ
ἀρθήσεται ἀπ' αὐτοῦ.	ἀπ' αὐτοῦ om.

Here, in all three places, it is plain that St. Luke has improved the text linguistically; as regards the sense, *περισσευθήσεται* was superfluous.

There are only about thirty-four instances in which we have found sometimes strong, sometimes weak, grounds for conjecturing that the text of St. Matthew is secondary to that of St. Luke, but these instances are still further reduced in number when we pass judgment upon them in combination. It is, namely, (1) by no means certain that the *ἀμήν* of viii. 10, x. 15, xi. 11, and xiii. 17, is an interpolation of St. Matthew's, for in St. Matt. xxiv. 47 St. Luke represents it by *ἀληθῶς* (and in St. Matt. xxiii. 36 by *ναί*); it may therefore very well have also occurred in Q in the other passages, and St. Luke may have left it untranslated, seeing that he avoids un-Hellenic words. The same may be said (2) of the solemn *λέγω ὑμῖν* of

xi. 22; St. Luke often gives it in his text of Q (*vide* St. Luke x. 12, 24; xi. 51; xv. 7, &c.); it thus stood in Q, and it is therefore possible that it was also omitted by St. Luke here and there. (3) It cannot be proved that St. Matthew in iii. 9 replaced *ἄρξησθε* by *δόξητε*, and it is quite improbable that he inserted *εἰς μετάνοιαν* in iii. 11.

In regard to the remaining instances, thirteen affect the *introductions* to the discourses (not the discourses themselves), or contain insignificant stylistic alterations. The discourse, St. Matt. viii. 19 f., is introduced by the words: *καὶ προσελθὼν εἷς γραμματεύς*, and in the same passage (verse 21) *τῶν μαθητῶν*[1] is added to *ἕτερος*, together with the addition of the vocatives *διδάσκαλε, κύριε*. Here also (verse 22), and in xi. 4, 7, *ὁ Ἰησοῦς* is inserted, and in xi. 25 *ἀποκριθεὶς ὁ Ἰησοῦς*. The discourse of xii. 38 ff. is introduced by the words: *τότε ἀπεκρίθησαν αὐτῷ τινες τῶν γραμματέων καὶ Φαρισαίων λέγοντες*, and the discourse of xii. 22 ff. by *τότε προσηνέχθη αὐτῷ δαιμονιζόμενος*; lastly, the parable of xiii. 33 by the words *ἄλλην παραβολὴν ἐλάλησεν αὐτοῖς*. *Τότε* (a favourite particle with St. Matthew, occurring in his gospel ninety times, in St. Mark six times, in St. Luke fourteen times) is inserted in ix. 37, and perhaps in xii. 44. One cannot be quite certain whether in St. Matt. xi. 16 the words *καὶ τίνι εἰσὶν ὅμοιοι* are omitted, or whether St. Luke has added them. The former alternative is probable, because also in the case of St. Matt. xiii. 33, St. Luke exceeds St. Matthew in reading the words:

[1] It is questionable whether in St. Matt. ix. 37 *τοῖς μαθηταῖς αὐτοῦ* is an interpolation; it may also be original.

τίνι ὁμοιώσω τὴν βασιλείαν τοῦ θεοῦ; though he elsewhere shows a dislike for rhetorical questions. In xii. 39 *τοῦ προφητοῦ* is added to Ἰωνᾶ, and in xii. 22 the dumb man is both blind and dumb—similar amplifications occur in St. Matthew's treatment of the Markan text.

The group that is now left (about fifteen instances) comprise changes made in the actual fabric of the discourses themselves. Here we must at once agree that St. Matthew has a distinct preference for the expression "your (the) Heavenly Father," or for the epithet "Heavenly," and for the substitution of "Heaven" for "God," of which preference the exciting cause does not seem to have been found in Q. Thus in vi. 26, *ὁ πατὴρ ὑμῶν ὁ οὐράνιος* is substituted for *ὁ θεός*, in vi. 32, *ὁ οὐράνιος* is added to *ὁ πατὴρ ὑμῶν*, in vii. 11, *ὁ πατὴρ ὑμῶν ὁ ἐν τοῖς οὐρανοῖς* is written instead of *ὁ πατὴρ ὁ ἐξ οὐρανοῦ*, and in xi. 11, *τ. βασ. τῶν οὐρανῶν* instead of *τ. βασ. τ. θεοῦ*. It is evident that in these cases the text of this gospel is secondary, seeing that these terms also appear in passages which are not dependent upon Q. Again, this evangelist has also a preference for the conception *δίκαιος* (*δικαιοσύνη*). In vi. 33, *καὶ τὴν δικαιοσύνην* is certainly an addition—and a by no means unimportant one!—and in xiii. 17, the *βασιλεῖς* are certainly more original than the *δίκαιοι*. One may perhaps discern imitation of sacred Biblical phraseology in vi. 26 (*τὰ πετεινὰ τοῦ οὐρανοῦ* for *τοὺς κόρακας*), in vi. 28 (*τὰ κρίνα τοῦ ἀγροῦ* for *τὰ κρίνα*), and in vi. 30 (*τὸν χόρτον τοῦ ἀγροῦ* for *ἐν ἀγρῷ τον χόρτον*), yet here we cannot be certain.

The expression of St. Luke (xii. 30) τὰ ἔθνη τοῦ κόσμου (in St. Matt. vi. 32, τοῦ κόσμου is wanting), which does not occur elsewhere in the New Testament nor in the LXX, may be original (an Aramaic phrase); St. Matthew may have omitted τοῦ κόσμου as superfluous.[1] There remain a few passages of greater weight and significance. In vi. 33 St. Matthew has inserted πρῶτον, and has thus limited the exclusiveness of the command to seek after the kingdom of God; in vii. 12 he has added to the Golden Rule the words: οὗτος γάρ ἐστιν ὁ νόμος καὶ οἱ προφῆται. He has given a complete twist to the passage concerning Jonah, in that he has applied to the simile a new *tertium comparationis* (Jonah's three days' abode in the whale's belly), and thus has interpreted it of our Lord's abode in Hades; the present tense in xi. 27 is probably due to him, as well as the conclusion of xii. 32.

On the whole it may be said St. Matthew has treated the discourses with great respect, and has edited them in a very conservative spirit. Seeing that the more important corrections are so few in number, it is absurd to attempt to deduce from them the permanent motives which guided the evangelist in making them. The alteration in the terms for "God," or for "the Kingdom," was no correction in his eyes; still less perhaps the summary phrase, "This is the Law and the Prophets." Thus, there remain only the addition of "Righteousness" and "πρῶτον," and the transformation of the "Sign of

[1] One cannot be sure of Q's term for the Last Day in St. Matt. x. 15 and xi. 22 (*i.e.* whether ἡ ἡμέρα κρίσεως is original or not).

Jonah," which transformation may have been found by him already carried out in his exemplar of Q.

In contrast with these few instances of correction on the part of St. Matthew, we reckon *nearly one hundred and fifty instances of correction by St. Luke; but these are all, with very few exceptions, of a stylistic character*. St. Luke's interest in style manifests itself in detail in the most varied directions, and yet it remains consistent with itself. Let us here give a summary of its most important manifestations:—

1. He replaces vulgar expressions by those that are more refined, and substitutes more appropriate for inappropriate words.

2. He replaces simple by compound verbs.

3. He replaces conjunctions by the relative.

4. He replaces καί with the finite verb by δέ (or by the participle, or by a final sentence); but, on the other hand, he also inserts καί when it makes the passage run more smoothly.

5. He improves the arrangement of the words.

6. He makes a more logical use of tenses and numbers, and is fond of participial constructions.

7. He prunes away superfluous pronouns which easily crept into translations from Semitic languages, and, moreover, into the language of the common people.

8. He varies the monotonous use of ἐάν by other constructions (ὅστις ἄν by πᾶς).

9. He corrects too great circumstantiality of language; but, on the other hand, he explains obscure expressions.

10. He reduces the number of rhetorical questions.

11. He introduces the construction of ἐγένετο with the gen. abs. followed by a finite verb.

12. He multiplies the instances where ἦν is used in construction with the participle.

Beyond these stylistic motives which have led him to make corrections,[1] no definite bias of any kind can be discovered in his treatment of the sections which we have considered — with *one* exception, namely, the introduction of the Holy Spirit into the passage parallel to St. Matt. vii. 11. The omission of the clothing in the passage parallel to St. Matt. vi. 28, 31, and the corresponding recasting of the words, is a somewhat drastic change, but in so far as it displays bias, the bias is very innocent. When he replaces "bread and stone" by "egg and scorpion," he may be dependent upon another traditional form of the saying which was perhaps influenced by a current proverb (*vide supra* on St. Matt. vii. 9). He has indulged in a fairly long interpolation in the words: σὺ δὲ ἀπελθὼν διάγγελλε τὴν βασιλείαν τοῦ θεοῦ (ix. 60, *cf.* St. Matt. viii. 22); but the interpolation is, so to speak, neutral in character. Again, in order to give greater liveliness of form, he interpolates into the discourse of St. Matt. xxiv. 43 ff., after verse 44, the words: εἶπεν δὲ ὁ Πέτρος· κύριε πρὸς ἡμᾶς τὴν παραβολὴν ταύτην λέγεις ἢ καὶ πρὸς πάντας; καὶ εἶπεν ὁ κύριος. Lastly, he has ventured to give some sort of a paraphrase of the saying of St. Matt. xi. 12, which was

[1] Also the omission of ἔρημος is probably to be explained from motives of style (*vide supra* on St. Matt. xxiii. 38).

evidently unintelligible even to himself, in his balder version: ἀπὸ τότε ἡ βασιλεία τοῦ θεοῦ εὐαγγελίζεται, καὶ πᾶς εἰς αὐτὴν βιάζεται.

If we neglect these few instances, in which indeed it is possible that another text of Q than that used by St. Matthew may have lain before St. Luke, then we may say that in regard to the rest of the text (that is, the text as a whole), *one and the same text lies behind St. Luke and St. Matthew.* It further follows that the connection between these two gospels, of which neither is the source of the other, must be a *literary* connection—*i.e.* the dependence of each upon common oral sources is not a sufficient explanation.

Having gained this firm standpoint, we now proceed to the investigation of those sections common to St. Matthew and St. Luke in which the differences are greater.

II

St. Matt. iii. 7[a]: ἰδὼν δὲ πολλοὺς τῶν Φαρισαίων καὶ Σαδδουκαίων ἐρχομένους ἐπὶ τὸ βάπτισμα εἶπεν αὐτοῖς·	St. Luke iii. 7[a]: ἔλεγεν δὲ [οὖν ?] τοῖς ἐκπορευομένοις ὄχλοις βαπτισθῆναι ὑπ' [ἐνώπιον] αὐτοῦ.

It is no longer possible to determine exactly what stood in Q, certainly not "the Pharisees and Sadducees" (they are characteristic of St. Matthew), nor the imperfect ἔλεγεν (for it is characteristic of St. Luke), nor the infinitive βαπτισθῆναι, which is likewise characteristic of St. Luke; perhaps, however, Q had *πολλοί* with the genitive, for it is never found elsewhere in St. Matthew (see, however, St. Luke i. 16),[1] probably also the word *αὐτοῖς*. The source may have run somewhat in this way: *ἰδὼν πολλοὺς . . . ἐρχομένους ἐπὶ τὸ βάπτισμα εἶπεν αὐτοῖς*. From St. Matthew verse 5 = St. Luke verse 3, it follows that *πᾶσα ἡ περίχωρος τοῦ Ἰορδάνου* stood in Q.

St. Matt. iv. 1 f.:	St. Luke iv. 1–13.
Τότε ὁ Ἰησοῦς ἀνήχθη εἰς τὴν ἔρημον ὑπὸ τοῦ πνεύματος πειρασθῆναι ὑπὸ τοῦ διαβόλου, (2) καὶ νηστεύσας ἡμέρας μ' καὶ νύκτας μ' ὕστερον ἐπείνασεν.	Ἰησοῦς δὲ πλήρης πνεύματος ἁγίου ὑπέστρεψεν ἀπὸ τοῦ Ἰορδάνου, καὶ ἤγετο ἐν τῷ πνεύματι ἐν τῇ ἐρήμῳ ἡμέρας μ' πειραζόμενος ὑπὸ τοῦ διαβόλου. καὶ οὐκ ἔφαγεν οὐδὲν ἐν ταῖς ἡμέραις ἐκείναις, καὶ συντελεσθεισῶν αὐτῶν ἐπείνασεν.
(3) καὶ προσελθὼν ὁ πειράζων εἶπεν αὐτῷ· εἰ υἱὸς εἶ τοῦ θεοῦ, εἰπὲ ἵνα οἱ λίθοι οὗτοι ἄρτοι γένωνται.	εἶπεν δὲ αὐτῷ ὁ διάβολος· εἰ υἱὸς εἶ τοῦ θεοῦ, εἰπὲ τῷ λίθῳ τούτῳ ἵνα γένηται ἄρτος.
(4) ὁ δὲ ἀποκριθεὶς εἶπεν· γέγραπται· οὐκ ἐπ' ἄρτῳ μόνῳ ζήσεται ὁ ἄνθρωπος, ἀλλ' ἐπὶ παντὶ	καὶ ἀπεκρίθη πρὸς αὐτὸν ὁ Ἰησοῦς· γέγραπται ὅτι οὐκ ἐπ' ἄρτῳ μόνῳ ζήσεται ὁ ἄνθρωπος.

[1] Yet it is also possible that ὄχλοι occurred in Q, since the word is also found elsewhere in that source.

ῥήματι (ἐκπορευομένῳ διὰ στόματος) θεοῦ.	
(5) τότε παραλαμβάνει αὐτὸν ὁ διάβολος εἰς τὴν ἁγίαν πόλιν, καὶ ἔστησεν αὐτὸν ἐπὶ τὸ πτερύγιον τοῦ ἱεροῦ, (6) καὶ λέγει αὐτῷ· εἰ υἱὸς εἶ τοῦ θεοῦ, βάλε σεαυτὸν	The verses 5–7 come in St. Luke after 8–9. ἤγαγεν δὲ αὐτὸν εἰς Ἱερουσαλήμ. What follows is identical, yet om. αὐτόν. εἶπεν (f. λέγει)
κάτω· γέγραπται γὰρ ὅτι τοῖς ἀγγέλοις αὐτοῦ ἐντελεῖται περὶ	ἐντεῦθεν [κάτω]
σοῦ, καὶ ἐπὶ χειρῶν ἀροῦσίν σε, μή ποτε προσκόψῃς πρὸς λίθον τὸν πόδα σου.	περὶ σοῦ τοῦ διαφυλάξαι σε, καὶ ὅτι ἐπὶ
(7) ἔφη αὐτῷ ὁ Ἰησοῦς· πάλιν γέγραπται· οὐκ ἐκπειράσεις κύριον τὸν θεόν σου.	καὶ ἀποκριθεὶς ὁ Ἰησοῦς εἶπεν αὐτῷ (ὅτι) εἴρηται
(8) πάλιν παραλαμβάνει αὐτὸν ὁ διάβολος εἰς ὄρος ὑψηλὸν λίαν, καὶ	καὶ ἀναγαγὼν αὐτὸν (ὁ διαβ. . . . λίαν om.) καὶ om.
δείκνυσιν αὐτῷ πάσας τὰς βασιλείας τοῦ κόσμου καὶ τὴν δόξαν αὐτῶν, (9) καὶ εἶπεν αὐτῷ· ταῦτά σοι πάντα δώσω, ἐὰν πεσὼν προσκυνήσῃς μοι. (10) τότε λέγει αὐτῷ ὁ Ἰησοῦς· ὕπαγε, σατανᾶ· γέγραπ-	ἔδειξεν τῆς οἰκουμένης (f. τ. κόσμ.), καὶ τ. δόξαν αὐτῶν om., ἐν στιγμῇ χρόνου add., perhaps πρὸς αὐτὸν, add. ὁ διάβολος, σοὶ δώσω τὴν ἐξουσίαν ταύτην ἅπασαν [καὶ τὴν δόξαν αὐτῶν], ὅτι ἐμοὶ παραδέδοται καὶ ᾧ ἂν θέλω

ται γάρ· κύριον τὸν θεόν σου προσκυνήσεις καὶ αὐτῷ μόνῳ λατρεύσεις.	δίδωμι αὐτήν· σὺ οὖν ἐὰν προσκυνήσῃς ἐνώπιον ἐμοῦ, ἔσται σοῦ πᾶσα. καὶ ἀποκριθεὶς ὁ Ἰησοῦς εἶπεν αὐτῷ· What follows is identical, but without ὕπαγε, σατανᾶ and γάρ.
(11) τότε ἀφίησιν αὐτὸν ὁ διάβολος, καὶ ἰδοὺ ἄγγελοι προσῆλθον καὶ διηκόνουν αὐτῷ.	καὶ συντελέσας πάντα πειρασμὸν ὁ διάβολος ἀπέστη ἀπ' αὐτοῦ ἄχρι καιροῦ.

In the above passage I have indicated by spaced type all the words which are common, or which closely correspond to one another, in the two gospels. It is at once seen that we have here an essentially identical text. The chief difference is that in St. Luke the third temptation has become the second. It is in favour of the order of St. Matthew that the temptation on the mountain is undoubtedly the chief temptation; here it is no longer a question of the Divine Sonship being put to the test, but of its renunciation: the Son of God is tempted to enter into the service of Satan. It is in favour of St. Luke's order, that according to it the scene of the temptations changes only at the last temptation, that the devil makes his final assault with a temptation actually based upon the words of Scripture, and that our Lord's answer forbids further temptation. It is not possible to give a certain decision on the point, but probability is on the side of the order of St. Matthew. Nothing can be built upon the ὕπαγε Σατανᾶ of St. Matthew, for these words can scarcely be original. If they were, what reason could St. Luke have had for omitting them? (ὑπάγειν is indeed a rare word with him, never occurring in the Acts and only once in the gospel, while it is found twenty times in St. Matthew, fifteen times in St. Mark, and thirty-three times in St. John). Besides, the phrase occurs again in St. Matt. xvi. 23, and may therefore, perhaps, have been inserted from the latter passage (where St. Mark viii. 33 also has it).

The wide divergence at the beginning and end is partly due to the influence of the Markan text. Hence it is that St. Matthew derives the episode "ἄγγελοι διηκόνουν αὐτῷ" (προσῆλθον belongs to the style of St. Matthew, the word is found more than fifty times in this gospel). It is from St. Mark that St. Luke derives "ἡμέρας μ' πειραζόμενος ὑπὸ τοῦ διαβόλου" (St. Mark: μ' ἡμέρας πειραζόμενος ὑπὸ τοῦ Σατανᾶ). All further deviations of St. Luke from St. Matthew in the introduction are likewise secondary, so that we must recognise the pure text of Q in the version of St. Matthew; for (1) in place of the representation of the Spirit as the active subject St. Luke writes in accordance with his style and mode of thinking: πλήρης πνεύματος ἁγίου and ἐν τῷ πνεύματι, (2) he inserts ὑπέστρεψεν ἀπὸ τ. Ἰορδ. (ὑποστρέφειν is found twenty-two times in the gospel and eleven times in the Acts, never in St. Mark or St. Matthew); (3) he writes the imperfect ἤγετο for ἀνήχθη (the use of the imperfect is almost peculiar to St. Luke; moreover, ἀνήχθη is certainly original, for it is found in St. Matthew only in this passage, and it gives a correct touch of local colouring [the wilderness is on the high ground] —elsewhere in St. Luke the word occurs frequently; it is dropped here because the evangelist did not understand its significance); (4) he omits the forty nights as superfluous (agreeing with St. Mark); (5) he replaces the clumsy ὕστερον by the good Greek phrase συντελεσθεισῶν αὐτῶν, (6) he mistakes the technical νηστεύειν, and replaces it by the extravagant οὐκ ἔφαγεν οὐδέν, (7) by his corrections, or through the influence of the Markan text, he has made it appear doubtful whether the temptations occurred during the forty days or first after that period had passed.

St. Matt. 3: προσελθών is added by St. Matthew (*vide supra*); δέ is put for καί by St. Luke; ὁ πειράζων is most probably the original word.

St. Matt. 3: The one stone of St. Luke, and the address to the stone, seem to me secondary, just because they better suit the situation. Why should St. Matthew have changed them?

St. Matt. 4: ὁ δὲ ἀποκριθεὶς εἶπεν is characteristic of St. Matthew's solemn style, but πρὸς αὐτὸν is Lukan, likewise ὅτι.

St. Matt. 4: ἀλλ' ἐπὶ παντὶ ῥήματι θεοῦ (with or without ἐκπορευομένῳ διὰ στόματος, words which have weak attestation) is an interpolation of St. Matthew, who completes the quotation from the LXX.

St. Matt. 5: The historic present is here, as always, avoided by St. Luke; likewise παραλαμβάνειν εἰς (also in verse 8, again in St. Matt. xxvii. 27) was distasteful to him.

St. Matt. 5: St. Matthew has replaced "Jerusalem" by "the holy city" (see also xxvii. 53); for the gospel of the Hebrews also read "Jerusalem."

St. Matt. 5: St. Luke avoids the Semitic repetition of *αὐτόν*.

St. Matt. 5: *ἐντεῦθεν* is a Lukan interpolation; the word is found elsewhere in St. Luke, never however in St. Matthew and St. Mark.

St. Matt. 6: *τοῦ διαφυλάξαι σε* is an interpolation of St. Luke's (according to the LXX), so also *ὅτι* here and in verse 7.

St. Matt. 7: Here St. Luke with *καὶ ἀποκριθεὶς ὁ Ἰησοῦς εἶπεν αὐτῷ* is the more circumstantial of the two, so also in St. Matt. 10.

St. Matt. 7: The *πάλιν* of St. Matthew is original; St. Luke avoids *πάλιν* (see also St. Matt. 8); it is found about seventeen times in St. Matthew, twenty-nine times in St. Mark, forty-seven times in St. John; on the other hand, only two (three) times in St. Luke's gospel and five times in the Acts.—*γέγραπται*, not *εἴρηται*, is original, for the latter (together with *τὸ εἰρημένον*) is peculiar to St. Luke—*vide* ii. 24; Acts ii. 16, xiii. 40; elsewhere only in Rom. iv. 18.

St. Matt. 8, 9: *ὅρος ὑψηλόν*, perhaps also attested by the gospel of the Hebrews; St. Luke rationalises and leaves the scene somewhat in shadow (he would probably have us suppose that our Lord was raised up into the air so as to be able to see everything).—The word *οἰκουμένη* is Lukan (used by St. Luke eight times, once by St. Matthew, never by St. Mark and St. John);

ἐν στιγμῷ χρόνου is of course interpolated by St. Luke (the words καὶ τὴν δόξαν αὐτῶν have either been displaced in St. Luke or should be omitted altogether). St. Luke's theological opinions have likewise led him to amplify the devil's address to our Lord by the long interpolation: σοὶ (set at the beginning, *cf.* the ἐμοὶ and σὺ in what follows) δώσω τὴν ἐξουσίαν ταύτην ἅπασαν, ὅτι ἐμοὶ παραδέδοται καὶ ᾧ ἂν θέλω δίδωμι αὐτήν· σὺ οὖν . . . ἔσται σοι πᾶσα.—ἐνώπιον is Lukan (occurring in St. Luke thirty-six times, never in St. Mark and St. Matthew); on the other hand, πεσών is an interpolation in the style of St. Matthew (*cf.* ii. 11; xviii. 26, 29).

St. Matt. 10: Concerning ὕπαγε Σατανᾶ (whence the inserted γάρ which follows), *vide supra.*

St. Matt. 11: καὶ συντελ. π. πειρ. is added by St. Luke (συντελεῖν is wanting in St. Matthew, occurs twice elsewhere in St. Luke).—ἀφίησιν stood in Q; ἀφιστάναι is found ten times in St. Luke, never in St. Matthew, St. Mark, and St. John.—ἄχρι καιροῦ is a Lukan interpolation which weakens the unique significance of these temptations. The expression occurs again in the New Testament only in Acts xiii. 11.

The text of the story of the Temptation, as it stood in Q, can therefore in my opinion be still restored with almost perfect certainty; almost everywhere the matter which is peculiar to either of our two authorities shows itself to be secondary. The genuine text is the shortest, and St. Matthew approaches nearer to it than does St. Luke. Q here ran somewhat as follows:—

Ὁ Ἰησοῦς ἀνήχθη εἰς τὴν ἔρημον ὑπὸ τοῦ πνεύματος

πειρασθῆναι ὑπὸ τοῦ διαβόλου, καὶ νηστεύσας ἡμέρας μ' καὶ νύκτας μ' ὕστερον ἐπείνασεν, καὶ ὁ πειράζων εἶπεν αὐτῷ· εἰ υἱὸς εἶ τοῦ θεοῦ, εἰπὲ ἵνα οἱ λίθοι οὗτοι ἄρτοι γένωνται, καὶ ἀπεκρίθη· γέγραπται· οὐκ ἐπ' ἄρτῳ μόνῳ ζήσεται ὁ ἄνθρωπος. παραλαμβάνει δὲ αὐτὸν εἰς Ἱερουσαλὴμ καὶ ἔστησεν αὐτὸν ἐπὶ τὸ πτερύγιον τοῦ ἱεροῦ καὶ λέγει αὐτῷ· εἰ υἱὸς εἶ τοῦ θεοῦ, βάλε σεαυτὸν κάτω· γέγραπται γὰρ ὅτι τοῖς ἀγγέλοις αὐτοῦ ἐντελεῖται περὶ σοῦ, καὶ ἐπὶ χειρῶν ἀροῦσίν σε, μή ποτε προσκόψῃς πρὸς λίθον τὸν πόδα σου. ἔφη αὐτῷ ὁ Ἰησοῦς· πάλιν γέγραπται· οὐκ ἐκπειράσεις κύριον τὸν θεόν σου. πάλιν παραλαμβάνει αὐτὸν εἰς ὄρος ὑψηλὸν λίαν καὶ δείκνυσιν αὐτῷ πάσας τὰς βασιλείας τοῦ κόσμου καὶ τὴν δόξαν αὐτῶν, καὶ εἶπεν αὐτῷ· ταῦτά σοι πάντα δώσω, ἐὰν προσκυνήσῃς μοι. καὶ λέγει αὐτῷ ὁ Ἰησοῦς· γέγραπται· κύριον τὸν θεόν σου προσκυνήσεις καὶ αὐτῷ μόνῳ λατρεύσεις. καὶ ἀφίησιν αὐτὸν ὁ διάβολος.

St. Matt. v. 3, 4, 6, 11, 12.	St. Luke vi. 20[b], 21–23.
(3) Μακάριοι οἱ πτωχοὶ τῷ πνεύματι, ὅτι αὐτῶν ἐστιν ἡ βασιλεία τῶν οὐρανῶν.	τῷ πνεύματι om. ὑμετέρα (f. αὐτῶν) τοῦ θεοῦ (f. τ. οὐρ.)
(4) μακάριοι οἱ πενθοῦντες, ὅτι αὐτοὶ παρακληθήσονται.[1]	These two verses are transposed in St. Luke. κλαίοντες νῦν (f. πενθ.) γελάσετε (f. αὐτ. παρακλ.)

[1] The beatitude which immediately follows in the ordinary text (its position varies in the MSS.): μακάριοι οἱ πραεῖς, ὅτι αὐτοὶ κληρονομήσουσιν τὴν γῆν (=Ps. xxxvii. 11), is probably a later interpolation; *vide* Wellhausen on this passage.

(6) μακάριοι οἱ πεινῶντες καὶ διψῶντες τὴν δικαιοσύνην, ὅτι αὐτοὶ χορτασθήσονται.	νῦν (post πεινῶντες) καὶ . . . δικαιοσ. om. αὐτοί om. χορτασθήσεσθε
(11) μακάριοί ἐστε ὅταν ὀνειδίσωσιν ὑμᾶς καὶ διώξωσιν καὶ εἴπωσιν πᾶν πονηρὸν καθ' ὑμῶν ψευδόμενοι [ἕνεκεν ἐμοῦ]. (12) χαίρετε καὶ ἀγαλλιᾶσθε, ὅτι ὁ μισθὸς ὑμῶν πολὺς ἐν τοῖς οὐρανοῖς· οὕτως γὰρ ἐδίωξαν τοὺς προφήτας τοὺς πρὸ ὑμῶν.	ἔσεσθε (?) ὅταν μισήσωσιν ὑμάς οἱ ἄνθρωποι καὶ ὅταν ἀφορίσωσιν ὑμᾶς [καὶ ὀνειδίσωσιν ?] καὶ ἐκβάλωσιν τὸ ὄνομα ὑμῶν ὡς πονηρὸν ἕνεκα τοῦ υἱοῦ τοῦ ἀνθρώπου. χάρητε ἐν ἐκείνῃ τῇ ἡμέρᾳ καὶ σκιρτήσατε· ἰδοὺ γὰρ ὁ μισθὸς ὑμῶν πολὺς ἐν τῷ οὐρανῷ· κατὰ τὰ αὐτὰ γὰρ ἐποίουν τοῖς προφήταις οἱ πατέρες αὐτῶν.

It is still possible practically to settle the question of the original text of verses 3, 4, 6.[1] As (καὶ διψῶντες) τὴν δικαιοσύνην is added by St. Matthew, so also with the greatest probability we may decide similarly concerning τῷ πνεύματι (the simple πτωχοὶ is also found in St. Matt. xi. 5: πτωχοὶ εὐαγγελίζονται). On the other hand, κλαίοντες (for πενθοῦντες) is certainly a correction of St. Luke, who

[1] Apart from the order, and perhaps also the question whether the first or third person is original. The pronoun ὑμέτερος is certainly Lukan (*vide* a Concordance); but it may stand for an original ὑμῶν. Wellhausen and others decide for St. Luke. But the repetition of the pleonastic αὐτοί gives an impression of originality, and St. Luke also elsewhere (*cf.* St. Matt. xi. 18) transforms the third person into the second.

is fond of using κλαίειν (eleven times in the gospel, in St. Matthew only two occurrences and one of these in a quotation, *cf.* St. Luke vii. 32 = St. Matt. xi. 17); κλαίειν then brought about the γελάσετε in the following clause (St. Luke is fond of strong expressions, γελᾶν occurs again with him only in vi. 25, never elsewhere in the New Testament), Ps. cxxvi. may have influenced the evangelist here. The twofold νῦν is of course also interpolated by St. Luke (νῦν occurs thirty-seven times in the gospel and Acts, four times in St. Matthew).

St. Matthew 11 and St. Luke 22 look like two separate translations, yet are not so, as is shown by St. Matthew 12 = St. Luke 23. We must start from the consideration of this verse and it will then appear that St. Luke is almost everywhere secondary. Ἐν ἐκείνῃ τῇ ἡμέρᾳ is as secondary as νῦν; the imperative aorists are an improvement in style; σκιρτήσατε (for ἀγαλλιᾶσθε) is a genuinely Lukan exaggeration (*vide supra* γελάσετε); σκιρτᾶν is peculiar to St. Luke in the New Testament (*vide* i. 41, 44), likewise ἰδοὺ γὰρ (never found in St. Matthew and St. Mark, six times in St. Luke); St. Luke does not care for the plural οὐρανοῖς, and (κατὰ) τὰ αὐτά is Lukan (elsewhere in the New Testament only in St. Luke vi. 26 and Acts xv. 27). Ἐποίουν for ἐδίωξαν was written by St. Luke, because in the preceding clauses not only persecutions but also other trials are mentioned. A genuine translation-variant appears to stand at the conclusion. Wellhausen says: "St. Luke has read 'their forefathers' as the subject of the verb; St. Matthew has read 'your forefathers' in apposition to the Prophets. The difference in

Aramaic is only that of *daq'damaihôn* (οἱ πατέρες αὐτῶν) from *daq'damaikôn* (τοὺς πρὸ ὑμῶν)." But there is yet another explanation of this variation—namely, that St. Luke is here influenced by his reminiscence of the familiar invective against the Pharisees (St. Matt. xxiii. 29 f. = St. Luke xi. 47 f.); in that passage the prophets and the fathers are spoken of together, and thence he has derived "the fathers" here. This may have happened the more easily since the words in St. Matthew (*i.e.* in Q), τοὺς πρὸ ὑμῶν, appeared liable to misinterpretation (Apostles = Prophets), or as an unnecessary addition which of itself cried out for some better substitute.

It accordingly follows that St. Matthew 12 presents the original text of Q, which has been altered by St. Luke. Then, however, it is possible that also St. Matthew 11 = St. Luke 22 are not two different translations of a common original; rather it is probable that here again St. Luke has deliberately altered—in fact, has transformed—the whole verse. This, in the first place, shows itself in the stylistic variants. In place of πονηρὸν . . . ψευδόμενοι (the very fact that ψευδόμενοι does not occur elsewhere in the synoptists shows that it probably belongs to Q) he writes the excellent Greek phrase ὡς πονηρόν, and supplies the subjectless verbs with the subject οἱ ἄνθρωποι. One of the principal differences is that St. Matthew has ὀνειδίσωσιν, διώξωσιν, εἴπωσιν πᾶν πονηρὸν καθ' ὑμῶν ψευδόμενοι, while St. Luke writes μισήσωσιν, ἀφορίσωσιν, ἐκβάλωσιν τ. ὄνομα ὑμῶν ὡς πονηρόν. The order in St. Matthew is not quite logical, in St. Luke it is strictly logical:

hatred is followed by excommunication, excommunication by the general defamation of the name. Besides, we find that St. Luke uses *μισεῖν* also in other places where it does not occur in the parallel passage of St. Matthew (vi. 27, xiv. 26), and that *ἐκβάλλειν*, in the metaphorical sense = "to defame" (here only in the New Testament), is good Greek, whereas *εἰπεῖν πᾶν πονηρόν* is not Greek at all. Accordingly, here also the text of St. Matthew is everywhere to be preferred. It must remain an open question whether, in the places where St. Matthew is secondary, the corrections are due to the evangelist himself or whether a secondary text already lay before him. The Beatitudes certainly circulated in various recensions from an early period, indeed from the beginning. Thus Polycarp (Epist. 2) quotes as follows: *μακάριοι οἱ πτωχοὶ καὶ οἱ διωκόμενοι ἕνεκεν δικαιοσύνης, ὅτι αὐτῶν ἐστιν ἡ βασιλεία τοῦ θεοῦ.* This looks like a combination of the texts of St. Matthew and St. Luke; perhaps, however, it is a combination of these two and of the source, or perhaps it is another version of the source.

A word must be said concerning [*ἕνεκεν ἐμοῦ*] in St. Matthew and *ἕνεκα τοῦ υἱοῦ τοῦ ἀνθρώπου* in St. Luke. St. Matthew's phraseology here is somewhat redundant; many authorities have therefore omitted *ψευδόμενοι*; but this word seems to me to be supported by the *ὡς πονηρόν* of St. Luke (*vide supra*). On the other hand, *ἕνεκεν ἐμοῦ* should be omitted from the text of St. Matthew, for a succession of ancient Western authorities do not read it; others read *ἕνεκεν δικαιοσύνης* (Da.b.c.g′.k); the ancient Syriac reads *ἕνεκεν τοῦ ὀνόματός μου*. If these words were wanting in St. Matthew then the *ἕνεκ. τ. υἱοῦ τ. ἀνθρ.* of St. Luke most certainly did not stand in Q. This phrase stands in close connection with *τὸ ὄνομα ὑμῶν*, which also does not belong to Q (*vide supra*). If, nevertheless, the critic asserts that *ἕνεκεν* must belong to Q, it is no longer possible to ascertain what word came after this preposition in the source.

St. Matt. v. 13, 15, 18, 25, 26, 32.	St. Luke xiv. 34, 35; xi. 33; xvi. 17; xii. 58, 59; xvi. 18.
(13) ὑμεῖς ἐστε τὸ ἅλας τῆς γῆς· ἐὰν δε τὸ ἅλας μωρανθῇ, ἐν τίνι ἁλισθήσεται; εἰς οὐδὲν ἰσχύει ἔτι εἰ μὴ βληθὲν ἔξω καταπατεῖσθαι ὑπὸ τῶν ἀνθρώπων.	καλὸν οὖν τὸ ἅλας· ἐὰν δὲ καὶ τὸ ἅλας μωρανθῇ, ἐν τίνι ἀρτυθήσεται; οὔτε εἰς γῆν οὔτε εἰς κοπρίαν εὔθετόν ἐστιν· ἔξω βάλλουσιν αὐτό.
(15) οὐδὲ καίουσιν λύχνον καὶ τιθέασιν αὐτὸν ὑπὸ τὸν μόδιον, ἀλλ' ἐπὶ τὴν λυχνίαν, καὶ λάμπει πᾶσιν τοῖς ἐν τῇ οἰκίᾳ.	οὐδεὶς λύχνον ἅψας εἰς κρυπτὴν τίθησιν [οὐδὲ ὑπὸ τὸν μόδιον], ἀλλ' ἐπὶ τὴν λυχνίαν, ἵνα οἱ εἰσπορευόμενοι τὸ φῶς βλέπωσιν.
(18) ἀμὴν γὰρ λέγω ὑμῖν, ἕως ἂν παρέλθῃ ὁ οὐρανὸς καὶ ἡ γῆ, ἰῶτα ἓν ἢ μία κεραία οὐ μὴ παρέλθῃ ἀπὸ τοῦ νόμου, ἕως ἂν πάντα γένηται.	εὐκοπώτερον δέ ἐστιν τὸν οὐρανὸν καὶ τὴν γῆν παρελθεῖν ἢ τοῦ νόμου μίαν κεραίαν πεσεῖν.

(25) ἴσθι εὐνοῶν τῷ ἀντιδίκῳ σου ταχὺ ἕως ὅτου εἶ μετ' αὐτοῦ ἐν τῇ ὁδῷ· μήποτέ σε παραδῷ ὁ ἀντίδικος τῷ κριτῇ καὶ ὁ κριτὴς τῷ ὑπηρέτῃ, καὶ εἰς φυλακὴν βληθήσῃ· (26) ἀμὴν λέγω σοι, οὐ μὴ ἐξέλθῃς ἐκεῖθεν ἕως ἂν ἀποδῷς τὸν ἔσχατον κοδράντην.	ὡς γὰρ ὑπάγεις μετὰ τοῦ ἀντιδίκου σου ἐπ' ἄρχοντα, ἐν τῇ ὁδῷ δὸς ἐργασίαν ἀπηλλάχθαι ἀπ' αὐτοῦ, μήποτε κατασύρῃ σε πρὸς τὸν κριτήν, καὶ ὁ κριτής σε παραδώσει τῷ πράκτορι, καὶ ὁ πράκτωρ σε βαλεῖ εἰς φυλακήν· λέγω σοι, οὐ μὴ ἐξέλθῃς ἐκεῖθεν ἕως καὶ τὸ ἔσχατον λεπτὸν ἀποδῷς.
(32) ἐγὼ δὲ λέγω ὑμῖν ὅτι πᾶς ὁ ἀπολύων τὴν γυναῖκα αὐτοῦ παρεκτὸς λόγου πορνείας ποιεῖ αὐτὴν μοιχευθῆναι, καὶ ὃς ἐὰν ἀπολελυμένην γαμήσῃ, μοιχᾶται.	πᾶς ὁ ἀπολύων τὴν γυναῖκα αὐτοῦ καὶ γαμῶν ἑτέραν μοιχεύει, καὶ ὁ ἀπολελυμένην ἀπὸ ἀνδρὸς γαμῶν μοιχεύει.

The first saying also stood in St. Mark (ix. 50) in the form: *καλὸν τὸ ἅλας· ἐὰν δὲ τὸ ἅλας ἄναλον γένηται, ἐν τίνι αὐτὸ ἀρτύσετε; ἔχετε ἐν ἑαυτοῖς ἅλα.*

The saying in Q ran: *ὑμεῖς ἐστε τὸ ἅλας τῆς γῆς* [in this form or in a similar form St. Luke must have read it in Q, for the context in which he gives the saying shows that he referred it, like St. Matthew, to the disciples; but as in cases of doubt he often prefers St. Mark to Q, so here also he has chosen the form of St. Mark]· *ἐὰν δὲ τὸ ἅλας μωρανθῇ, ἐν τίνι ἁλισθήσεται* [here also St. Luke uses the *ἀρτύειν* of St. Mark]; *εἰς οὐδὲν ἰσχύει ἔτι* [St. Luke replaces this expression by οὐκ εὔθετος (εὔθετος and ἀνεύθετος are peculiar to St. Luke, *cf.* xiv. 35 and Acts xxvii. 12), and reinforces it according to his custom with the phrase οὔτε εἰς γῆν οὔτε εἰς κοπρίαν (κοπρία only in St. Luke, *vide* xiii. 8), which also replaces the word καταπατεῖσθαι] εἰ μὴ βληθὲν ἔξω καταπατεῖσθαι ὑπὸ τῶν ἀνθρώπων [that βληθὲν ἔξω is original is shown by the fact that St. Luke did not like to sacrifice it, but let it hobble behind the main body of the saying]. Thus the verse stood in Q in the form in which it is preserved in St. Matthew.

In the second saying, ἅπτειν and ἀνάπτειν (for "fire" and "light"), are Lukan, so that the verdict here must be given for St. Matthew; the participial construction is Lukan; the οὐδείς for an indefinite third person plural is a stylistic improvement. Ὑπὸ τὸν μόδιον is probably an interpolation from St. Matthew into the Lukan text; St. Luke says εἰς κρυπτήν. Οἱ εἰσπορευόμενοι is Lukan, *vide* viii. 16; Acts iii. 2, xxviii. 30.—The saying occurs four times in the gospels (twice in St. Luke). In St. Mark iv. 21 it runs: μήτι ἔρχεται ὁ λύχνος ἵνα ὑπὸ τὸν μόδιον τεθῇ ἢ ὑπὸ τὴν κλίνην, οὐχ ἵνα ἐπὶ τὴν λυχνίαν τεθῇ; in Q it ran as St. Matthew gives it. St. Luke gives it both times (*vide* viii. 16) with the same traits which can be easily explained as peculiarities of his own; in viii. 16, however, he inserts the "bed" from St. Mark, and replaces the "bushel" not by εἰς κρυπτήν but by the general phrase καλύπτει αὐτὸν σκεύει (for this word see Acts ix. 15; x. 11, 16; xi. 5; xxvii. 17). In making the lamp give light, not to those within the house but to those entering in, St. Luke evidently intends to improve the sense of the passage; he perhaps also thinks of the missionary aspect of the gospel (though this is doubtful).

The third saying in Q ran as follows: ἕως ἂν παρέλθῃ ὁ οὐρανὸς καὶ ἡ γῆ, ἰῶτα ἓν ἢ μία κεραία οὐ μὴ παρέλθῃ ἀπὸ τοῦ νόμου. In regard to form, St. Luke has improved the clumsy construction, but he has also altered the thought by the εὐκοπώτερον which he has adopted from other sayings (*vide* St. Matt. ix. 5 *cum parall.*; xix. 24 *cum parall.*). According to St. Matthew, the Law abides as long as Heaven and Earth remain; according to St. Luke, it lasts longer than they. Here we discern St. Luke's genuinely Hellenic reverence for the Old Testament—a reverence which could be so deep, because the writer stood remote from the controversies concerning the application of the precepts of the Law to the daily life. The converse hypothesis (Wellhausen) that St. Matthew has attenuated the thought is unacceptable from considerations both of matter and style. St. Luke has introduced πεσεῖν in order to avoid the double παρέλθῃ (πεσεῖν in the metaphorical sense is not found in the gospels, but *cf.* Rom. xi. 11, 22; xiv. 4; 1 Cor. x. 12; xiii. 8; Heb. iv. 11), and he has omitted the ἰῶτα ἓν as superfluous and somewhat singular. In St. Matthew the opening words ἀμὴν γ. λ. ὑμῖν and the concluding clause ἕως ἂν πάντα γέν. are perhaps secondary. The latter was probably added because the preceding passage in St. Matthew speaks of "fulfilling"; the evangelist may, besides, have been influenced by a reminiscence of St. Mark xiii. 30.

Close consideration of the fourth saying also shows that St. Matthew has excellently preserved the text of Q (perhaps *ἀμήν* is secondary). The temporal *ὡς* at the beginning is specifically Lukan (references are here unnecessary); *ἐπ' ἄρχοντα* is an explanatory interpolation, and *ἴσθι εὐνοῶν* (here only in the New Testament) seemed to St. Luke too weak—he replaced it by the transparently clear phrase *δὸς ἐργασίαν ἀπηλλάχθαι ἀπ' αὐτοῦ* (*ἐργασία* is not found elsewhere in the four gospels, see however Acts xvi. 16, 19; xix. 24, 25; Ephes. iv. 19; neither is *ἀπαλλάσσειν* found elsewhere in the four gospels, see however Acts xix. 12: *ἀπαλλάσσεσθαι ἀπ' αὐτῶν*). St. Luke has just as happily avoided the awkward phrase *ταχὺ ἕως ὅτου εἶ μετ' αὐτοῦ* (he places the *μετά* at the very beginning), as well as the unnecessary repetition of *ὁ ἀντίδικος*. Moreover, his sense of style would not allow him to describe the action of the adversary and the judge with one and the same word (St. Matthew uses *παραδοῦναι* in both cases); he writes here *κατασύρειν* and *παραδοῦναι* (*κατασύρειν* does not occur elsewhere in the New Testament, but *σύρειν* [of men] is peculiar to St. Luke, occurring indeed three times in the Acts). St. Luke has replaced the very indefinite word *ὑπηρέτης* by the technical term *ὁ πράκτωρ*, and the vulgar *κοδράντης* by *λεπτόν*. In all these cases it is simply inconceivable that St. Matthew had before him, and has altered, the text presented in St. Luke.

In the fifth saying St. Luke is evidently dependent not only upon Q but also upon St. Mark x. ii. (*ὃς ἂν ἀπολύσῃ τὴν γυναῖκα αὐτοῦ καὶ γαμήσῃ ἄλλην, μοιχᾶται ἐπ' αὐτήν· καὶ ἐὰν αὐτὴ ἀπολύσασα τὸν ἄνδρα αὐτῆς* [*vel ἐὰν γυνὴ ἐξέλθῃ ἀπὸ τοῦ ἀνδρὸς αὐτῆς καὶ*] *γαμήσῃ ἄλλον, μοιχᾶται*). Accordingly, in St. Matthew we have only to omit the introduction and the phrase *παρεκτὸς λόγου πορνείας*. In St. Luke *καὶ γαμῶν ἑτέραν* comes from another source—in fact, from St. Mark—and by its insertion the sense of the saying is altogether changed (that St. Luke's correcting hand was at work here is also evident from the substitution of the participle for *ὃς ἐὰν γαμήσῃ*). In Q the saying gave expression to the austere thought: "He who divorces his wife causes her to commit adultery: both she and her new husband are guilty of adultery." St. Luke has completely changed this thought.

St. Matt. v. 39, 40, 42, 44–48.	St. Luke vi. 29, 30, 27, 28, 35[b], 32, 33, 36.
(39) *Ὅστις σε ῥαπίζει εἰς τὴν* [*δεξιὰν*] *σιαγόνα* (*σου*), *στρέψον αὐτῷ καὶ τὴν ἄλλην,*	*τῷ τύπτοντί σε εἰς* [*ἐπὶ*] *τὴν σιαγόνα, πάρεχε καὶ τὴν ἄλλην,*
(40) *καὶ τῷ θελοντί σοι κριθῆναι καὶ τὸν χιτῶνά σου λαβεῖν, ἄφες αὐτῷ καὶ τὸ ἱμάτιον.*	*καὶ ἀπὸ τοῦ αἴροντός σου τὸ ἱμάτιον καὶ τὸν χιτῶνα μὴ κωλύσῃς.*
(42) *τῷ αἰτοῦντί σε δός, καὶ τὸν θέλοντα ἀπὸ σοῦ δανίσασθαι μὴ ἀποστραφῇς.*	*παντὶ αἰτοῦντί σε δίδου, καὶ ἀπὸ τοῦ αἴροντος τὰ σὰ μὴ ἀπαίτει* [*cf.* v. 35: *καὶ δανείζετε μηδὲν ἀπελπίζοντες*].
(44) *ἐγὼ δὲ λέγω ὑμῖν· ἀγαπᾶτε τοὺς ἐχθροὺς*	*ὑμῖν λέγω τοῖς ἀκούουσιν· ἀγαπ. τ. ἐχθρ. ὑμ., καλῶς*

ὑμῶν καὶ προσεύχεσθε ὑπὲρ τῶν διωκόντων ὑμᾶς,	ποιεῖτε τοῖς μισοῦσιν ὑμᾶς, εὐλογεῖτε τοὺς καταρωμένους ὑμᾶς, προσεύχεσθε περὶ τῶν ἐπηρεαζόντων ὑμᾶς,
(45) ὅπως γένησθε υἱοὶ τοῦ πατρὸς ὑμῶν τοῦ ἐν οὐρανοῖς, ὅτι τὸν ἥλιον αὐτοῦ ἀνατέλλει ἐπὶ πονηροὺς καὶ ἀγαθοὺς καὶ βρέχει ἐπὶ δικαίους καὶ ἀδίκους.	καὶ ἔσεσθε υἱοὶ ὑψίστου, ὅτι αὐτὸς χρηστός ἐστιν ἐπὶ τοὺς ἀχαρίστους καὶ πονηρούς.
(46) ἐὰν γὰρ ἀγαπήσητε τοὺς ἀγαπῶντας ὑμᾶς, τίνα μισθὸν ἔχετε; οὐχὶ καὶ οἱ τελῶναι τὸ αὐτὸ ποιοῦσιν;	καί εἰ ἀγαπᾶτε τοὺς ἀγαπῶντας ὑμᾶς, ποία ὑμῖν χάρις [ἐστίν]; καὶ γὰρ οἱ ἁμαρτωλοὶ τοὺς ἀγαπῶντας αὐτοὺς ἀγαπῶσιν.
(47) καὶ ἐὰν ἀσπάσησθε τοὺς ἀδελφοὺς ὑμῶν μόνον, τί περισσὸν ποιεῖτε; οὐχὶ καὶ οἱ ἐθνικοὶ τὸ αὐτὸ ποιοῦσιν;	καὶ [γὰρ] ἐὰν [εἰ] ἀγαθοποιῆτε [-εῖτε] τοὺς ἀγαθοποιοῦντας ὑμᾶς, ποία ὑμῖν χάρις [χάρις ὑμ.] ἐστίν; καὶ οἱ ἁμαρτωλοὶ τὸ αὐτὸ ποιοῦσιν.
(48) ἔσεσθε οὖν ὑμεῖς τέλειοι ὡς ὁ πατὴρ ὑμῶν ὁ οὐράνοις τέλειός ἐστιν.	γίνεσθε οἰκτίρμονες, καθὼς ὁ πατὴρ ὑμῶν οἰκτίρμων ἐστίν [οἰκτείρει].

There can be no question that in the two first verses St. Matthew has preserved the original text; St. Luke has (1) introduced the participial construction; he has (2) replaced the vulgar ῥαπίζειν by τύπτειν, the equally vulgar στρέψον by πάρεχε, the awkward un-Hellenic and diffuse *τῷ θέλοντί σοι κριθῆναι καὶ . . . λαβεῖν* by *ἀπὸ τοῦ αἴροντος* (in the latter instance he has transformed a command relating to behaviour in case of a judicial action into a general maxim; hence *μὴ κωλύσῃς* for the more positive *ἄφες*. St. Matthew says: "He who wishes to sue thee for thy coat, allow him to take also thy cloak"; St. Luke says: "He who takes thy cloak, hinder him not from taking also thy coat"). *Ῥαπίζειν* is found in the New Testament only in St. Matthew (viz. once again in xxvi. 67); *στρέφειν* is used by St. Luke only in the form *στραφείς*, notice also the Semitic repetition of the dative in *αὐτῷ* (D. has avoided this by writing *ὁ θέλων*). In the order, "cloak"—"coat," St. Luke might seem to represent the original; "for the coat is nearer to the body than the cloak." But St. Luke was obliged to begin with the cloak, for the robber catches hold of the cloak, not the undergarment; we can thus easily understand that the Lukan text is secondary in its origin, but we cannot explain a secondary origin of the text of St. Matthew.

The Lukan insertion of *παντί* in St. Matthew verse 42, is also found in the Lukan version of the fifth petition of the Lord's Prayer and elsewhere in St. Luke; likewise the substitution of *δίδου* for *δός* also occurs in the fourth petition of that prayer. *Δίδου* is more correct Greek, seeing that the command is general. In what follows, the words *ἀπαιτεῖν* (note the play upon *αἰτεῖν* and *ἀπαιτεῖν*) and *ἀπελπίζειν* of themselves show classical feeling; the possessive pronoun (*τὰ σά*) is also Lukan; the whole clause, *καὶ ἀπὸ τοῦ αἴροντος . . . ἀπαίτει*, is interpolated by

St. Luke. On the other hand, verse 42^b in St. Matthew is original, for the thought is expressed in St. Luke 35, and the construction in St. Matthew is clumsy (the middle ἀποστρέφεσθαι is not found in St. Luke).

In verse 44 St. Luke has, as is so often the case, omitted the superfluous pronominal subject, and has added τοῖς ἀκούουσιν (influenced by what precedes in this gospel). In this verse the two exhortations peculiar to St. Luke can scarcely be original; what reason could St. Matthew have had for omitting them? Besides, St. Luke is fond of the words μισεῖν and εὐλογεῖν (οἱ μισοῦντες ἡμᾶς, in the literature of the post-apostolic epoch, is indeed almost a technical term with Christians for their adversaries). The four verbs ἀγαπᾶν, καλῶς ποιεῖν, εὐλογεῖν, προσεύχεσθαι form a premeditated climax which is not to be compared for originality with the simple combination of ἀγαπᾶν and προσεύχεσθαι. St. Luke has already avoided the word διώκειν in St. Matt. v. 11, 12 (*vide supra*)—why, I know not; ἐπηρεάζειν occurs again only in 1 Pet. iii. 16, and does not belong to the vocabulary of common speech (*vide* Aristotle's definition).

In verse 45 the peculiarly Lukan ὕψιστος (without ὁ and without θεός) shows that St. Luke has made changes; ὅπως is not frequent in St. Luke (it is found only seven times in the gospel), elsewhere also its use is avoided by this evangelist. Χρηστός ἐστιν ἐπὶ τοὺς ἀχαρίστους has too much of the flavour of the literary style to be original. It is difficult to say why St. Luke has done away with the beautiful simile of

St. Matthew. Did he think that it did not express the thought clearly enough? That he had it before him in his source seems to follow from πονηρούς, which comes in haltingly at the close (the δίκαιος and ἄδικος of St. Matthew are suspicious; the former being a favourite word with this evangelist). "Your Father in Heaven," in St. Matthew, is almost always suspicious. At the very least, "in Heaven" is to be omitted.

In verse 46 τίνα μισθὸν ἔχετε is certainly original; for χάρις, given by St. Luke, is a specifically Lukan word (found twenty-five times in the gospel and the Acts, never occurring in St. Matthew and St. Mark). The question in 46[b] is also original; for καὶ γάρ is Lukan (*vide* the fifth petition of the Lord's Prayer in St. Luke, where St. Matthew has ὡς καί, in St. Matthew καὶ γάρ occurs twice, in St. Luke's gospel nine times), and St. Luke has often removed rhetorical questions from Q. Again, the τελῶναι must be more original than the more general term οἱ ἁμαρτωλοί. St. Luke perhaps did not wish to repeat the phrase τὸ αὐτὸ ποιοῦσιν (*vide* verse 47), therefore he develops it here. The εἰ here and in the following verse is certainly secondary; in Q, ἐάν is very much more frequent than εἰ. Also in other passages St. Luke has changed ἐάν into εἰ.

In verse 47 St. Luke understood ἀσπάζεσθαι to mean "to be friendly disposed towards anyone," "to devote oneself in love towards anyone" (probably rightly), and has accordingly rendered it by ἀγαθοποιεῖν, it is obvious that St. Matthew is original here. The μόνον of St. Matthew is also original; St. Luke avoids this use of the word (only once in the gospel [viii. 50]—and that from St. Mark—while in St. Matthew it often occurs; it also occurs only once in the Acts). For *ποία ὑμῖν χάρις*, *vide supra* on verse 46; the fact that the corresponding words of St. Matthew (*τί περισσὸν ποιεῖτε*) are a vulgarism is in their favour. For *καὶ οἱ ἁμαρτωλοί*, *vide supra* on verse 46; "*ἐθνικοί*" is not found at all in St. Luke—the word would have been almost unintelligible to his readers.

In verse 48 St. Luke has again erased the superfluous pronominal subject (*cf.* verse 44). In replacing (*ὅπως*) *γένησθε* by *ἔσεσθε* in verse 45, and *ἔσεσθε* by *γίνεσθε* in verse 48, he has in both cases improved the logic of the passage. Likewise in writing *καθώς* for *ὡς* he has improved the style. It is, however, difficult to decide whether *τέλειοι* or *οἰκτίρμονες* is the original word. Wellhausen describes the latter as "much the more genuine." *Τέλειος* is indeed found in the gospels only here and in St. Matt. xix. 21. To assign the idea to Q or to our Lord on the evidence of these two passages is hazardous. *Οἰκτίρμων* is found nowhere else in the gospels. Nevertheless, I am inclined to prefer the latter word—at least so far as significance is concerned. Perhaps *ἐλεήμονες* stood in Q and has been replaced in St. Luke by the more refined word.

St. Matt. vi. 9: *Πάτερ ἡμῶν ὁ ἐν τοῖς οὐρανοῖς· ἁγιασθήτω τὸ ὄνομά σου·* (10) *ἐλθάτω ἡ βασιλεία*	St. Luke xi. 2–4. *ἡμῶν . . . οὐραν.* om. The first three petitions are probably wanting; read

σου· γενηθήτω τὸ θέλημά σου, ὡς ἐν οὐρανῷ καὶ ἐπὶ γῆς·	in their place: ἐλθέτω τὸ ἅγιον πνεῦμά σου ἐφ᾽ ἡμᾶς καὶ καθαρισάτω ἡμᾶς.
(11) τὸν ἄρτον ἡμῶν τὸν ἐπιούσιον δὸς ἡμῖν σήμερον·	(ἡμῶν om.?) δίδου τὸ καθ᾽ ἡμέραν (f. σήμερον)
(12) καὶ ἄφες ἡμῖν τὰ ὀφειλήματα ἡμῶν, ὡς καὶ ἡμεῖς ἀφήκαμεν τοῖς ὀφειλέταις ἡμῶν·	τὰς ἁμαρτίας καὶ γὰρ αὐτοὶ (f. ἡμεῖς) ἀφίομεν παντὶ ὀφείλοντι ἡμῖν·
(13) καὶ μὴ εἰσενέγκῃς ἡμᾶς εἰς πειρασμόν, ἀλλὰ ῥῦσαι ἡμᾶς ἀπὸ τοῦ πονηροῦ.	ἀλλὰ . . . πονηρ. om.

It is certain that the two forms of the prayer depend upon one original form and one original translation, and it is just as certain that St. Luke could not have known the prayer as the customary congregational prayer in the communities with which he was acquainted, otherwise he would not have revised its language so drastically. The form transmitted to him contained only the vocative πάτερ (*cf.* St. Paul) and the so-called fourth, fifth, and sixth petitions. All the other clauses found in St. Matthew are either accretions which attached themselves to the common prayer during the process of transformation into a solemn congregational prayer in the primitive Jewish Christian communities and under the dominating influence of the prayers of the Synagogue, or they were added by St. Matthew himself. With the correction δίδου compare St.

Luke's similar correction of St. Matt. v. 42. St. Matthew gives the prayer as it was meant to be, and as indeed it was, used daily; St. Luke gives it as an instruction in prayer, therefore the present tense. This also explains the substitution of τὸ καθ' ἡμέραν for σήμερον, as to which it is to be noted that τ. καθ' ἡμέραν occurs elsewhere in the New Testament only in St. Luke (xix. 47; Acts xvii. 11). 'Οφείλημα was most probably distasteful to St. Luke because it belonged to the vulgar idiom—there is no doubt that it is the original word; ἡμεῖς is replaced by αὐτοί in order to avoid the threefold repetition of the same word (St. Luke is also fond of omitting the pronominal subject before the verb—*vide supra* on St. Matt. v. 44, 48, and elsewhere); καὶ γάρ also is a phrase that St. Luke uses elsewhere (*vide supra* on St. Matt. v. 46). The perfect ἀφήκαμεν is certainly as original as the ὡς (*vide* St. Matt. v. 23); St. Luke has here attenuated the full and important significance of the petition. Lastly, the interpolation of παντί (with participle instead of substantive) is also Lukan—*vide supra* on St. Matt. v. 42 and elsewhere. The question whether the amplification of the prayer is due to St. Matthew himself, or whether he adopted it in the form it had already taken in the Church (*vide supra*), is one that cannot be definitely settled (πάτερ ἡμῶν ὁ ἐν τ. οὐρ. seems to betray the style of St. Matthew). An original form ("πάτερ" and the fourth, fifth, and sixth petitions) must have existed, and there is nothing to say against its having stood in Q. The seventh petition like the first three has strong points of resemblance with the prayers of the Synagogue, and it is certain that St. Luke would not have passed over this petition if it had existed in his exemplar.

St. Matt. vi. 20: *θησαυρίζετε δὲ ὑμῖν θησαυροὺς ἐν οὐρανῷ, ὅπου οὔτε σὴς οὔτε βρῶσις ἀφανίζει καὶ ὅπου κλέπται οὐ διορύσσουσιν οὐδὲ κλέπτουσιν.*	St. Luke xii. 33[b]: *θησαυρὸν ἀνέκλειπτον ἐν τοῖς οὐρανοῖς ὅπου κλέπτης οὐκ ἐγγίζει οὐδὲ σὴς διαφθείρει.*

Taking also into consideration verse 19 of St. Matthew and verse 33[a] of St. Luke, it is at once seen that St. Matthew gives a saying which is complete in itself, while St. Luke adopts, as it were, only a reminiscence of this saying, which he binds up with the command to sell all things and give alms (*cf.* his enthusiasm for this ideal in the Acts). Moreover, the phraseology and the selection of words betray the deliberate choice, and thus the secondary character of St. Luke. *Διαφθείρειν* (also *φθείρειν*) does not belong to the vocabulary of the gospels, but is classical; the thief and the moth are not easily understood apart from St. Matt. vi. 19; *ἐγγίζειν* is a feeble word which St. Luke was fond of using (it is not found in St. John, occurs three times in St. Mark, six or seven times in St. Matthew, twenty-four times in St. Luke), and *ἀνέκλειπτος* also belongs to the language of literature (St. Luke loves such formations, *cf.* xvii. 1: *ἀνένδεκτος*; xi. 46: *δυσβάστακτος*; Acts xxvii. 12: *ἀνεύθετος*). Accordingly, the plural *οὐρανοῖς*, which is much rarer in St. Luke than in St. Matthew, can alone be claimed for Q, wherein verse 19 must also have stood, as is shown by the δέ of verse 20. Verse 19 runs: *μὴ θησαυρίζετε ὑμῖν θησαυροὺς ἐπὶ τῆς γῆς, ὅπου σὴς καὶ βρῶσις ἀφανίζει, καὶ ὅπου κλέπται διορύσσουσιν καὶ κλέπτουσιν.* Only, if reference had been made to treasures upon earth, do the moth and the thief explain themselves.

St. Matt. vii. 13:	St. Luke xiii. 24:
Εἰσέλθατε διὰ τῆς στενῆς πύλης· ὅτι πλατεῖα [ἡ πύλη] καὶ εὐρύχωρος ἡ ὁδὸς ἡ ἀπάγουσα εἰς τὴν ἀπώλειαν, καὶ πολλοί εἰσιν οἱ εἰσερχόμενοι δι' αὐτῆς· (14) ὅτι στενὴ ἡ πύλη καὶ τεθλιμμένη ἡ ὁδὸς ἡ ἀπάγουσα εἰς τὴν ζωήν, καὶ ὀλίγοι εἰσὶν οἱ εὑρίσκοντες αὐτήν.	ἀγωνίζεσθε εἰσελθεῖν διὰ τῆς στενῆς θύρας, ὅτι πολλοί, λέγω ὑμῖν, ζητήσουσιν εἰσελθεῖν καὶ οὐκ ἰσχύσουσιν.

As in the former passage, so here St. Luke gives only an extract, wherein, however, he develops the teaching by means of *ἀγωνίζεσθε* and *ζητήσουσιν* (*ἀγωνίζεσθαι*, a classical word not found elsewhere in the gospels, though it occurs in St. Paul; St. Luke also writes *ἐζητήσαμεν ἐξελθεῖν* in Acts xvi. 10, and a *ζητεῖν* which is not given in St. Matthew is also found in St. Luke's parallel to St. Matt. x. 39; with *οὐκ ἰσχύειν*, compare also St. Luke vi. 48, viii. 43, xiv. 6, xiv. 30, xvi. 3, xx. 26; Acts vi. 10, xxv. 7). The converse theory that St. Matthew here, and in vi. 19 f., has worked up a shorter text (Wellhausen), is absolutely incapable of proof. St. Luke has written *θύρα* for *πύλη*, because he omitted "the way," so that *θύρα* would more naturally suggest itself. St. Luke thinks of the door of a house (*vide* also the following verse 25); Q and St. Matthew think of the gate of a city.

St. Matt. vii. 16: ἀπὸ τῶν καρπῶν ἐπιγνώσεσθε αὐτούς· μήτι συλλέγουσιν ἀπὸ ἀκανθῶν σταφυλὰς ἢ ἀπὸ τριβόλων σῦκα; (17) οὕτως πᾶν δένδρον ἀγαθὸν καρποὺς καλοὺς ποιεῖ, τὸ δὲ σαπρὸν δένδρον καρποὺς πονηροὺς ποιεῖ. (18) οὐ δύναται δένδρον ἀγαθὸν καρποὺς πονηροὺς ἐνεγκεῖν, οὐδὲ δένδρον σαπρὸν καρποὺς καλοὺς ποιεῖν.

Cf. also St. Matt. xii. 33: ἢ ποιήσατε τὸ δένδρον καλὸν καὶ τὸν καρπὸν αὐτοῦ καλόν, ἢ ποιήσατε τὸ δένδρον σαπρὸν καὶ τὸν καρπὸν αὐτοῦ σαπρόν· ἐκ γὰρ τοῦ καρποῦ τὸ δένδρον γινώσκεται.

St. Luke vi. 44, 43: ἕκαστον δένδρον ἐκ τοῦ ἰδίου καρποῦ γινώσκεται· οὐ γὰρ ἐξ ἀκανθῶν συλλέγουσιν σῦκα, οὐδὲ ἐκ βάτου σταφυλὴν τρυγῶσιν. (43) οὐ[γάρ] ἐστιν δένδρον καλὸν ποιοῦν καρπὸν σαπρόν, οὐδὲ [πάλιν] δένδρον σαπρὸν ποιοῦν καρπὸν καλόν.

St. Matthew found the saying in two sources, and therefore gives it twice, probably intermingling the two forms. Which of the two sources is Q, is to be determined by comparison with St. Luke. (In regard to the order of the clauses—whether St. Luke verse 44, stood before verse 43—we are no longer in a position to say anything definite.) We may be sure that Q had the words ἐκ τοῦ καρποῦ τὸ δένδρον γινώσκεται (ἕκαστον was probably added by St. Luke—an interpolation of the same character as the πᾶς which he is so fond of inserting in the text—likewise ἰδίου, which is, moreover, wanting in D). Also the rhetorical question of St. Matthew 16[b] is original; St. Luke has often removed such rhetorical questions (*vide supra* on St. Matt. v. 46, 47). Βάτος is a more choice expression than τρίβολος, and is therefore secondary, and the Lukan distinction between συλλέγειν and τρυγᾶν is certainly appropriate, but for that very reason it can scarcely be original. St. Luke chose the singular σταφυλήν, because he had also replaced the plural τριβ. by the singular βάτος. The 17th verse of St. Matthew is wanting in St. Luke; the latter may have considered it superfluous. (It is nevertheless a Semitic practice to give positive and negative expression to the same thought in adjacent clauses.) For οὐ δύναται . . . ἐνεγκεῖν . . . ποιεῖν, St. Luke reads: οὐκ ἔστιν . . . ποιοῦν . . . ποιοῦν—this participial construction is Lukan; the evangelist probably also wished to avoid an infinitive aorist and present in close connection. It is, moreover, noteworthy that neither ἤνεγκον nor any of its derivatives are found in St. Luke's gospel. The singular καρπόν in St. Luke and St. Matt. xii. 33, together with the adjectives καλός and *σαπρός* (see likewise St. Matt. xii. 33) must have stood in Q.

St. Matt. vii. 21: *οὐ πᾶς ὁ λέγων μοι κύριε κύριε εἰσελεύσεται εἰς τὴν βασιλείαν τῶν οὐρανῶν, ἀλλ' ὁ ποιῶν τὸ θέλημα τοῦ πατρός μου τοῦ ἐν τοῖς οὐρανοῖς.*	St. Luke vi. 46–49; vii. 1: *τί δέ με καλεῖτε κύριε κύριε, καὶ οὐ ποιεῖτε ἃ λέγω;*
(24) *πᾶς οὖν ὅστις ἀκούει μου τοὺς λόγους τούτους καὶ ποιεῖ αὐτούς ὁμοιωθήσεται ἀνδρὶ φρονίμῳ ὅστις ᾠκοδόμησεν αὐτοῦ τὴν οἰκίαν ἐπὶ τὴν πέτραν.* (25) *καὶ κατέβη ἡ βροχὴ καὶ ἦλθον οἱ ποταμοὶ καὶ ἔπνευσαν οἱ ἄνεμοι καὶ προσέπεσαν τῇ οἰκίᾳ ἐκείνῃ, καὶ οὐκ ἔπεσεν· τεθεμελίωτο γὰρ ἐπὶ τὴν πέτραν.* (26) *καὶ πᾶς ὁ ἀκούων μου τοὺς λόγους τούτους καὶ μὴ ποιῶν αὐτοὺς ὁμοιωθήσεται ἀνδρὶ μωρῷ, ὅστις ᾠκοδόμησεν αὐτοῦ τὴν οἰκίαν ἐπὶ τὴν ἄμμον.* (27) *καὶ κατέβη ἡ βροχὴ καὶ ἦλθον οἱ ποταμοὶ καὶ ἔπνευσαν οἱ ἄνεμοι καὶ προσέκοψαν τῇ οἰκίᾳ ἐκείνῃ, καὶ ἔπεσεν,*	(47) *πᾶς οὖν ἐρχόμενος πρός με καὶ ἀκούων μου τῶν λόγων καὶ ποιῶν αὐτούς, ὑποδείξω ὑμῖν τίνι ἐστὶν ὅμοιος.* (48) *ὅμοιός ἐστιν ἀνθρώπῳ οἰκοδομοῦντι οἰκίαν, ὃς ἔσκαψεν καὶ ἐβάθυνεν καὶ ἔθηκεν θεμέλιον ἐπὶ τὴν πέτραν. πλημμύρης δὲ γενομένης προσέρηξεν ὁ ποταμὸς τῇ οἰκίᾳ ἐκείνῃ καὶ οὐκ ἴσχυσεν σαλεῦσαι αὐτὴν διὰ τὸ καλῶς οἰκοδομῆσθαι αὐτήν.* (49) *ὁ δὲ ἀκούσας καὶ μὴ ποιήσας ὅμοιός ἐστιν ἀνθρώπῳ οἰκοδομήσαντι οἰκίαν ἐπὶ τὴν γῆν χωρὶς θεμελίου, ᾗ προσέρηξεν ὁ ποταμός, καὶ εὐθὺς συνέπεσεν, καὶ ἐγένετο τὸ ῥῆγμα τῆς οἰκίας ἐκείνης μέγα.*

καὶ ἦν ἡ πτῶσις αὐτῆς μεγάλη.

(vii. 28, viii. 5) καὶ ἐγένετο ὅτε ἐτέλεσεν ὁ Ἰησοῦς τοὺς λόγους τούτους . . . εἰσελθόντος δὲ αὐτοῦ εἰς Καφαρναούμ . . .

(vii. 1) ἐπειδὴ ἐπλήρωσεν πάντα τὰ ῥήματα αὐτοῦ . . . εἰσῆλθεν εἰς Καφαρναούμ.

It may be questioned whether St. Matt. vii. 21 and St. Luke vi. 46 are really derived from Q. The common source perhaps lies far in the background of time, and we may not with absolute certainty claim the verse for Q. If, however, an attempt is made to reconstruct Q, then ὁ λέγων μοι κύριε is, in respect of originality, certainly to be preferred to καλεῖν με κύριε, and "to do the will of my Father" to "my words." St. Matt. 22, 23 and St. Luke xiii. 26, 27 are quite independent of one another (I have therefore refrained from printing these verses in the above passage), even though here also a common source lies far in the background. It is most probable that we have here genuine instances of translation-variants—compare ὁμολογήσω αὐτοῖς ὅτι οὐδέποτε ἔγνων ὑμᾶς· ἀποχωρεῖτε ἀπ' ἐμοῦ οἱ ἐργαζόμενοι τὴν ἀνομίαν with λέγω ὑμῖν, οὐκ οἶδα πόθεν ἐστέ· ἀπόστητε ἀπ' ἐμοῦ πάντες ἐργάται ἀδικίας. In regard to the parable which certainly stood in the common source, Wellhausen has remarked that in St. Luke it is more lifelike, and that its reference to the different characters of the Christian community is more obvious and distinct. Even if this were so, it would have little weight in determining the superior originality of St. Luke's version. But I cannot share Wellhausen's impression, except perhaps in the case of the very descriptive words: ὃς ἔσκαψεν καὶ ἐβάθυνεν καὶ ἔθηκεν θεμέλιον. St. Matthew often omits such descriptions, so that these words are perhaps original (yet, on the other hand, we have ground for hesitation in the fact that the first two verbs are found in the New Testament only in St. Luke; σκάπτειν again in xiii. 8 and xvi. 3; I shall, however, return to this point). As for the rest, the text of St. Matthew for the most part deserves the preference (with perhaps the exception of ὑποδείξω κτλ. in St. Luke, for this ὑποδείξω receives a certain attestation from another passage in Q, viz. St. Matt. iii. 7 = St. Luke iii. 7, and is once again omitted by St. Matthew in x. 28, *cf.* St. Luke xii. 5). The introduction of the parable accordingly ran perhaps somewhat as follows: πᾶς οὖν ὅστις ἀκούει μου τοὺς λόγους τούτους καὶ ποιεῖ αὐτούς, ὑποδείξω ὑμῖν τίνι ἐστὶν ὅμοιος. ὅμοιός ἐστιν κτλ. And yet it may very well be that ὑποδείξω was inserted by St. Luke, and that the somewhat illogical future passive ὁμοιοθήσεται has in this case a claim to originality. St. Matthew writes: πᾶς οὖν ὅστις ἀκούει καὶ ποιεῖ, St. Luke in better Greek: πᾶς οὖν (ἐρχόμενος πρός με καὶ) ἀκούων καὶ ποιῶν. St. Matthew writes: ἀνδρὶ ὅστις ᾠκοδόμησεν, St. Luke: ἀνθρώπῳ οἰκοδομοῦντι. St. Matthew, αὐτοῦ τὴν οἰκίαν, St. Luke in better Greek: οἰκίαν. St. Matthew: καὶ κατέβη ἡ βροχή, St. Luke avoids the vulgar βροχή, and writes in the genitive absolute πλημμύρης γενομένης. St. Matthew thinks of storms of rain and wind, but to St. Luke it seemed improbable that these could overturn a house, and he therefore supplies a flooded river. For οὐκ ἴσχυσεν, as Lukan, *vide supra* on St. Luke xiii. 24. St. Matthew writes: πᾶς ὁ ἀκούων καὶ μὴ ποιῶν, St. Luke more correctly: ὁ δὲ ἀκούσας καὶ μὴ ποιήσας. St. Matthew writes: ἐπὶ τὴν ἄμμον, St. Luke—because he saw that a man could build a house firmly even on sand—writes: ἐπὶ τὴν γῆν χωρὶς θεμελίου. As these words are certainly added by St. Luke, it is therefore improbable that the "ἔθηκεν θεμέλιον" occurring in a former verse stood in Q. This, however, also renders "ἔσκαψεν καὶ ἐβάθυνεν" very doubtful. The original parable simply distinguished between the house on the rock and the house on the sand, just as St. Matthew gives it. The thought that a good foundation depends *upon labour* is first introduced by St. Luke, and was suggested by the words in Q: τεθεμελίωτο ἐπὶ τὴν πέτραν, where, however, the emphasis rests upon πέτραν. Why indeed should St. Matthew have omitted this trait if he had found it in his exemplar? On the other hand, it is quite intelligible that the simple contrast of "rock and sand" did not seem sufficient to a later writer, who reflected that still everything depended upon the laying a good foundation, whatever the nature of the soil might be. Moreover, συμπίπτειν is certainly less original than the simple πίπτειν, and it is very clear that the words speaking of a great breach are a correction; for "the falling was great" is a solecism. In St. Matthew φρόνιμος and μωρός alone cannot be claimed for Q; for μωρός is exclusively confined to St. Matthew among the four evangelists (occurring seven times in the first gospel), and φρόνιμος also occurs in this gospel seven times (never in St. Mark, twice in St. Luke).

It is a most important point that St. Matt. vii. 28 and viii. 5 have a parallel in St. Luke vii. 1; for from this it follows with certainty that even in Q large portions of the Sermon on the Mount occurred together, and that the Sermon was followed by the Cure of the Centurion's Servant in Capernaum. But both evangelists have altered the wording here; for ἐγένετο ὅτε ἐτέλεσεν is a phrase that is often repeated by St. Matthew (*vide* xi. 1, xiii. 53, xix. 1, xxvi. 1), and the genitive absolute (εἰσελθόντος αὐτοῦ), which is added, likewise shows the secondary character of the text of St. Matthew at this point. But the Lukan text is shown to be secondary by ἐπειδή (never occurring in St. Matthew, St. Mark, and St. John; five times, however, in St. Luke's gospel and Acts), as well as by πάντα τὰ ῥήματα (never occurring in St. Matthew, St. Mark, and St. John; thrice again in St. Luke). There seems, therefore, no hope of recovering the original wording of the source before the words εἰσῆλθεν εἰς Καφαρναούμ.

St. Matt. viii. 5:	St. Luke vii. 1–10. . . .
Εἰσελθόντος δὲ αὐτοῦ εἰς Καφαρναοὺμ προσῆλθεν αὐτῷ ἑκατόνταρχος παρακαλῶν αὐτὸν (6) καὶ λέγων· κύριε, ὁ παῖς μου βέβληται ἐν τῇ οἰκίᾳ παραλυτικός, δεινῶς βασανιζόμενος. (7) λέγει	εἰσῆλθεν εἰς Καφαρναούμ. (2) ἑκατοντάρχου δέ τινος δοῦλος κακῶς ἔχων ἤμελλεν τελευτᾶν, ὃς ἦν αὐτῷ ἔντιμος. (3) ἀκούσας δὲ περὶ τοῦ Ἰησοῦ ἀπέστειλεν πρὸς αὐτὸν πρεσβυτέρους τῶν Ἰου-

αὐτῷ· ἐγὼ ἐλθὼν θεραπεύσω αὐτόν. (8) ἀποκριθεὶς δὲ ὁ ἑκατόνταρχος ἔφη· κύριε, οὐκ εἰμὶ ἱκανὸς ἵνα μου ὑπὸ τὴν στέγην εἰσέλθῃς· ἀλλὰ μόνον εἰπὲ λόγῳ, καὶ ἰαθήσεται ὁ παῖς μου. (9) καὶ γὰρ ἐγὼ ἄνθρωπός εἰμι ὑπὸ ἐξουσίαν, ἔχων ὑπ' ἐμαυτὸν στρατιώτας, καὶ λέγω τούτῳ· πορεύθητι, καὶ πορεύεται, καὶ ἄλλῳ· ἔρχου, καὶ ἔρχεται, καὶ τῷ δούλῳ μου· ποίησον τοῦτο, καὶ ποιεῖ. (10) ἀκούσας δὲ ὁ Ἰησοῦς ἐθαύμασεν καὶ εἶπεν τοῖς ἀκολουθοῦσιν· ἀμὴν λέγω ὑμῖν, οὐδὲ ἐν τῷ Ἰσραὴλ τοσαύτην πίστιν εὗρον.

(13) καὶ εἶπεν ὁ Ἰησοῦς τῷ ἑκατοντάρχῃ· ὕπαγε, ὡς ἐπίστευσας γενηθήτω σοι· καὶ ἰάθη ὁ παῖς ἐν τῇ ὥρᾳ ἐκείνῃ.

δαίων, ἐρωτῶν αὐτὸν ὅπως ἐλθὼν διασώσῃ τὸν δοῦλον αὐτοῦ. (4) οἱ δὲ παραγενόμενοι πρὸς τὸν Ἰησοῦν παρεκάλουν αὐτὸν σπουδαίως, λέγοντες ὅτι ἄξιός ἐστιν ᾧ παρέξῃ τοῦτο. (5) ἀγαπᾷ γὰρ τὸ ἔθνος ἡμῶν καὶ τὴν συναγωγὴν αὐτὸς ᾠκοδόμησεν ἡμῖν. (6) ὁ δὲ Ἰησοῦς ἐπορεύετο σὺν αὐτοῖς. ἤδη δὲ αὐτοῦ οὐ μακρὰν ἀπέχοντος ἀπὸ τῆς οἰκίας, ἔπεμψεν φίλους ὁ ἑκατοντάρχης λέγων αὐτῷ· κύριε, μὴ σκύλλου· οὐ γὰρ ἱκανός εἰμι ἵνα ὑπὸ τὴν στέγην μου εἰσέλθῃς· (7) διὸ οὐδὲ ἐμαυτὸν ἠξίωσα πρὸς σὲ ἐλθεῖν· ἀλλὰ εἰπὲ λόγῳ, καὶ ἰαθήτω ὁ παῖς μου. (8) καὶ γὰρ ἐγὼ ἄνθρωπός εἰμι ὑπὸ ἐξουσίαν τασσόμενος, ἔχων ὑπ' ἐμαυτὸν στρατιώτας, καὶ λέγω τούτῳ· πορεύθητι, καὶ πορεύεται, καὶ ἄλλῳ· ἔρχου, καὶ ἔρχεται, καὶ τῷ δούλῳ μου· ποίησον τοῦτο, καὶ ποιεῖ. (9)

ἀκούσας δὲ ταῦτα ὁ Ἰησοῦς ἐθαύμασεν αὐτόν, καὶ στραφεὶς τῷ ἀκολουθοῦντι αὐτῷ ὄχλῳ εἶπεν· λέγω ὑμῖν, οὐδὲ ἐν τῷ Ἰσραὴλ τοσαύτην πίστιν εὗρον.

(10) καὶ ὑποστρέψαντες εἰς τὸν οἶκον οἱ πεμφθέντες εὗρον τὸν δοῦλον ὑγιαίνοντα.

In this section at least it is obvious that all traits in St. Luke different from or in addition to St. Matthew do not proceed from Q, and that St. Matthew thus transmits the source in the more original form. The two deputations to our Lord (in place of the personal interview of the centurion) are a later addition. This is strikingly shown (1) by the fact that the long speech which St. Luke assigns to the friends is intelligible and appropriate only if it was spoken by the centurion himself, and (2) because also in St. John (iv. 46 ff.) the centurion (βασιλικός) comes himself. An attempt to distinguish between that portion of the additional matter in St. Luke which perhaps came to him through tradition, and that for which he himself is solely responsible, is under such circumstances unnecessary. I would only remark that ἔντιμος (verse 2), οἱ παραγενόμενοι (verse 4), σπουδαίως (verse 4), μακρὰν ἀπέχειν (verse 6), διό (verse 7), ἀξιοῦν (verse 7), the passive τάσσεσθαι (verse 8) are, as far as the gospels are concerned, exclusively Lukan (διό alone occurs once in St. Matthew); and, again, that it is in the style of St. Luke to supply objects to the verbs (*cf.* St. Matthew verse 10 and St. Luke verse 9), and likewise to add τὶς (*cf.* St. Matthew verse 5 and St. Luke verse 2). Again, διασώζειν can be claimed as Lukan, as well as the alternation between ἀπέστειλεν (verse 3) and ἔπεμψεν (verse 6), and the pleonastic στραφείς (verse 9). It cannot be shown that St. Matthew has altered the text of Q (note among other things the ἐγώ of verse 7, which is so characteristic of Q); moreover, traces of this text still appear throughout St. Luke's version, even at the beginning of the narrative where the transformation is so complete (*vide* also παῖς of St. Luke verse 7, while δοῦλος is used in verse 2). Thus τοῖς ἀκολουθοῦσιν (St. Luke, τῷ ἀκολουθοῦντι αὐτῷ ὄχλῳ) is also original, probably also the ἀμήν. With the μὴ σκύλλου of St. Luke verse 6, compare St. Luke viii. 49 (St. Mark v. 35). The concluding verse has a completely different form in St. Matthew and St. Luke. Later I shall give what I believe to be sufficient justification for the bold hypothesis that this verse did not stand in Q. Here I would only point out that St. Matt. viii. 13 is almost exactly like St. Matt. xv. 28 (Canaanitish woman), while St. Luke winds up the passage with a conclusion of conventional character.

St. Matt. viii. 11:	St. Luke xiii. 28, 29:
Λέγω δὲ ὑμῖν ὅτι πολλοὶ ἀπὸ ἀνατολῶν καὶ δυσ-	ἐκεῖ ἔσται ὁ κλαυθμὸς καὶ ὁ βρυγμὸς τῶν

μῶν ἥξουσιν καὶ ἀνακλιθήσονται μετὰ Ἀβραὰμ καὶ Ἰσαὰκ καὶ Ἰακὼβ ἐν τῇ βασιλείᾳ τῶν οὐρανῶν· (12) οἱ δὲ υἱοὶ τῆς βασιλείας ἐκβληθήσονται [ἐξελεύσονται] εἰς τὸ σκότος τὸ ἐξώτερον· ἐκεῖ ἔσται ὁ κλαυθμὸς καὶ ὁ βρυγμὸς τῶν ὀδόντων.

ὀδόντων, ὅταν ὄψεσθε Ἀβραὰμ καὶ Ἰσαὰκ καὶ Ἰακὼβ καὶ πάντας τοὺς προφήτας ἐν τῇ βασιλείᾳ τοῦ θεοῦ, ὑμᾶς δὲ ἐκβαλλομένους ἔξω. (29) καὶ ἥξουσιν ἀπὸ ἀνατολῶν καὶ δυσμῶν καὶ [ἀπὸ] βορρᾶ καὶ νότου, καὶ ἀνακλιθήσονται ἐν τῇ βασιλείᾳ τοῦ θεοῦ.

If we represent the order of the component clauses of St. Matthew's version of the saying by the series 1, 2^a, 2^b, 2^c, 3, 4, then the order of St. Luke is given by the series 4, 2^b, 2^c, 3, 1, 2^a, 2^c. It is here evident that 4 occupies a false position at the beginning, for ἐκεῖ is thus out of connection (it does not connect with xiii. 27); hence 4 after 3, the order of St. Matthew, is original; 2^c (ἐν τῇ βασιλείᾳ τ. θ.) occurs twice in St. Luke, which of itself shows that $2^{a,b,c}$ belong together, and that 2^a (καὶ ανακλιθήσονται) is thus in place at the beginning, coming after 1. The order of St. Matthew is accordingly original. The change of order in St. Luke is due to the transposition of 4 (ἐκεῖ κτλ.) to the beginning, for which the reason is not obvious. This required further transpositions and also the interpolation of ὄψεσθε (so that the thought of the passage now reminds us of the Rich Man in Hades). Πάντας τοὺς προθήτας is also secondary; also ὄψεσθε with double accusative is Lukan. If in St. Matthew, ἐξελεύσονται is the right reading, as is probable, it is then the translation of the Aramaic *N'phaq*, which acts as the passive to *Appeq* (ἐκβάλλειν)—*vide* Wellhausen; but St. Luke here has not given a new and better translation of the Aramaic word, but has simply replaced the poor Greek ἐξελεύσονται by ἐκβαλλομένους. The phrase εἰς τ. σκότος τ. ἐξώτερον occurs in the New Testament only in St. Matthew, and that thrice (*vide* xxii. 13, xxv. 30). Here also it is inserted by the evangelist, who again probably introduced πολλοί at the beginning (elsewhere it is not unusual for St. Luke to supply subjects to subjectless verbs). On the other hand, *Borras* and *Notos* certainly belong to the Hellenic evangelist.

[St. Matt. x. 7: πορευόμενοι δὲ κηρύσσετε λέγοντες ὅτι ἤγγικεν ἡ βασιλεία τῶν οὐρανῶν.]	[St. Luke ix. 2: ἀπέστειλεν αὐτοὺς κηρύσσειν τὴν βασιλείαν τοῦ θεοῦ καὶ ἰᾶσθαι].
(12) εἰσερχόμενοι δὲ εἰς τὴν οἰκίαν ἀσπάσασθε αὐτήν· (13) καὶ ἐὰν μὲν ᾖ ἡ οἰκία ἀξία, ἐλθάτω ἡ εἰρήνη ὑμῶν ἐπ' αὐτήν· ἐὰν δὲ μὴ ᾖ ἀξία, ἡ εἰρήνη ὑμῶν πρὸς ὑμᾶς ἐπιστραφήτω.	(x. 5): εἰς ἣν δ' ἂν εἰσέλθητε οἰκίαν, πρῶτον λέγετε· εἰρήνη, τῷ οἴκῳ τούτῳ. (6) καὶ ἐὰν ᾖ ἐκεῖ υἱὸς εἰρήνης, ἐπαναπαήσεται ἐπ' αὐτὸν ἡ εἰρήνη ὑμῶν· εἰ δὲ μήγε, ἐφ' ὑμᾶς ἀνακάμψει.
(24) οὐκ ἔστιν μαθητὴς ὑπὲρ τὸν διδάσκαλον οὐδὲ δοῦλος ὑπὲρ τὸν κύριον αὐτοῦ. (25) ἀρκετὸν τῷ μαθητῇ, ἵνα γένηται ὡς ὁ διδάσκαλος αὐτοῦ, καὶ ὁ δοῦλος ὡς ὁ κύριος αὐτοῦ.	(vi. 40): οὐκ ἔστιν μαθητὴς ὑπὲρ τὸν διδάσκαλον· κατηρτισμένος δὲ πᾶς ἔσται ὡς ὁ διδάσκαλος αὐτοῦ.

St. Luke has transformed the direct discourse of St. Matt. x. 7 into narrative. The words καὶ ἰᾶσθαι are a Lukan interpolation, as is suggested by the fact that our Lord's work of healing is the chief point of interest with St. Luke. He also delights to give special emphasis to the *Mission* of the disciples. Again, the record that the Kingdom was the subject of their preaching is of later character than the tradition that it consisted of the proclamation "ἤγγικεν." It is, however, very questionable whether we are at all justified in assigning this clause to Q.

The conjunctive relative (St. Luke x. 5) is a construction which is very frequent in St. Luke, belonging to the characteristics which distinguish his style from those of the other evangelists, with whom it is of rare occurrence. Εἰσέλθητε is a grammatical improvement upon εἰσερχόμενοι. St. Luke has also avoided ἀσπάζεσθαι in St. Matt. v. 47; he substitutes the words of the greeting itself, deriving them from what follows. It is also undoubtedly due to later reflexion that the worthiness of a single inhabitant of the house replaces the worthiness of the whole house. Moreover, St. Luke elsewhere uses the phrases, "sons of light" (xvi. 8), "of this generation" (*l.c.* and xx. 34), "of consolation" (Acts iv. 36), "of the Resurrection" (St. Luke xx. 36). Nothing similar is found in St. Matthew. Ἄξιος, used absolutely, is also found in St. Matt. x. 11 and xxii. 8; St. Luke has avoided it (on linguistic grounds rightly). Ἐπαναπαήσεται (for ἐλθάτω ἐπ' αὐτήν) is found again in the New Testament only in Rom. ii. 17, and shows by the repeated preposition that it is alien to the simple language of the source. St. Luke reads εἰ for ἐάν, as (*vide supra*) in St. Matt. v. 46, 47 (εἰ is rare in Q). The middle ἐπιστρέφεσθαι is avoided by St. Luke in the gospel and the Acts (see, on the other hand, St. Matt. ix. 22; St. Mark v. 30, viii. 33; St. John xxi. 20); it probably belonged to the vulgar idiom.

In St. Matt. x. 24 f., St. Luke seems to me to have omitted the clause concerning the lord and the servant because it was superfluous and sounded quite trivial. That the second half of the verse in St. Luke proceeds from the same source as St. Matthew, is shown by the words ὡς ὁ διδάσκαλος αὐτοῦ. It is therefore impossible to accept Wellhausen's theory that we have here an instance of faulty translation from the Aramaic, and that πᾶς must be taken adverbially (= perfectly). St. Luke has often inserted πᾶς, and the reason why he has here made such drastic changes is easily seen. Verse 25 in St. Matthew (*i.e.* in the source) sounded as if every scholar could without difficulty become as his master; St. Luke somewhat pedantically wished to make such an inference impossible. Also κατηρτισμένος, which does not occur elsewhere in the gospels, though indeed in St. Paul (Rom. ix. 22; 1 Cor. i. 10; 2 Cor. xiii. 11; *cf.* Heb. xi. 3), is a word of somewhat choice character, and hence points to the style of St. Luke. Ἀρκετόν occurs once again in St. Matt. vi. 34, otherwise not in the New Testament (St. Matt. vi. 34 also comes probably from Q, but the parallel is wanting in St. Luke). The text of St. Matthew in this passage shows no trace of secondary elements. Even the ἤγγικεν of verse 7 is original; the narrative form of the parallel verse in St. Luke made it not very easy to include this word, *vide supra.*

St. Matt. x. 27: ὃ λέγω ὑμῖν ἐν τῇ σκοτίᾳ, εἴπατε ἐν τῷ φωτί· καὶ ὃ εἰς τὸ οὖς ἀκούετε, κηρύξατε ἐπὶ τῶν δωμάτων. (28) καὶ μὴ φοβεῖσθε ἀπὸ τῶν ἀποκτεννόντων τὸ σῶμα, τὴν δὲ ψυχὴν μὴ δυναμένων ἀποκτεῖναι· φοβεῖσθε δὲ μᾶλλον τὸν δυνάμενον καὶ ψυχὴν καὶ σῶμα ἀπολέσαι ἐν γεέννῃ. (29) οὐχὶ δύο στρουθία ἀσσαρίου πωλεῖται; καὶ ἓν ἐξ αὐτῶν οὐ πεσεῖται ἐπὶ τὴν γῆν ἄνευ τοῦ πατρὸς ὑμῶν. (30) ὑμῶν δὲ καὶ αἱ τρίχες τῆς κεφαλῆς πᾶσαι ἠριθμημέναι εἰσίν. (31) μὴ οὖν φοβεῖσθε· πολλῶν στρουθίων διαφέρετε ὑμεῖς. (32) πᾶς οὖν ὅστις ὁμολογήσει ἐν ἐμοὶ ἔμπροσθεν τῶν ἀνθρώπων, ὁμολογήσω κἀγὼ ἐν αὐτῷ ἔμπροσθεν τοῦ πατρός μου τοῦ ἐν τοῖς οὐρανοῖς. (33) ὅστις δὲ ἀρνήσηταί με ἔμπροσθεν τῶν ἀνθρώπων, ἀρνήσομαι

St. Luke xii. 3: ὅσα ἐν τῇ σκοτίᾳ εἴπατε, ἐν τῷ φωτὶ ἀκουσθήσεται, καὶ ὃ πρὸς τὸ οὖς ἐλαλήσατε ἐν τοῖς ταμείοις, κηρυχθήσεται ἐπὶ τῶν δωμάτων. (4) λέγω δὲ ὑμῖν τοῖς φίλοις μου, μὴ φοβηθῆτε ἀπὸ τῶν ἀποκτεννόντων τὸ σῶμα καὶ μετὰ ταῦτα μὴ ἐχόντων περισσότερόν τι ποιῆσαι· (5) ὑποδείξω δὲ ὑμῖν τίνα φοβηθῆτε· φοβήθητε τὸν μετὰ τὸ ἀποκτεῖναι ἔχοντα ἐξουσίαν ἐμβαλεῖν εἰς τὴν γέενναν· ναί, λέγω ὑμῖν, τοῦτον φοβήθητε. (6) οὐχὶ πέντε στρουθία πωλοῦνται ἀσσαρίων δύο; καὶ ἓν ἐξ αὐτῶν οὐκ ἔστιν ἐπιλελησμένον ἐνώπιον τοῦ θεοῦ. (7) ἀλλὰ καὶ αἱ τρίχες τῆς κεφαλῆς ὑμῶν πᾶσαι ἠρίθμηνται. μὴ φοβεῖσθε· πολλῶν στρουθίων διαφέρετε. (8) λέγω δὲ ὑμῖν, πᾶς ὃς ἂν ὁμολογήσῃ ἐν ἐμοὶ ἔμπροσθεν τῶν ἀνθρώπων, καὶ ὁ υἱὸς τοῦ ἀνθρώπου κἀγὼ αὐτὸν ἔμπροσθεν τοῦ πατρός μου τοῦ ἐν τοῖς οὐρανοῖς.

ὁμολογήσει ἐν αὐτῷ ἔμ-
προσθεν τῶν ἀγγέλων τοῦ
θεοῦ. (9) ὁ δὲ ἀρνησά-
μενός με ἐνώπιον τῶν
ἀνθρώπων ἀπαρνηθήσεται
ἐνώπιον τῶν ἀγγέλων τοῦ
θεοῦ.

Wellhausen recognises, in his remarks on St. Matthew verse 7, that St. Luke is here secondary. Probably he wished that our Lord should not appear as a mystagogue.—As he had already used εἴπατε in the protasis he wrote ἀκουσθήσεται in the apodosis, and then he was again obliged to alter ἀκούετε and to replace it by ἐλαλήσατε; moreover, ἀκούειν with εἰς τὸ οὖς offended his sense of style as an uncouth construction; St. Luke substitutes the more correct λαλεῖν πρὸς τὸ οὖς. Again, ὅσα is more correct than ὅ. Then κηρύξατε is changed into κηρυχθήσεται parallel to ἀκουσθήσεται. Finally, the contrast, "ear and housetop," was too grotesque for the Hellenic artist; he therefore softened it by interpolating "in the secret chambers."

Coming to St. Matthew verse 28, we see that the λέγω ὑμῖν τοῖς φίλοις μου can scarcely be original. St. Luke felt the faulty connection of the two verses, and therefore begins a new paragraph; moreover, "φίλοι" is a characteristic word which belongs both to the Lukan and the Johannine writings. Μὴ φοβηθῆτε is more elegant than μὴ φοβεῖσθε (St. Luke has allowed the present in St. Matthew verse 31 to stand). St. Luke says nothing concerning "the slaying of the soul"; it is not clear for what reason (he also omits "the soul" in verse 5). I conjecture that "the slaying of the soul" was a monstrous idea to the Hellenic evangelist (and besides περισσότερόν τι betrays the Lukan style). The ὑποδείξω of St. Luke may be original, but need not be so (*vide* on St. Matt. vii. 24); it stands in place of μᾶλλον, which is incorrect Greek. Again, ἀπολέσαι ἐν γεέννῃ is bad Greek; St. Luke substitutes ἐμβαλεῖν εἰς. By the repetition of λέγω and φοβήθητε at the close of the verse, St. Luke yet again points to its importance. Naturally this emphasis is not original.

The existence of the variants, "two sparrows for a farthing" and "five sparrows for two farthings" (verse 29[a]), is an enigma. Had sparrows become cheaper? In 29[b] no one will doubt that St. Matthew has the original text. This is shown also in the phraseology: ἐνώπιον is peculiar to St. Luke among the synoptists (it does not occur in St. Matthew and St. Mark), and οὐκ ἔστιν ἐπιλελησμ. is the language of literature. St. Matthew's πατὴρ ὑμῶν for θεός (*vide supra* on St. Matt. vi. 26) is alone secondary.

In St. Matthew verse 30, St. Luke's arrangement of the words is grammatically more correct, but that of St. Matthew better suits the sense, and is accordingly more original; ἠρίθμηνται is of course a correction for ἠριθμημέναι εἰσίν. St. Luke replaces the weak δέ by the stronger word ἀλλά.

In St. Matthew verse 31, Wellhausen is right in asserting that we have here an instance of false translation from the Aramaic (πολλῶν in place of πολλῷ); but the error already occurred in Q, for St. Luke also gives a similar text. The pronominal subject (ὑμεῖς) is omitted by St. Luke, as is so often the case. The οὖν in St. Matthew is doubtful.

St. Matt. 32 f.: St. Luke again marks the new thought by introducing the words λέγω δὲ ὑμῖν. "Son of Man," which he reads in his version of verse 32, cannot be original; for in verse 33 he also has the "I" (like St. Matthew in both places). However, ἔμπροσθεν τ. ἀγγέλων is certainly original (*vide* St. Mark viii. 38); here again we find support for the theory that St. Matthew has probably often inserted the phrases, "my Father which is in heaven," "the Father which is in heaven," into his source. In verse 33 both the participle ὁ ἀρνησάμενος as well as ἐνώπιον and ἀπαρνηθήσεται (for ἀρνήσομαι κἀγὼ αὐτόν) are Lukan (St. Luke uses the passive more frequently than the other evangelists).

St. Matt. x. 34: μὴ νομίσητε ὅτι ἦλθον βαλεῖν εἰρήνην ἐπὶ τὴν γῆν· οὐκ ἦλθον βαλεῖν εἰρήνην ἀλλὰ μάχαιραν. (35) ἦλθον γὰρ διχάσαι ἄνθρωπον κατὰ τοῦ πατρὸς αὐτοῦ καὶ θυγατέρα κατὰ τῆς μητρὸς αὐτῆς καὶ νύμφην κατὰ τῆς πενθερᾶς αὐτῆς. [(37) ὁ φιλῶν πατέρα ἢ μητέρα ὑπὲρ ἐμὲ οὐκ ἔστιν μου ἄξιος· καὶ ὁ φιλῶν υἱὸν ἢ

St. Luke xii. 51: δοκεῖτε ὅτι εἰρήνην παρεγενόμην δοῦναι ἐν τῇ γῇ; οὐχί, λέγω ὑμῖν, ἀλλ' ἢ διαμερισμόν. (53) διαμερισθήσονται πατὴρ ἐπὶ υἱῷ καὶ υἱὸς ἐπὶ πατρί, μήτηρ ἐπὶ θυγατέρα καὶ θυγάτηρ ἐπὶ τὴν μητέρα, πενθερὰ ἐπὶ τὴν νύμφην αὐτῆς καὶ νύμφη ἐπὶ τὴν πενθεράν. [(xiv. 26) εἴ τις ἔρχεται πρός με καὶ οὐ μισεῖ τὸν

θυγατέρα ὑπὲρ ἐμὲ οὐκ ἔστιν μου ἄξιος.]	πατέρα αὐτοῦ καὶ τὴν μητέρα καὶ τὴν γυναῖκα καὶ τὰ τέκνα καὶ τοὺς ἀδελφοὺς καὶ τὰς ἀδελφάς, ἔτι τε καὶ τὴν ἑαυτοῦ ψυχήν, οὐ δύναται εἶναί μου μαθητής.]
(38) καὶ ὃς οὐ λαμβάνει τὸν σταυρὸν αὐτοῦ καὶ ἀκολουθεῖ ὀπίσω μου, οὐκ ἔστιν μου ἄξιος.	(xiv. 27) ὅστις οὐ βαστάζει τὸν σταυρὸν ἑαυτοῦ καὶ ἔρχεται ὀπίσω μου, οὐ δύναται εἶναί μου μαθητής.
(39) ὁ εὑρὼν τὴν ψυχὴν αὐτοῦ ἀπολέσει αὐτήν, καὶ ὁ ἀπολέσας τὴν ψυχὴν αὐτοῦ ἕνεκεν ἐμοῦ εὑρήσει αὐτήν.	(xvii. 33) ὃς ἐὰν ζητήσῃ τὴν ψυχὴν αὐτοῦ περιποιήσασθαι ἀπολέσει αὐτήν, ὃς δ' ἂν ἀπολέσει ζωογονήσει αὐτήν.
(40) ὁ δεχόμενος ὑμᾶς ἐμὲ δέχεται, καὶ ὁ ἐμὲ δεχόμενος δέχεται τὸν ἀποστείλαντά με.	(x. 16) ὁ ἀκούων ὑμῶν ἐμοῦ ἀκούει, καὶ ὁ ἀθετῶν ὑμᾶς ἐμὲ ἀθετεῖ· ὁ δὲ ἐμὲ ἀθετῶν ἀθετεῖ τὸν ἀποστείλαντά με.

In St. Matthew verse 34, we find that St. Luke has again inserted λέγω ὑμῖν. Μὴ νομίσητε ὅτι ἦλθον occurs also in St. Matt. v. 17; δοκεῖτε is found in Q (St. Matt. xxiv. 44 = St. Luke xii. 44); yet there is some doubt whether this verse belongs to Q. As, however, St. Luke has here the interrogative form, which he has often obliterated elsewhere, we must decide in his favour. Εἰρήνην δοῦναι ἐν τῇ γῇ is certainly an improvement in style; παρεγενόμην is a choicer word than ἦλθον, and διαμερισμόν (here only in the New Testament) than μάχαιραν, lastly, the arrangement of the words in St. Luke shows more artistic skill. The same stands good of St. Matthew verse 35 = St. Luke verse 53: διαμερισμός was the cause of the substitution of διαμερισθήσονται for ἦλθον διχάσαι (the latter word is wanting in the LXX, and may also have been disliked by St. Luke); πατὴρ ἐπὶ υἱῷ καὶ υἱὸς ἐπὶ πατρὶ is more correct than the awkward ἄνθρωπον κατὰ τοῦ πατρὸς αὐτοῦ. For symmetry St. Luke also repeated the "mother and daughter," and the "mother-in-law and daughter-in-law."

It is difficult to come to a definite decision concerning the relationship of St. Matthew verse 37 to St. Luke xiv. 26. It may be doubted whether Q is here the common source, however certain it is that some such source lies in the ultimate background. It is probable that St. Luke is strongly influenced by St. Mark x. 29, that μισεῖν, and likewise ἔτι τε καὶ (τε is Lukan), must be assigned to him, that he has formed the conclusion of this verse after the pattern of the one which follows, and that St. Matthew has preserved the text of Q unaltered. (This may also be true of St. Matthew verse 36, which is not printed above: καὶ ἐχθροὶ τοῦ ἀνθρώπου [*vide* ἄνθρωπος in verse 35] οἱ οἰκιακοὶ αὐτοῦ. St. Luke omitted the whole verse because it seemed to him quite superfluous after verse 35.)

The saying of St. Matthew verse 38, occurs twice in both St. Matthew and St. Luke and once in St. Mark. The two forms printed above are derived from a single source, since they are both negative in form, while the other three begin with εἴ τις θέλει. Again it is the original form of the negative version which occurs in St. Matthew: this evangelist writes ὅς, while St. Luke, in better Greek, writes ὅστις, the former speaks of "taking" the cross, St. Luke of "bearing" ("taking," of course, is intended to mean "bearing"). St. Matthew writes pleonastically (according to Semitic idiom) ἀκολουθεῖν ὀπίσω, St. Luke corrects it into ἔρχεσθαι ὀπίσω. On each occasion St. Luke writes οὐ δύναται εἶναί μου μαθητής for οὐκ ἔστιν μου ἄξιος. One understands how the former phrase could have taken the place of the latter, but not how the latter could have replaced the former (concerning the avoidance of ἄξιος, *vide supra* on St. Matt. x. 13).

The saying of St. Matt. x. 39 is one of the two sayings of our Lord which is found in all four gospels (twice in St. Matthew and St. Luke). St. Matt. xvi. 25 and St. Luke ix. 26 are derived from St. Mark viii. 35; thus St. Matt. x. 39 and St. Luke xvii. 33 come from Q (in all the six versions the expression ἀπολλύειν τὴν ψυχήν is found).

St. Luke here uses the words περιποιεῖσθαι (*vide* Acts xx. 28; 1 Tim. iii. 13) and ζωογονεῖν (*vide* Acts vii. 19; 1 Tim. vi. 13), which are wanting elsewhere in the gospels—they are doubtless secondary; in sense they are identical with σώζειν—that is, with the Aramaic "aḥi" (*vide* Wellhausen). Moreover, the ζητήσῃ of St. Luke is very suspicious; for in St. Matt. vii. 13 (St. Luke xiii. 24) this evangelist has again interpolated ζητήσουσιν. St. Luke evidently regarded the expression τὴν ψυχὴν εὑρεῖν as not clear enough; St.

John also has replaced it by φιλεῖν τὴν ψυχήν. Only we are surprised to find that in this verse St. Matthew has the participle and St. Luke the finite verb (with ὃς ἐάν); elsewhere almost always the reverse is the case. St. Luke was probably influenced by his version of St. Mark which he had given previously in ix. 24. Ἕνεκεν ἐμοῦ is interpolated by St. Matthew (from St. Mark).

St. Matt. x. 40: The second half of this saying is the other of the two utterances of our Lord which are found in all four gospels. In St. Mark ix. 37 we find the saying concerning the reception of the little child (in whom Jesus Himself is received), which concludes: καὶ ὃς ἂν ἐμὲ δέχηται, οὐκ ἐμὲ δέχεται ἀλλὰ τὸν ἀποστείλαντά με. Upon this passage are dependent St. Matt. xviii. 5 (but without the second half) and St. Luke ix. 48: καὶ ὃς ἂν ἐμὲ δέξηται, δέχεται τὸν ἀποστείλαντά με. In the three other passages (the two printed above and St. John xiii. 20: ὁ λαμβάνων ἄν τινα πέμψω ἐμὲ λαμβάνει, ὁ δὲ ἐμὲ λαμβάνων λαμβάνει τὸν πέμψαντά μέ) the reference is to the reception of those who preach the gospel. The agreement of St. Matthew and St. John in this saying (St. Matthew δέχεσθαι and ἀποστεῖλαι, St. John λαμβάνειν and πέμψαι — genuine translation-variants) suggests the conclusion that St. Luke has here arbitrarily altered and amplified. The motive is clear from the slight alteration made by St. John. In St. Matthew (Q) the saying applies to the reception of the direct apostles of our Lord. This application no longer suited the circumstances of a later time, and more particularly of the Diaspora. Therefore we read in St. John ὁ λαμβάνων ἄν τινα πέμψω, and St. Luke changes "reception" into "hearing" (in the sense of "obeying"), with its contrast "setting at nought." For ἀθετεῖν in St. Luke, *vide* 1 Thess. iv. 8: ὁ ἀθετῶν οὐκ ἄνθρωπον ἀθετεῖ ἀλλὰ τὸν θεόν (and St. Luke vii. 30: τὴν βουλὴν τοῦ θεοῦ ἠθέτησαν); for the thought in St. Luke, *vide* Acts ix. 4: Σαούλ, τί με διώκεις. It is thus proved that in the two last verses of this section the Lukan text is again secondary, although, owing to the marked difference between St. Matt. x. 40 and St. Luke x. 16, it must remain doubtful whether this very widely circulated saying occurred in Q.

St. Matt. xi. 2: Ὁ δὲ Ἰωάννης ἀκούσας ἐν τῷ δεσμωτηρίῳ τὰ ἔργα τοῦ Χριστοῦ, πέμψας διὰ τῶν μαθητῶν αὐτοῦ εἶπεν αὐτῷ·	St. Luke vii. 18, 19: καὶ ἀπήγγειλαν Ἰωάννει οἱ μαθηταὶ αὐτοῦ περὶ πάντων τούτων. καὶ προσκαλεσάμενος δύο τινὰς τῶν μαθητῶν αὐτοῦ ὁ Ἰωάννης ἔπεμψεν πρὸς τὸν κύριον λέγων·

St. Luke has already told us (iii. 20) that St. John the Baptist had been imprisoned, it was not therefore necessary to mention this again; but something of the sort must have been mentioned in Q; hence the ἐν τῷ δεσμωτηρίῳ of St. Matthew is original. "To hear the works" is an awkward expression—on the other hand, the corresponding passag of St. Luke is of the conventional type; likewise, πέμψαι διά gives an impression of greater originality than the προσκαλεσάμενος (ἔπεμψεν) of the formal gospel style. Lastly, the interpolation of τινὲς and ὁ κύριος is Lukan, and the repetition of the name John shows that the version in verse 18 is not original. St. Matthew has thus preserved the text of Q.

St. Matt. xvii. 20b: Ἐὰν ἔχητε πίστιν ὡς κόκκον σινάπεως, ἐρεῖτε τῷ ὄρει τούτῳ· μετάβα ἔνθεν ἐκεῖ καὶ μεταβήσεται·	St. Luke xvii. 6: εἰ ἔχετε πίστιν ὡς κόκκον σινάπεως, ἐλέγετε ἂν τῇ συκαμίνῳ (ταύτῃ)· ἐκριζώθητι καὶ φυτεύθητι ἐν τῇ θαλάσσῃ· καὶ ὑπήκουσεν ἂν ὑμῖν.

St. Luke, as is often the case, has written εἰ for ἐάν. The commentators recognise that St. Luke has replaced "the mountain" by "the fig tree"—a reminiscence of the "Cursing of the fig tree," which he omitted.

St. Matt. xviii. 12: τί ὑμῖν δοκεῖ; ἐὰν γένηταί τινι ἀνθρώπῳ ἑκατὸν πρόβατα καὶ πλανηθῇ ἓν ἐξ αὐτῶν, οὐχὶ ἀφήσει τὰ ἐνενήκοντα ἐννέα ἐπὶ τὰ ὄρη καὶ πορευθεὶς ζητεῖ τὸ πλανώμενον; (13) καὶ ἐὰν γένηται εὑρεῖν αὐτό, ἀμὴν λέγω ὑμῖν, ὅτι χαίρει ἐπ' αὐτῷ μᾶλλον ἢ ἐπὶ τοῖς ἐνενήκοντα ἐννέα τοῖς μὴ πεπλανημένοις.	St. Luke xv. 4: τίς ἄνθρωπος ἐξ ὑμῶν ἔχων ἑκατὸν πρόβατα καὶ ἀπολέσας ἐξ αὐτῶν ἓν οὐ καταλείπει τὰ ἐνενήκοντα ἐννέα ἐν τῇ ἐρήμῳ καὶ πορεύεται ἐπὶ τὸ ἀπολωλὸς ἕως εὕρῃ αὐτό; (5) καὶ εὑρὼν ἐπιτίθησιν ἐπὶ τοὺς ὤμους αὐτοῦ χαίρων, (6) καὶ ἐλθὼν εἰς τὸν οἶκον συνκαλεῖ τοὺς φίλους καὶ τοὺς γείτονας, λέγων αὐτοῖς· συνχάρητέ

μοι, ὅτι εὗρον τὸ πρόβατόν μου τὸ ἀπολωλός. (7) λέγω ὑμῖν ὅτι οὕτως χαρὰ ἔσται ἐν τῷ οὐρανῷ ἐπὶ ἑνὶ ἁμαρτωλῷ μετανοοῦντι ἢ ἐπὶ ἐνενήκοντα ἐννέα δικαίοις, οἵτινες οὐ χρείαν ἔχουσιν μετανοίας.

St. Matthew has the principal interrogative clause in the apodosis; St. Luke by using the participial construction (as so often) makes the whole into one interrogative sentence. The former is original, likewise the awkward γίνεσθαι (St. Luke ἔχειν). The ἐξ ὑμῶν of St. Luke is out of good connection. St. Luke writes ἀπολέσας for πλανηθῇ, because with his construction he was compelled to avoid the change of subject. Καταλείπει is an evident correction for the clumsy ἀφήσει. Ἐπὶ τὰ ὄρη and ἐν τῇ ἐρήμῳ might be regarded as translation-variants, if it were probable from other passages that St. Luke had knowledge of the Aramaic original of Q; St. Luke has here replaced the special by the more general term. Again, he writes τὸ ἀπολωλός, because he had already written ἀπολέσας, St. Matthew gives τὸ πλανώμενον (in accordance with the πλανηθῇ of his text). Πορεύεται ἐπὶ τό is good Greek for πορευθεὶς ζητεῖ. The un-Hellenic phrase ἐὰν γένηται εὑρεῖν is replaced by the correct εὑρών. Here, therefore, the text of St. Luke is shown to be everywhere secondary.

St. Luke verse 6, and indeed the principal part of verse 5, have no parallel in St. Matthew. They may have stood in Q, and St. Matthew may have omitted them because they only give colour and finish to the parable; however, nothing certain can be said upon the point. Συνκαλεῖν is found eight times in the New Testament, including seven times in St. Luke; also "neighbours" (St. Luke xiv. 12, xv. 9) and "friends" have a Lukan flavour; *συνχαίρειν* is in the gospels exclusively Lukan (i. 58, xv. 9); and τὸ ἀπολωλός cannot have stood in Q, seeing that in a preceding verse it has been traced to St. Luke's correcting hand.

St. Matthew verse 13: Here the λέγω ὑμῖν, which also stands in St. Luke verse 7, is important, because it shows that this asseveration also occurred in Q; it does not, however, follow from this that it is always original when it is given by St. Matthew or St. Luke. St. Matthew asserts that the owner rejoices more over the one sheep than over the ninety-nine that had not wandered; St. Luke gives the spiritual application and interpolates the idea of repentance (*vide infra* St. Luke xvii. 3, 4 = St. Matt. xviii. 21, 22). There is no doubt as to which of these versions is the original. Thus here also St. Matthew has the ancient text.

St. Matt. xviii. 15: Ἐὰν δὲ ἁμαρτήσῃ ὁ ἀδελφός σου, ὕπαγε ἔλεγξον αὐτὸν μεταξὺ σοῦ καὶ αὐτοῦ μόνου. ἐάν σου ἀκούσῃ, ἐκέρδησας τὸν ἀδελφόν σου.	St. Luke xvii. 3: ἐὰν ἁμάρτῃ ὁ ἀδελφός σου, ἐπιτίμησον αὐτῷ, καὶ ἐὰν μετανοήσῃ, ἄφες αὐτῷ. (4) καὶ ἐὰν ἑπτάκις τῆς ἡμέρας ἁμαρτήσῃ εἰς σὲ καὶ ἑπτάκις ἐπιστρέψῃ

πρὸς σὲ λέγων· μετανοῶ, ἀφήσεις αὐτῷ.

(21) τότε προσελθὼν ὁ Πέτρος εἶπεν αὐτῷ· κύριε, ποσάκις ἁμαρτήσει εἰς ἐμὲ ὁ ἀδελφός μου καὶ ἀφήσω αὐτῷ; ἕως ἑπτάκις; (22) λέγει αὐτῷ ὁ Ἰησοῦς· οὐ λέγω σοι ἕως ἑπτάκις, ἀλλὰ ἕως ἑβδομηκοντάκις ἑπτά.

At the first glance the text in St. Luke, because it is the shorter, seems to be therefore the more original in form; as a matter of fact, it presents to a certain extent the longer form, and besides rests upon a conflation of ideas. It is the longer in that St. Luke alone gives τῆς ἡμέρας and speaks of repentance (just as in xv. 7), of which nothing is said in St. Matthew verses 21 f. In St. Luke the point upon which emphasis is laid is the sinner's repentance; while St. Matthew (*i.e.* Q) is concerned with the question of unconditional forgiveness, not in the case of sins in general but in the case of personal injury. St. Luke confuses the two cases. Here, however, St. Matthew too is not original, for his version in verse 15 is already determined by the subject-matter of the following verses (16 and 17). The text must have run: ἐὰν ἁμαρτήσῃ (ἁμάρτῃ of St. Luke is a grammatical improvement) ὁ ἀδελφός σου, ἔλεγξον αὐτὸν (ὕπαγε belongs perhaps to the style of St. Matthew; the rare ἔλεγξον is certainly more original than the frequent ἐπιτίμησον). The saying is, however, still imperfect, hence we cannot do without the following clause: ἐάν σου ἀκούσῃ ἐκέρδησας τὸν ἀδελφόν σου.

The other saying in St. Matthew verses 21 and 22 is quite independent of the previous one which St. Luke has blended with it. The absolutely un-Hellenic construction of its clauses, the equally un-Hellenic ἕως, and the ἑπτά (for ἑπτάκις) at the close, are enough to prove its originality—although the introduction of St. Peter may be secondary. The ἑβδομηκοντάκις ἑπτά probably seemed to St. Luke too paradoxical.

St. Matt. xix. 28: ὑμεῖς οἱ ἀκολουθήσαντές μοι . . . καθίσεσθε ἐπὶ δώδεκα θρόνους κρίνοντες τὰς δώδεκα φυλὰς τοῦ Ἰσραήλ.	St. Luke xxii. 28, 30: ὑμεῖς δέ ἐστε οἱ διαμεμενηκότες μετ' ἐμοῦ ἐν τοῖς πειρασμοῖς μου . . . καὶ καθήσεσθε ἐπὶ θρόνων κρίνοντες τὰς δώδεκα φυλὰς τοῦ Ἰσραήλ.

It is obvious that the introduction in St. Matthew is more original—besides, διαμένειν only occurs once again in the gospels, and that in St. Luke (i. 22); and the plural πειρασμοί is not found anywhere else in the gospels, though it occurs in Acts xx. 19. The rest is identical in the two versions; the number "twelve," twice repeated, must be regarded as original.

St. Matt. xxiii. 4: Δεσμεύουσιν δὲ φορτία βαρέα καὶ ἐπιτιθέασιν ἐπὶ	St. Luke xi. 46: καὶ ὑμῖν τοῖς νομικοῖς οὐαί· φορτίζετε τοὺς ἀνθρώπους

τοὺς ὤμους τῶν ἀνθρώπων, αὐτοὶ δὲ τῷ δακτύλῳ αὐτῶν οὐ θελουσιν κινῆσαι αὐτά.	φορτία δυσβάστακτα, καὶ αὐτοὶ ἑνὶ τῶν δακτύλων ὑμῶν οὐ προσψαύετε τοῖς φορτίοις.
(13) οὐαὶ δὲ ὑμῖν, γραμματεῖς καὶ Φαρισαῖοι ὑποκριταί, ὅτι κλείετε τὴν βασιλείαν τῶν οὐρανῶν ἔμπροσθεν τῶν ἀνθρώπων· ὑμεῖς γὰρ οὐκ εἰσέρχεσθε οὐδὲ τοὺς εἰσερχομένους ἀφίετε εἰσελθεῖν.	xi. 52: οὐαὶ ὑμῖν τοῖς νομικοῖς, ὅτι ἤρατε [ἔχετε] τὴν κλεῖδα τῆς γνώσεως· αὐτοὶ οὐκ εἰσήλθατε καὶ τοὺς εἰσερχομένους ἐκωλύσατε.
(23) οὐαὶ ὑμῖν, γραμματεῖς καὶ Φαρισαῖοι ὑποκριταί, ὅτι ἀποδεκατοῦτε τὸ ἡδύοσμον καὶ τὸ ἄνηθον καὶ τὸ κύμινον, καὶ ἀφήκατε τὰ βαρύτερα τοῦ νόμου, τὴν κρίσιν καὶ τὸ ἔλεος καὶ τὴν πίστιν. ταῦτα δὲ ἔδει ποιῆσαι κἀκεῖνα μὴ ἀφεῖναι.	xi. 42: οὐαὶ ὑμῖν τοῖς Φαρισαίοις, ὅτι ἀποδεκατοῦτε τὸ ἡδύοσμον καὶ τὸ πήγανον καὶ πᾶν λάχανον, καὶ παρέρχεσθε τὴν κρίσιν καὶ τὴν ἀγάπην τοῦ θεοῦ. [ταῦτα ἔδει ποιῆσαι κἀκεῖνα μὴ παρεῖναι.]
(25) οὐαὶ ὑμῖν, γραμματεῖς καὶ Φαρισαῖοι ὑποκριταί, ὅτι καθαρίζετε τὸ ἔξωθεν τοῦ ποτηρίου καὶ τῆς παροψίδος, ἔσωθεν δὲ γέμουσιν ἐξ ἁρπαγῆς καὶ ἀκρασίας.[1]	xi. 39: νῦν ὑμεῖς οἱ Φαρισαῖοι τὸ ἔξωθεν τοῦ ποτηρίου καὶ τοῦ πίνακος καθαρίζετε, τὸ δὲ ἔσωθεν ὑμῶν γέμει ἁρπαγῆς καὶ πονηρίας.

[1] St. Matthew verse 26 and St. Luke verse 41 are not without connection, yet do not lend themselves easily to comparison. In the first place, St. Luke 41a (οὐχ ὁ ποιήσας τὸ ἔξωθεν καὶ τὸ ἔσωθεν

[(27) οὐαὶ ὑμῖν, γραμματεῖς καὶ Φαρισαῖοι ὑποκριταί, ὅτι παρομοιάζετε τάφοις κεκονιαμένοις, οἵτινες ἔξωθεν μὲν φαίνονται ὡραῖοι, ἔσωθεν δὲ γέμουσιν ὀστέων νεκρῶν καὶ πάσης ἀκαθαρσίας.]

[xi. 44: οὐαὶ ὑμῖν, ὅτι ἐστὲ ὡς τὰ μνημεῖα τὰ ἄδηλα, καὶ οἱ ἄνθρωποι οἱ περιπατοῦντες ἐπάνω οὐκ οἴδασιν.]

(29) οὐαὶ ὑμῖν, γραμματεῖς καὶ Φαρισαῖοι ὑποκριταί, ὅτι οἰκοδομεῖτε τοὺς τάφους τῶν προφητῶν καὶ κοσμεῖτε τὰ μνημεῖα τῶν δικαίων, (30) καὶ λέγετε· εἰ ἤμεθα ἐν ταῖς ἡμέραις τῶν πατέρων ἡμῶν, οὐκ ἂν ἤμεθα αὐτῶν κοινωνοὶ ἐν τῷ αἵματι τῶν προφητῶν. (31) ὥστε μαρτυρεῖτε ἑαυτοῖς ὅτι υἱοί ἐστε τῶν φονευσάντων τοὺς προφήτας. (32) καὶ ὑμεῖς πληρώσατε τὸ μέτρον τῶν πατέρων ὑμῶν.

xi. 47: οὐαὶ ὑμῖν, ὅτι οἰκοδομεῖτε τὰ μνημεῖα τῶν προφητῶν, οἱ δὲ πατέρες ὑμῶν ἀπέκτειναν αὐτούς. (48) ἄρα μάρτυρές ἐστε καὶ συνευδοκεῖτε τοῖς ἔργοις τῶν πατέρων ὑμῶν, ὅτι αὐτοὶ μὲν ἀπέκτειναν αὐτούς, ὑμεῖς δὲ οἰκοδομεῖτε.

ἐποίησεν;) has not any parallel in St. Matt. 26; the same is the case with the vocative, Φαρισαῖε τυφλέ, of St. Matt. 26. Whether the words καθάρισον πρῶτον τὸ ἐντὸς τοῦ ποτηρίου and πλὴν τὰ ἐνόντα δότε ἐλεημοσύνην go back to *one* Aramaic source (wherein "dakki" was confounded with "zakki") is doubtful. The latter halves of the verses, ἵνα γένηται καὶ τὸ ἐκτὸς αὐτοῦ καθαρόν and καὶ ἰδοὺ πάντα καθαρὰ ὑμῖν ἐστιν, are alone really related to one another. If, however, a single source was here really used, then St. Matthew has the more original text.

(34) διὰ τοῦτο ἰδοὺ ἐγὼ ἀποστελλω πρὸς ὑμᾶς προφήτας καὶ σοφοὺς καὶ γραμματεῖς· ἐξ αὐτῶν ἀποκτενεῖτε καὶ σταυρώσετε καὶ ἐξ αὐτῶν μαστιγώσετε ἐν ταῖς συναγωγαῖς ὑμῶν καὶ διώξετε ἀπὸ πόλεως εἰς πόλιν· (35) ὅπως ἔλθῃ ἐφ' ὑμᾶς πᾶν αἷμα δίκαιον ἐκχυννόμενον ἐπὶ τῆς γῆς ἀπὸ τοῦ αἵματος Ἄβελ τοῦ δικαίου ἕως τοῦ αἵματος Ζαχαρίου υἱοῦ Βαραχίου, ὃν ἐφονεύσατε μεταξὺ τοῦ ναοῦ καὶ τοῦ θυσιαστηρίου. (36) ἀμὴν λέγω ὑμῖν, ἥξει ταῦτα πάντα ἐπὶ τὴν γενεὰν ταύτην.

xi. 49: διὰ τοῦτο καὶ ἡ Σοφία τοῦ θεοῦ εἶπεν· ἀποστελῶ εἰς αὐτοὺς προφήτας καὶ ἀποστόλους, καὶ ἐξ αὐτῶν ἀποκτενοῦσιν καὶ ἐκδιώξουσιν, (50) ἵνα ἐκζητηθῇ τὸ αἷμα πάντων τῶν προφητῶν τὸ ἐκχυννόμενον ἀπὸ καταβολῆς κόσμου ἀπὸ τῆς γενεᾶς ταύτης, (51) ἀπὸ αἵματος Ἄβελ ἕως αἵματος Ζαχαρίου τοῦ ἀπολομένου μεταξὺ τοῦ θυσιαστηρίου καὶ τοῦ οἴκου· ναί, λέγω ὑμῖν, ἐκζητηθήσεται ἀπὸ τῆς γενεᾶς ταύτης.

St. Matt. xxiii. 4: For δεσμεύειν φορτία, which is scarcely intelligible Greek, St. Luke has written φορτίζειν φορτία (*cf.*, in this evangelist, xvii. 24: ἀστραπὴ ἀστράπτουσα, Acts xxviii. 10: τιμαῖς ἐτίμησαν, Acts iv. 17: ἀπειλῇ ἀπειλησώμεθα, Acts v. 28: παραγγελίᾳ παρηγγείλαμεν, St. Luke xxii. 15: ἐπιθυμίᾳ ἐπεθύμησα, xxiii. 46: φωνήσας φωνῇ [likewise Acts xvi. 28], vi. 8: ἀναστὰς ἔστη, Acts v. 4: μένον ἔμενεν, St. Luke ii. 8: φυλάσσοντες φυλακάς). The construction of φορτίζειν with a double accusative filled the place of ἐπιτιθέασιν.—

δυσβάστακτος is literary Greek and Lukan, *vide supra* the remarks on St. Matt. vi. 20=St. Luke xii. 33.—ἑνὶ τ. δακτ. is a stylistic correction of, and lends emphasis to, τῷ δακτύλῳ.—προσψαύειν (for κινεῖν), because it is a compound, is shown to be a correction.—In St. Luke this verse stands among the Woes against the scribes; this may be correct. St. Matthew introduced the verse into a description of the Pharisees which he had taken from a separate source, and so was able to arrange a list of seven Woes. And yet it may well have been otherwise (*vide infra* on verse 25); it is evident that in Q part of the subject-matter occurred in a description of the Pharisees, part in the form of Woes.—Νομικός is found six times in St. Luke, never in St. Mark, St. John, and St. Paul, once in St. Matthew (xxii. 35), but the latter occurrence is doubtful. The word, therefore, certainly did not stand in the source; St. Luke has substituted it for "Pharisees," or has combined it or used it alternately with the latter word (*vide* xi. 39, 42, 43), perhaps in order to remind his uninstructed readers who the Pharisees were (*cf.* Acts xxiii. 8 f.). The καί of St. Luke, verse 46, is probably to be counted original.

St. Matt. xxiii. 13: The combination of scribes and Pharisees is also found four times in St. Luke (v. 30, vi. 7, xi. 53, xv. 2). If he had found it here he would certainly have given it in his text. Since, however, he writes νομικοί, we must suppose that only "Pharisees" stood in Q (*vide supra* on verse 4).—ὑποκριταί is much more frequent in St. Matthew than in St. Luke; and in St. Matt. xxiv. 51, St.

Luke has replaced it by ἄπιστοι. Whether it stood in Q in the passages we are now considering cannot be certainly determined; probably Q ran: οὐαὶ ὑμῖν τοῖς Φαρισαίοις.—It is obvious that "to hold the key of knowledge" is the correction, and "to close the kingdom of Heaven" is the original; moreover, the verb εἰσέρχεσθαι does not suit well with γνῶσις, which word occurs only once again in the gospels, and that also in St. Luke (i. 77, γνῶσις σωτηρίας).—St. Luke puts αὐτοί in the place of ὑμεῖς, for he does not like the personal pronominal subject expressed with the verb.—St. Luke gives the aorist εἰσήλθατε instead of the present because, as a matter of fact, the "lawyers" did not possess the γνῶσις.—St. Luke omits γάρ because its connection with the context is not clear, and he simply writes ἐκωλύσατε instead of the circumstantial οὐκ αφίετε εἰσελθεῖν, just as in the case of St. Matt. v. 40 he replaces ἄφες αὐτῷ by μὴ κωλύσῃς (κωλύειν once in St. Matthew, 6 + 6 times in the Lukan writings).

St. Matthew xxiii. 23: Concerning the introduction, compare what has been said above on verse 13.—"Anise and cummin" (St. Matthew), "Rue and every herb" (St. Luke); the former is original (Nestle, "Expos. Times," xv. 528; "Ztschr. f. Neutestamentl," Wissensch. 1906, s. 10, believes that cummin and rue correspond to שבתא and שברא).—τὰ βαρύτερα τοῦ νόμου is difficult of interpretation and seems to conflict with verse 4, according to which the very charge brought against the Pharisees is that they impose the heavy burden; the words are therefore omitted by St. Luke.—

παρέρχεσθε is a more elegant word than ἀφήκατε.—It follows from ἔλεος—the middle of the three words in St. Matthew—that here conduct towards the neighbour is spoken of (Wellhausen); St. Luke, however, alters this and reads, "Ye pass by the judgment and the love of God." The conclusion of the verse found in many manuscripts of St. Luke is an interpolation from St. Matthew. It can scarcely have stood in Q, for it is in accordance with the tendency of St. Matthew. Moreover, the preceding words καὶ τὴν πίστιν are very doubtful.

St. Matt. xxiii. 25: Here, in contrast to St. Matthew verse 4, St. Matthew has the woe and St. Luke the simple description (*vide supra*); the νῦν, which is found only here, seems to be original; St. Luke has substituted the more general word πίναξ (*cf.* St. Mark vi. 25) for παροψίς. He has also correctly interpreted the somewhat dubious ἔσωθεν by τὸ ἔσωθεν ὑμῶν, and has replaced ἀκρασία, which seemed too special a word here, by the more general πονηρία.

St. Matt. xxiii. 27: Wellhausen thinks that the text of St. Matthew is here more diffuse and less original than that of St. Luke. But the sayings are absolutely different: in St. Matthew the Pharisees are compared to whitewashed sepulchres (whitened, in order that they might be seen of men); in St. Luke, on the other hand, they are compared to just the opposite, to sepulchres which cannot be seen. The latter simile is only intelligible from Num. xix. 16: those who walked over the sepulchre were rendered unclean. The Jewish ordinance which lies at the background of the version in St. Luke vouches for the originality of this text. And yet the text of St. Matthew can scarcely be due to intentional alteration. If, however, we are not allowed to assume that both verses belonged to Q, then St. Luke must have the preference, seeing that St. Matthew verse 27 does not carry us much farther than verse 25. Only, the more elegant and appropriate *μνημεῖον* (for *τάφος*) is due to the correcting hand of St. Luke (*τάφος* is not found anywhere in St. Mark and St. Luke)—see also the remarks on St. Matthew verse 29.

St. Matt. xxiii. 29–32 = St. Luke xi. 47, 48. Does St. Luke here give an extract or the original? We may confidently affirm the former alternative, because of the cold, matter-of-fact tone of St. Luke's version. Moreover, its secondary character is also shown by *ἀποκτείνειν* for *φονεύειν* and by *συνευδοκεῖν*, which is peculiar to St. Luke and St. Paul (*vide* Acts viii. 1, xxii. 20; Rom. i. 32; 1 Cor. vii. 12, 13), as well as by *μάρτυς*, which occurs thirteen times in the Acts (*μαρτυρεῖν* is found in St. Matthew only in this passage). St. Luke also avoids *ὥστε* in the sense of *itaque*. However, the scribes and Pharisees are interpolated here by St. Matthew (*vide* Wellhausen on this passage) as well as the words *καὶ κοσμεῖτε τὰ μνημεῖα τῶν δικαίων*. St. Matthew often concerns himself with "the righteous" (side by side with prophets and such like people). We, moreover, note that the prophets alone are mentioned afterwards. Again, verse 32 is perhaps original—*cf.* the clumsy phrase *πληροῦν τὸ μέτρον τῶν πατέρων* (on the other hand, verse 33 is an appendix which has been fashioned after the pattern of iii. 7).

St. Matt. xxiii. 34–36. We discover from St. Luke alone that our Lord here quotes an authority which He regards as inspired. The fact that we do not know what this authority was, is no reason for asserting that the passage in question is not a quotation, especially seeing that we read εἶπεν (not the present), and that our Lord could not possibly have said, "I send prophets, wise men and scribes." We can easily understand that the dislike to represent our Lord as quoting from an apocryphal book, or some other motive, led St. Matthew to erase the quotation formula (his ἰδού is, as it were, a substitute for what has been omitted, and διὰ τοῦτο has good sense only in St. Luke). That St. Luke has interpolated here is inconceivable. St. Luke has made drastic corrections in detail. As usual, he has omitted ἐγώ before the verb; he has transformed the wise men and scribes[1] into apostles! (just as in 1 Clem. 42, Deacons are interpolated); he has changed ἀποστέλλω into ἀποστελῶ (because of the conclusion of the discourse); he has inserted καί before ἐξ αὐτῶν (pr.); he has replaced διώκειν by ἐκδιώκειν, and the uncouth (Semitic) phrase ἔλθῃ ἐφ' ὑμᾶς πᾶν αἷμα by ἐκζητηθῇ τὸ αἷμα πάντων (the passive is enough to betray his style, also ἐκζητεῖν occurs in St. Luke alone among the gospels), also ὅπως, as in several other passages, by ἵνα. For ἐπὶ

[1] This word is certainly original, seeing that in the context of St. Matthew the γραμματεῖς are denounced, so that the evangelist himself could not have inserted them here.

τῆς γῆς, which seemed superfluous, he has substituted ἀπὸ καταβολῆς κόσμου, words which seemed much less superfluous, and he has introduced γενεὰ αὕτη from verse 51 in order to lend greater precision to the solemn asseveration of the close of that verse. As in St. Matt. xxiii. 31, he avoids φονεύειν, replacing ὃν ἐφονεύσατε by the participle τοῦ ἀπολομένου. Concerning the variants εἰς αὐτούς and πρὸς ὑμᾶς I have nothing to say, the two prepositions occur in parallel passages of the two evangelists without any recognisable reason for their variation. In σταυρώσετε καὶ ἐξ αὐτῶν μαστιγώσετε ἐν ταῖς συναγωγαῖς ὑμῶν we probably have an addition by St. Matthew—*cf.* St. Matt. xx. 19, μαστιγῶσαι καὶ σταυρῶσαι—also ἀπὸ πόλεως εἰς πόλιν is probably interpolated in accordance with St. Matt. x. 23, likewise the two occurrences of "δίκαιον" (*vide supra* on xxiii. 29); St. Luke reads, but scarcely correctly, πάντων τῶν προφητῶν. Concerning υἱοῦ Βαραχίου, I would point out (1) that it is not quite certain that these words are original in St. Matthew; (2) that as St. Luke does not read them, and as the gospel of the Hebrews according to St. Jerome's testimony read "filium Joiadæ" [so also (in accordance with 2 Chron. xxiv. 20) a Greek scholion to St. Matthew], it is therefore very improbable that the words stood in Q. What reason could St. Luke have had for omitting them? Their historical control was not within his reach. We therefore here refrain from discussing what Zacharias is meant by St. Matthew or his interpolator. There is no reason for suspecting an historical hysteron-proteron. In place of the "Temple and the Altar," St. Luke writes with greater precision, "the Altar and the House (of the Temple)." Lastly, the ναί of St. Luke shows that ἀμήν stood in Q; ἐκζητηθήσεται ἀπό is substituted for ἥξει ἐπί in order to take up the ἐκζητηθῇ of the previous verse; this led to the omission of ταῦτα πάντα, which words indeed do not express the sense very clearly in the context of St. Matthew (the subject to ἐκζητ. in St. Luke is τὸ αἷμα). The absence of τοῦ twice before αἵματος in St. Luke is probably original.

St. Matt. xxiv. 26: Ἐὰν οὖν εἴπωσιν ὑμῖν· ἰδοὺ ἐν τῇ ἐρήμῳ ἐστίν, μὴ ἐξέλθητε· ἰδοὺ ἐν τοῖς ταμείοις, μὴ πιστεύσητε· (27) ὥσπερ γὰρ ἡ ἀστραπὴ ἐξέρχεται ἀπὸ ἀνατολῶν καὶ φαίνεται ἕως δυσμῶν, οὕτως ἔσται ἡ παρουσία τοῦ υἱοῦ τοῦ ἀνθρώπου· (28) ὅπου ἐὰν ᾖ τὸ πτῶμα, ἐκεῖ συναχθήσονται οἱ ἀετοί.

xxiv. 37: Ὥσπερ γὰρ αἱ ἡμέραι τοῦ Νῶε, οὕτως ἔσται ἡ παρουσία τοῦ υἱοῦ τοῦ ἀνθρώπου. (38) ὡς γὰρ ἦσαν ἐν ταῖς ἡμέραις [ἐκείναις] ταῖς πρὸ τοῦ κατακλυσμοῦ τρώγοντες καὶ πίνοντες, γαμοῦντες

St. Luke xvii. 23: καὶ ἐροῦσιν ὑμῖν· ἰδοὺ ἐκεῖ, ἰδοὺ ὧδε· μὴ ἀπέλθητε μηδὲ διώξητε. (24) ὥσπερ γὰρ ἡ ἀστραπὴ ἀστράπτουσα ἐκ τῆς ὑπὸ τὸν οὐρανὸν εἰς τὴν ὑπ' οὐρανὸν λάμπει, οὕτως ἔσται ὁ υἱὸς τοῦ ἀνθρώπου ἐν τῇ ἡμέρᾳ αὐτοῦ. (37) ὅπου τὸ σῶμα, ἐκεῖ καὶ οἱ ἀετοὶ ἐπισυναχθήσονται.

(26) καὶ καθὼς ἐγένετο ἐν ταῖς ἡμέραις Νῶε, οὕτως ἔσται καὶ ἐν ταῖς ἡμέραις τοῦ υἱοῦ τοῦ ἀνθρώπου· (27) ἤσθιον, ἔπινον, ἐγάμουν, ἐγαμίζοντο, ἄχρι ἧς ἡμέρας εἰσῆλθεν Νῶε εἰς τὴν κιβωτόν, καὶ ἦλθεν ὁ

καὶ γαμίζοντες, ἄχρι ἧς ἡμέρας εἰσῆλθεν Νῶε εἰς τὴν κιβωτόν, (39) *καὶ οὐκ ἔγνωσαν ἕως ἦλθεν ὁ κατακλυσμὸς καὶ ἦρεν ἅπαντας, οὕτως ἔσται ἡ παρουσία τοῦ υἱοῦ τοῦ ἀνθρώπου.*

κατακλυσμὸς καὶ ἀπώλεσεν πάντας.

(40) *τότε ἔσονται δύο ἐν τῷ ἀγρῷ, εἷς παραλαμβάνεται καὶ εἷς ἀφίεται.* (41) *δύο ἀλήθουσαι ἐν τῷ μύλῳ, μία παραλαμβάνεται καὶ μία ἀφίεται.*

(34) *λέγω ὑμῖν, ταύτῃ τῇ νυκτὶ ἔσονται δύο ἐπὶ κλίνης μιᾶς, ὁ εἷς παραλημφθήσεται καὶ ὁ ἕτερος ἀφεθήσεται·* (35) *ἔσονται δύο ἀλήθουσαι ἐπὶ τὸ αὐτό, ἡ μία παραλημφθήσεται, ἡ δὲ ἑτέρα ἀφεθήσεται.*

Clauses with *ἐάν* may be presumed to have stood in Q; St. Luke often uses such clauses, and, again, he often alters them. As for the rest, it is difficult in St. Matt. xxiv. 26 to determine whether St. Luke has abbreviated or St. Matthew has amplified. The former alternative seems to me more probable, especially as *διώκειν*, used in this sense, is a word characteristic of St. Luke and St. Paul. In verse 27 *ἀστραπὴ ἀστράπτουσα* is Lukan in style (*vide* note on St. Matt. xxiii. 4 = St. Luke xi. 46); the rest of the clause in St. Matthew is also original (St. Luke guards against the idea that lightning only passes from east to west; *cf.* a similar Lukan correction of St. Matt. viii. 11 = St. Luke xiii. 29). Also *ἡ παρουσία* must be regarded as the reading of Q; it is indeed only found in St. Matthew, but with the exception of xxiv. 3 (which passage may also be derived from Q), only in places dependent upon Q (*vide* xxiv. 37, 39). St. Luke has avoided the word, which belonged to the sphere of Jewish Messianic dogma and was an unsuitable term for that Second Coming in which Christians believed and which is here referred to—*vide* Wellhausen on St. Matt. xxiv. 3. St. Luke's λάμπει is a better word than φαίνεται, and is therefore a correction. Ἐν τῇ ἡμέρᾳ αὐτοῦ does not possess firm textual authority, but it is an indispensable element of St. Luke's vocabulary.—For the disagreeable word πτῶμα St. Luke has substituted the more elegant σῶμα, he has deleted ἐὰν ᾖ, has given smoothness to the clause by the addition of καί, and has replaced συναχθ. by the double compound ἐπισυναχθ.

St. Matt. xxiv. 37: On logical grounds St. Luke could not allow ὥσπερ αἱ ἡμέραι . . . οὕτως ἔσται ἡ παρουσία to remain unchanged (besides this he is not fond of ὥσπερ—on the other hand, he uses καθώς 16 + 12 times, while in St. Matthew it occurs only three times). In regard to ἡ παρουσία St. Matthew is again in the right (*vide supra* on St. Matt. xxiv. 27). In place of the double comparison (St. Matt. xxiv. 37 ff.)—one element stating the theme which the other develops—St. Luke only gives a simple comparison. The latter can scarcely be original; but St. Luke's unoriginality is also shown by the imperfects. The use of the imperfect is a speciality of St. Luke, and shows his better feeling for the niceties of the Greek language. Moreover, ἐγαμίζοντο is an improvement upon γαμίζοντες (*vide* Wellhausen), and is thus a correction. Here again, as before in other pages, we find that the shorter text of St. Luke is not original but a revision. It almost necessarily followed that St. Matthew verse 39ᵃ should fall a victim to the reviser's pruning-knife, nor indeed do we lose much thereby.

Wellhausen calls St. Matthew verse 40 a poor variant of St. Luke verse 34; but in comparing St. Matthew and St. Luke it often happens that the poorer version—*i.e.* the version which is less good in logic and sense—is the original. Here, moreover, the motive which led to St. Luke's alteration is quite clear. He wished by means of the examples given to express something which was not distinctly expressed in the original text—namely, that the Son of Man might come by night just as well as by day. Accordingly he changed τότε into ταύτῃ τῇ νυκτί and replaced ἐν τῷ ἀγρῷ by ἐπὶ κλίνης μιᾶς, again, he substituted for εἷς . . . εἷς the better Greek ὁ εἷς . . . ὁ ἕτερος (likewise for μία . . . μία the better Greek ἡ μία . . . ἡ ἑτέρα); lastly, he changed the present into the more correct future (so also in the following verse) and repeated the ἔσονται (in verse 35) which could not be dispensed with in correct composition. That the women grind "at the mill" (St. Matthew) was self-evident; it was not superfluous to mention that they grind ἐπὶ τὸ αὐτό. Hence St. Luke substitutes the latter phrase for the former.

There are thus about fifty variants in the case

of which we have found reason to question the originality of the text of St. Matthew; of these one-half coincide with the variants which we have characterised above (pp. 34 ff.). The ἀμὴν λέγω ὑμῖν in v. 18 may be original, likewise the ἀμήν in v. 26, the ἐγὼ λέγω ὑμῖν in v. 32, and the ἀμήν in viii. 10 (*vide supra*). On the other hand, τοῦ ἐν οὐρανοῖς with πατρός (v. 45), οὐρανῷ in place of οὐρανοῖς (vi. 20), and ὁ πατὴρ ὑμῶν for ὁ θεός (x. 29), are not original. We find circumstantial phrases, like those we have noticed above, in προσελθών (iv. 3), ὁ δὲ ἀποκριθεὶς εἶπεν for ἀπεκρίθη (iv. 4), and τότε προσελθὼν ὁ Πέτρος εἶπεν αὐτῷ (xviii. 21); we find interpolations in the "Pharisees and Sadducees" of chap. iii. 7, in the "scribes" in addition to the "Pharisees" of chap. xxiii. 23 (together with the "hypocrites"), and the "scribes and Pharisees" of chap. xxiii. 29. "The righteous" and "righteousness" also appear in these sections, *vide* v. 6 ("to hunger and thirst after righteousness"), xxiii. 29, 35 (*bis*), and probably also v. 45 (yet here "the righteous" may perhaps be original because of the parallelism). The ὕπαγε in all three cases of its occurrence (iv. 10, viii. 13, xviii. 15) is probably inserted by St. Matthew—on the other hand, one cannot be quite certain whether the ὑποδείξω of St. Luke, which does not appear in St. Matt. vii. 24 and x. 28, is original or not; it seems to me more probable that St. Matthew is in the right. No importance is to be attached to the slight stylistic variants in chap. iv. 9 (πεσών add.), viii. 5 (gen. abs. for finite verb), viii. 11 (πολλοί add.),

x. 31 (οὖν add.), xxiii. 4 (δέ for καί), xxiii. 25 (νῦν om.), xxiii. 35 (τοῦ add. *bis*). In these cases it is naturally impossible to give a definite verdict. It is probable that μὴ νομίσητε (x. 34), in place of the interrogative δοκεῖτε, is secondary (*vide supra* on δοκεῖν, St. Matt. iii. 9). Also the words μωρός and φρόνιμος, which expressly characterise the two builders of houses in chap. vii. 24, 26, are probably added by St. Matthew.

Besides these instances there are, however, several others in which the modification of the text is of noteworthy, and at times of considerable, importance. In chap. iv. 11, at the conclusion of the story of the Temptation, the words "καὶ ἰδοὺ ἄγγελοι προσῆλθον καὶ διηκόνουν αὐτῷ" are inserted. Before this we find that the quotation, "Man doth not live by bread alone," is continued ("but by every word, &c.," iv. 4). In chap. viii. 12, "εἰς τὸ σκότος τὸ ἐξώτερον" is a formula current with St. Matthew (for the simple ἔξω). But of considerably greater importance are the following instances, wherein we trace distinct bias of various kinds:—

1. Jerusalem is introduced as the "holy city" (iv. 5); here we recognise the bias of a Christian of Jerusalem (note, however, that the term does not occur in the reproduction of a discourse of our Lord).

2. The addition in chap. xxiii. 23 (ταῦτα ἔδει ποιῆσαι κἀκεῖνα μὴ παρεῖναι) displays a Jewish Christian reverence for ceremonial precepts.[1]

[1] The whole verse, xxiii. 27, is possibly an interpolation; one cannot come to a clear decision on this point.

3. The conception of τέλειος is introduced into chap. v. 48 (*cf.* the conception δίκαιος); a distinct ethical tendency is hereby indicated.

4. In chap. v. 32, in reference to the question of divorce, an important limitation is given in the interpolated phrase παρεκτὸς λόγου πορνείας.

5. Another limitation is given in the τῷ πνεύματι (with οἱ πτωχοί) of chap. v. 3.

6. The omission of the enigmatical quotation formula (xxiii. 34): καὶ ἡ Σοφία τοῦ θεοῦ εἶπεν, seems necessarily to presuppose the dogmatic bias of one who refused to recognise an uncanonical writing.

7. The substitution of "Father in heaven" for the "Angels of God" (x. 32, 33) is connected with the evangelist's Christological position.

8. The addition of ἕνεκεν ἐμοῦ in chap. x. 39 is likewise due to the influence of Christological dogma.

9. The addition of μεταξὺ σοῦ καὶ αὐτοῦ μόνου to ἔλεγξον αὐτόν (xviii. 15) points to the existence of a stereotyped gradation of disciplinary rule in the Christian community. But it is questionable whether this passage in its present form belongs to the original text of St. Matthew.

10. Lastly, in chap. xxiii. 34, St. Matthew has probably interpolated the words καὶ σταυρώσετε καὶ ἐξ αὐτῶν μαστιγώσετε ἐν ταῖς συναγωγαῖς ὑμῶν, and has added ἀπὸ πόλεως εἰς πόλιν to διώξετε.

Probably these are all variations which St. Matthew has allowed himself to make from the transmitted text of Q (add also the clause ἕως ἂν πάντα γένηται in chap. v. 18).[1] Taking into account the considerable size of Q, they are few in number and of slight importance. Yet, on the other hand, they are numerous enough to exclude the hypothesis that St. Luke did not follow a source common to himself and St. Matthew, but used the gospel of St. Matthew itself.

As for the variants of St. Luke, they are eight to ten times as numerous as those of St. Matthew. As in the case of the former group (pp. 38 ff.), so also here it can be clearly shown that these variants are almost exclusively of a stylistic character. The twelve categories of our former list are now increased by several others. The most important are the following:—

13. He introduces the imperfect, erases the hist. present, and makes a correct use of the participle, imperfect, and infinitive present and aorist.

14. He substitutes the infinitive of the verb for a prepositional clause.

[1] Concerning υἱοῦ βαραχίου (chap. xxiii. 35), see my remarks on the passage itself. If the words were added by St. Matthew himself, the question arises as to which Zacharias he was thinking of. In spite of Wellhausen's discussion of this question, the last word on the subject has not yet been said. The theory that it is the Zacharias who was slain in the Temple at Jerusalem in the year 67 or 68 A.D. is, in my opinion, impossible; for though St. Matthew could well put a detailed prophecy into the mouth of our Lord, yet he could not have let him say: ὃν ἐφονεύσατε. Since it follows from St. Luke that the saying in Q was not introduced as a word of the Lord, but as an utterance of the Sophia, this later Zacharias is absolutely excluded.—I do not wish here to go further into the question of the Lord's Prayer. The address as it appears in St. Matthew suggests that the evangelist himself was the editor; but there are other reasons leading to a contrary opinion.

15. He introduces the genit. abs.

16. He amplifies, exaggerates, emphasises, accentuates.

17. He writes λέγειν πρός, inserts τίς, completes objects, &c.

18. In some cases he alters the whole style of the narrative, changes the order (*vide* pp. 38 f. and elsewhere), amplifies, curtails; the stylistic motive is not always apparent (other motives also enter into play, such as those which led him to the addition of new traits which enrich a simple narrative).[1]

19. He has favourite words and particles which he interpolates, while on the contrary he avoids other words.

Alterations in the subject-matter of the source showing distinct motive and bias are extremely rare when compared with those stylistic changes which remind us of the corrections constantly made in our hymn-books. In what follows, I propose to deal with the most important of these material alterations:—

In the story of the Temptation (iv. 1–13) it is expressly stated that our Lord was in Himself πλήρης πνεύματος ἁγίου, and that He was led into the wilderness not ὑπὸ τοῦ πνεύματος but ἐν πνεύματι. Also an opportunity is taken to let the devil explain that all power over the world had been delivered to him, and that he could give it to whomsoever he willed.—The saying concerning divorce is altered: it is made clear that the one guilty of adultery is

[1] These variants, or, one may say, arbitrary alterations, range between those of the least and the greatest interference with the text. He even replaces a mountain by a fig-tree.

he who divorces his wife and marries another.—Into the beginning of the Lord's Prayer (xi. 2–4) there is inserted a petition for the gift of the Holy Spirit (ἐλθέτω τὸ ἅγιον πνεῦμά σου ἐφ' ἡμᾶς καὶ καθαρισάτω ἡμᾶς).—In the parable of the Two Houses (vi. 46–49), St. Luke has inserted the new thought that in building everything depends upon the careful and laborious preparation of a proper foundation.—In chap. ix. 2 he has set "healing" side by side with the preaching of the approaching kingdom as an equally important function of the disciples.—In chap. xii. 3 he shows a disposition to guard against our Lord being represented as an esoteric teacher; in the following verse he has introduced "οἱ φίλοι μου" as a designation which our Lord had applied to His disciples, and in the same passage he has omitted the expression "to kill the soul," because it seemed to him—the Hellene—to be too paradoxical.—In chap. x. 16 he does not suffer our Lord to speak of the "reception" of the apostles (into the house); for this, at the time of the writer, was no longer possible, but of "hearing" them.—Into the parable of the Lost Sheep (xv. 7), St. Luke has interpolated the trait of repentance, of which no mention was made in the text of the source (so also in xvii. 3, 4); in chap. xi. 52 he has substituted "gnosis" for the "kingdom"; in chap. xi. 42, τὴν ἀγάπην τοῦ θεοῦ for ἔλεος (and πίστις); in chap. xi. 49, "apostles" for "wise men and scribes"; and in chap. vi. 22 he has inserted ἕνεκεν τοῦ υἱοῦ τοῦ ἀνθρώπου.

These, so far as I can see, are all the corrections which display a distinct bias in regard to subject-matter. Such bias, therefore, has had no stronger influence with St. Luke than with St. Matthew—indeed, in the former case, its influence is somewhat weaker. In regard to style, however, St. Luke has thoroughly revised the text of the source, while St. Matthew in this respect has, as it seems, almost entirely refrained from correction. Yet although the stylistic corrections of St. Luke are so numerous, we cannot say that he has completely obliterated the characteristics of his exemplar. Indeed, in spite of all, we cannot but recognise that his work of revision is ever carried out in a conservative spirit, and that his readers receive from him a just impression of our Lord's style of discourse. In not a few passages we are left in darkness as to the reason why in one place he corrects and in another place he allows the transmitted text to stand in spite of its harshness; only in some passages can we explain St. Luke's version from his consideration of the parallel sections of St. Mark. In a few cases it is possible to doubt whether any common source lies at the background of St. Matthew and St. Luke (as in St. Luke vi. 46–49; vii. 1–10; xi. 41, 44; xiv. 26); yet there is an overbalancing weight of probability in favour of this hypothesis. We, however, almost always notice that short and pregnant utterances of our Lord, as compared with the longer discourses, have suffered least correction, and that the revision is most stringent in narrative and parable.

That one and the same Greek translation of an Aramaic original lies behind the two gospels is shown by the large number of parallel sections which are verbally alike. Yet it is impossible to say anything at all definite concerning the homogeneity and extent of this source.[1] The exemplar used by St. Matthew may have differed in this or that detail from the exemplar which lay before St. Luke—it is even probable from the nature of such texts that this was so—but we have found no sure criteria by which we can clearly distinguish the separate exemplars so that we can with any propriety speak of Q[1] and Q[2]. Even the translation-variants, to which Wellhausen, Nestle, and others have drawn attention, are not so certain as they appear at first sight; always, or almost always, they admit of other explanations. Nevertheless, I would not deny the possibility, and here and there even the probability, of such variants. That in many sentences the Aramaic original is discernible under the veil of the Greek text, is a fact which does not require to be specially pointed out.[2]

[1] Yet we may here remark that there is no basis for the hypothesis that the parts of the Sermon on the Mount, which are common to St. Matthew and St. Luke, are not dependent upon a common written source, but are derived from oral tradition. The situation here is not dissimilar to that of many other passages—*i.e.* it is beyond measure probable that St. Luke had before him a written text (the same which St. Matthew has used) which he has edited in accordance with his own stylistic principles.

[2] The result to which our investigation has brought us agrees in all important points with the results obtained by Wernle. This scholar, while rejecting the hypothesis that St. Luke was distinctly biassed in his reproduction of his sources, writes as follows ("Synopt. Frage," s. 88):—"St. Luke had before him the discourses of the Logia-source in the primary form, not in a secondary edition. He himself, in spite of his conservative attitude, submitted this source to a threefold redaction: (1) he corrected it in accordance with his own Greek style; (2) he arranged and furbished up the discourses so as to give them definite positions in the course

On the basis of the preceding investigations, I open the second chapter with a reconstruction of the text of Q. In not a few passages I am quite conscious of the hypothetical character of the text as it is printed. But without boldness it is impossible to make any advance in the solution of a problem such as this, and one must reckon with probabilities. However, I may claim no slight probability for the text I offer. But before we pass to the next chapter, I would add an appendix which is intended to justify my neglect of the sections, St. Matt. xxi. 32 (St. Luke vii. 29, 30), St. Matt. xxii. 2–11 (St. Luke xiv. 16–23), and St. Matt. xxv. 14–30 (St. Luke xix. 12–27), in my attempt to ascertain the contents and the text of Q.

of the narrative [this does not come out so clearly in the course of our investigations, because St. Luke's introductions to the discourses have from the first been excluded from consideration]; (3) he has edited them in accordance with the requirements of the times." Wernle is also correct in his further remark (s. 185): "Almost everywhere St. Matthew has preserved a better text than St. Luke;" yet he ought to have added that in St. Matthew there are to be found many alterations of the text of a very drastic nature—far more drastic than any St. Luke has allowed himself to make.

APPENDIX TO CHAPTER I

St. Matt. xxi. 32: ἦλθεν γὰρ Ἰωάννης πρὸς ὑμᾶς ἐν ὁδῷ δικαιοσύνης, καὶ οὐκ ἐπιστεύσατε [scil. οἱ ἀρχιερεῖς καὶ οἱ πρεσβύτεροι] αὐτῷ· οἱ δὲ τελῶναι καὶ αἱ πόρναι ἐπίστευσαν αὐτῷ· ὑμεῖς δὲ ἰδόντες οὐδὲ μετεμελήθητε ὕστερον τοῦ πιστεῦσαι αὐτῷ.

St. Luke vii. 29, 30: καὶ πᾶς ὁ λαὸς ἀκούσας καὶ οἱ τελῶναι ἐδικαίωσαν τὸν θεόν, βαπτισθέντες τὸ βάπτισμα Ἰωάννου· οἱ δὲ Φαρισαῖοι καὶ οἱ νομικοὶ τὴν βουλὴν τοῦ θεοῦ ἠθέτησαν εἰς ἑαυτούς, μὴ βαπτισθέντες ὑπ᾽ αὐτοῦ.

St. Matthew introduces this passage among the discourses with the Jewish authorities (at the conclusion of the parable of the Two Sons) after the entry into Jerusalem; in St. Luke it occurs very much earlier, in connection with the long discourse concerning St. John (that it does not fit into the context either at the one place or the other can be easily shown, *vide* Wellhausen on both passages). But one cannot but entertain serious doubt as to whether the passage belongs to Q—indeed whether the two versions are directly dependent upon any single common source. They are certainly derived from a common tradition—viz. some saying of our Lord to the effect, "The publicans followed the preaching of John, while the leaders of the people rejected him." But beyond this all is different. Moreover, both in St. Matthew and St. Luke there occur in these passages such strong traces of the characteristics of the respective evangelists, or such evident signs of dependence upon the context, that it is no longer possible to deduce from them the wording of the original tradition. "Οἱ τελῶναι καὶ αἱ πόρναι" in St. Matthew come from xxi. 31; "δικαιοσύνη" must as a rule be regarded as an interpolation by St. Matthew; "πιστεύειν αὐτῷ," thrice repeated, is derived from xxi. 25, and μεταμέλεσθαι from xxi. 29. The same is the case in St. Luke. "Πᾶς ὁ λαός" occurs a dozen times in this gospel (never in St. Mark, once in St. Matthew); the active δικαιοῦν is never found in St. Matthew and St. Mark, while it occurs thrice in St. Luke's gospel; βαπτισθέντες τὸ βάπτισμα is Lukan (*cf.* τιμαῖς ἐτίμησαν, ἀπειλῇ ἀπειλησώμεθα, παραγγελίᾳ παρηγγείλαμεν, ἐπιθυμίᾳ ἐπεθύμησα, φωνήσας φωνῇ, ἀναστὰς ἔστη, μενον ἔμενεν, φυλάσσοντες φυλακάς, ἀστραπὴ ἀστράπτουσα, φορτία φορτίζειν); likewise οἱ νομικοί in itself, and in conjunction with οἱ Φαρισαῖοι, is Lukan; "ἡ βουλή" does not occur in St. Matthew, St. Mark, and St. John, while it is used nine times by St. Luke; ἀθετεῖν (wanting in St. Matthew) is also inserted by St. Luke in x. 16 = St. Matt. x. 40; εἰς ἑαυτούς (ἑαυτόν) occurs only once again in the gospels, viz. in St. Luke xv. 17. Therefore we can say absolutely nothing concerning the form and origin of this saying.

St. Matt. xxii. 2–11 (the Great Supper)—St. Luke xiv. 16–24.

The skeleton is identical: A man who gives a feast; his first invitation (to those who are invited as a matter of course) is refused on the excuse of business of various kinds. The master becomes angry and invites the vagabonds. In detail some verbal, or almost verbal, coincidences are found: ἄνθρωπος (the giver of the feast), ἀπέστειλεν τὸν δοῦλον αὐτοῦ (τοὺς δούλους αὐτοῦ), οἱ κεκλημένοι, ἔρχεσθε . . . ἕτοιμά ἐστιν (ἡτοίμακα . . . δεῦτε), ἀγρὸν ἠγόρασα (εἰς τὸν ἴδιον ἀγρόν), ζεύγη βοῶν ἠγόρασα (εἰς τὴν ἐμπορίαν αὐτοῦ), ὀργισθείς (ὠργίσθη), εἶπεν τῷ δούλῳ αὐτοῦ (λέγει τοῖς δούλοις αὐτοῦ), ἔξελθε εἰς τὰς πλατείας καὶ ῥύμας τῆς πόλεως (πορεύεσθε ἐπὶ τὰς διεξόδους τῶν ὁδῶν), ἔξελθε εἰς τὰς ὁδούς (ἐξελθόντες εἰς τὰς ὁδούς).

But in contrast with these coincidences we find instances of great dissimilarity:—

1. In St. Matthew the host is a king (God).

2. The feast is a marriage-feast.

3. The marriage feast is given in honour of the son (Christ).

4. In St. Matthew several servants[1] are sent out with invitations, in St. Luke only one.[2]

5. In St. Matthew the first invited are invited twice (the second time other servants are sent); in St. Luke, after the invitation of the poor, homeless, &c., since there is still room, the invitation is extended to the utterly destitute.

6. In St. Matthew the second invitation to the first invited is amplified so as to attract them.

7. In St. Matthew it is only shortly stated what the first invited did instead of responding to the invitation; in St. Luke their excuses are given word for word (three cases are given in contrast to two in St. Matthew).

8. St. Matthew relates that some of the invited ill-treated and slew the inviting servants; St. Luke knows nothing of this.

9. St. Matthew relates that the king sent his armies against those murderers and destroyed them and burnt their city;[3] St. Luke tells us nothing of this.[4]

10. St. Matthew adds the story of the man without a wedding garment.

[1] The prophets are probably signified. I do not understand how Wellhausen has arrived at the conclusion that the apostles are meant.

[2] Perhaps our Lord Himself is signified; but this interpretation is by no means certain.

[3] The text here is, of course, doubtful; perhaps we ought to read "destroyed them and their cities."

[4] Taking together these new traits in St. Matthew, it is clear that the evangelist has amalgamated a second parable (B) with the main parable (A). B tells us of a king against whom his subjects revolted in his absence, and who punished them with a terrible vengeance. This parable was allied to the parable of the Vineyard.

There is no need of many words to prove that here St. Matthew is almost everywhere secondary; the only question is whether the distinction of two classes of poor, as well as the verbal report of the excuses in St. Luke, are primary. The former trait answers to this evangelist's warm interest in the very poorest, and the latter to that pictorial style which is a frequent characteristic of St. Luke. Nevertheless, in these traits he may also preserve the original text. The main distinction between the two versions is that St. Matthew has transformed a genuine parable[1] into an allegory with an historical motive.

Did, however, the text, as presented in St. Luke, form the exemplar of St. Matthew? and did it belong to Q? The first question should perhaps be answered in the affirmative: the exemplar of St. Matthew, so far as its essential content is concerned, would not have presented a very different appearance from the text given in St. Luke, which besides permits of easy translation back again into Aramaic.[2] The second question

[1] In the concluding verse in St. Luke (xiv. 24) our Lord Himself is represented as the host; but the introduction of this trait has not seriously affected the general character of the original parable.

[2] Note also that *δέ* is wanting, and that, on the other hand, ten clauses of the section begin with *καί* (the style is, however, Lukan in places; thus *τις*, verse 16; *παραγενόμενος*, verse 21; *ὥρα*, with gen., verse 17 [*vide* St. Luke i. 10; Acts iii. 1, x. 3, xvi. 33, xxiii. 23], *ἤρξαντο*, verse 18; *παραιτεῖσθαι*, verses 18 and 19 [wanting in the gospels; see, however, Acts xxv. 11]; *ἀνάπηρος*, verse 21 [only again in New Testament in St. Luke xiv. 13]). *'Απὸ μιᾶς*, verse 18, can scarcely be Semitic (Wellhausen), but is a vulgar abbreviation for *ἀπὸ μιᾶς γνώμης* (so once in Philo) *vel ψυχῆς*. The phrase: *ἔχω ἀνάγκην ἐξελθὼν ἰδεῖν αὐτόν* is good Greek. Is the phrase: *ἔχε με παρῃτημένον* ("habe me excusatum," Martial) a Latinism? We must of course become much more cautious in making such assumptions. It is also possible that St. Matthew has preserved a more faithful representation of the original text *if we subtract all the traits which are derived from the parable B.*

I am inclined to answer in the negative; for St. Matthew has upon no other occasion so freely edited or amalgamated with other material those sections which are derived from Q. We must therefore conjecture that either this section did not occur in Q, or that if it did, it had already received another form in Q before that source reached St. Matthew. In the first case, the section lies outside our sphere of investigation into the constitution of the text of Q; in the second case, it is difficult to determine whether we should claim for Q the Lukan text purified of its Lukan traits or the text of St. Matthew less those traits derived from the parable B. Hence we must disregard this section altogether.

St. Matt. xxv. 14–30 (the parable of the Talents)—St. Luke xix. 12–27.

Here the chief distinction between St. Matthew and St. Luke lies in the fact that St. Luke has amalgamated with the parable of the Talents (C) the afore-mentioned parable B (concerning the king taking vengeance upon his revolted subjects) which St. Matthew has combined with the parable (A) of the preceding section.[1] A very perplexing case! The parable B could not preserve its separate existence, and has been incorporated into the parable of the Great Supper (A) by St. Matthew, and into the parable of the Talents (C) by St. Luke—in both cases bringing into its new context a disturbing and incongruous element. In St. Luke the parable B^2 is given in clearer detail than B^1 in St. Matthew, but its connection with the context is even poorer here than in the latter gospel. It is noteworthy that St. Matthew has amalgamated with A yet a third parable D (the

[1] B in St. Matthew is not quite identical with B in St. Luke, yet they are closely allied. We must therefore distinguish them as B^1 and B^2.

Wedding Garment), and that C and D both conclude with the clause: ἐκβάλετε (αὐτὸν) εἰς τὸ σκότος τὸ ἐξώτερον· ἐκεῖ ἔσται ὁ κλαυθμὸς καὶ ὁ βρυγμὸς τῶν ὀδόντων. The parable B² also concluded with a terrifying command: κατασφάξατε αὐτοὺς ἔμπροσθέν μου,[1] and the parable A likewise concludes with a melancholy sentence (St. Luke xiv. 24): οὐδεὶς τῶν ἀνδρῶν ἐκείνων τῶν κεκλημένων γεύσεταί μου τοῦ δείπνου. There were thus four parables, all of which were originally concerned with the Parousia (the Judgment and the Kingdom); St. Matthew gives them in the order—first, A amalgamated with B¹ and with D as an appendix, then C; St. Luke gives first A, then C amalgamated with B². How this came to pass in the course of tradition it is no longer possible to discover; we must therefore refrain from attempting to ascertain whether these parables stood in Q, and in what form.[2]

Now in regard to C, we find that at the beginning of the parable the form in St. Matthew is different from that in St. Luke; on the other hand verbal, or almost verbal, coincidences are not wanting—indeed in the second part and in the dialogue—this is characteristic!—they become very strongly marked. *Cf.* ἄνθρωπος (both) — ἀποδημῶν [ἐπορεύθη εἰς χώραν μακράν] — ἐκάλεσεν [καλέσας] — τοὺς ἰδίους δούλους [δέκα δούλους] — ἔδωκεν αὐτοῖς (both) — εὖ, δοῦλε ἀγαθέ . . . ἐπὶ ὀλίγα ἦς πιστός, ἐπὶ πολλῶν σε καταστήσω [εὖγε, ἀγαθὲ δοῦλε, ὅτι ἐν ἐλαχίστῳ πιστὸς ἐγένου, ἴσθι ἐξουσίαν ἔχων κτλ.] — σκληρὸς εἶ ἄνθρωπος, θερίζων ὅπου οὐκ ἔσπειρας καὶ συνάγων ὅθεν οὐ διεσκόρπισας [ἄνθρωπος αὐστηρὸς εἶ, αἴρεις ὃ οὐκ ἔθηκας, καὶ θερίζεις ὃ οὐκ ἔσπειρας] — πονηρὲ δοῦλε . . . ᾔδεις ὅτι θερίζω ὅπου οὐκ

[1] *Cf.* B¹: ἀπώλεσεν τοὺς φονεῖς ἐκείνους καὶ τὴν πόλιν αὐτῶν ἐνέπρησεν [or in place of the last four words simply, τὰς πόλεις].

[2] A further amalgamation took place in the Gospel of the Hebrews; here the parable of the Prodigal Son is combined with C.

ἔσπειρα καὶ συνάγω ὅθεν οὐ διεσκόρπισα [πονηρὲ δοῦλε, ᾔδεις ὅτι . . . αἴρων ὃ οὐκ ἔθηκα καὶ θηρίζων ὃ οὐκ ἔσπειρα] — ἔδει σε οὖν βαλεῖν τὰ ἀργύριά μου τοῖς τραπεζείταις, καὶ ἐλθὼν ἐγὼ ἐκομισάμην ἂν τὸ ἐμὸν σὺν τόκῳ [καὶ διὰ τί οὐκ ἔδωκάς μου τὸ ἀργύριον ἐπὶ τράπεζαν; κἀγὼ ἐλθὼν σὺν τόκῳ ἂν αὐτὸ ἔπραξα] — ἄρατε οὖν ἀπ' αὐτοῦ τὸ τάλαντον καὶ δότε τῷ ἔχοντι τὰ δέκα τάλαντα [ἄρατε ἀπ' αὐτοῦ τὴν μνᾶν καὶ δότε τῷ τὰς δέκα μνᾶς ἔχοντι] — τῷ γὰρ ἔχοντι παντὶ δοθήσεται . . . τοῦ δὲ μὴ ἔχοντος καὶ ὃ ἔχει ἀρθήσεται ἀπ' αὐτοῦ [ὅτι παντὶ τῷ ἔχοντι δοθήσεται, ἀπὸ δὲ τοῦ μὴ ἔχοντος καὶ ὃ ἔχει ἀρθήσεται]. Here it is quite evident that there is, at the background, a single traditional source declaring itself even in details of phraseology.[1] Hence the differences proceed most probably from the hand of the final revisor—*i.e.* either St. Luke or St. Matthew have made corrections. Which of them was the corrector? We give the following table of comparison, wherein we of course entirely neglect those traits which St. Luke has derived from B[2]:—

St Matthew :—	St. Luke :—
Servants of an indefinite number,	Ten servants,
The lord on his departure commits all his possessions to his servants,	The lord on his departure commits to each only a pound, and expressly tells them to trade therewith.
and indeed to each according to his ability, to one five talents, to another two, to the third one (these are intended to serve as examples of the method of distribution),	

[1] The synonyms are not translation-variants, but are linguistic corrections made by St. Luke.

he who received five talents gains therewith other five talents, he who received two gains other two, he who received one buries it in the earth;	This information is not given expressly in the narrative but is communicated in what follows.
on his return the lord as a reward sets those who had received the five and the two talents over "many things" and adds, "Enter into the joy of thy lord"; the talent is taken from him who had buried it.	the first says that his pound has gained ten pounds, the second that his pound has gained five pounds; the first is set over ten cities, the second over five cities, another [the other] returns the pound which he had kept wrapped in a napkin;[1] it is taken from him.

In St. Matthew the lord divides what he leaves behind him among all his servants—leaving them to decide what they should do with it; in St. Luke he makes trial of ten of his servants, giving them an express direction as to their procedure. In St. Matthew he divides to each individually according to his ability, but gives the same reward to those who had laboured; in St. Luke he gives the same to all, but the reward varies in accordance with the performance of each.[2] It seems to me that the simpler version is that of St. Matthew. This impression,

[1] Σουδάριον in St. Luke is an obvious Latinism.

[2] In St. Matthew it is the servant who gains, in St. Luke it is the pound which each has received. The latter version is naturally secondary, because it betrays most reflexion. Lastly, there are still obvious traces in St. Luke that his exemplar mentioned not ten but, as in St. Matthew, three servants.

moreover, is confirmed by a glance at a passage in St. Mark. Here we read (xiii. 34): ὡς ἄνθρωπος ἀπόδημος (*cf.* St. Matthew verse 14: ὥσπερ ἄνθρωπος ἀποδημῶν, otherwise in St. Luke) ἀφεὶς τὴν οἰκίαν αὐτοῦ καὶ δοὺς τοῖς δούλοις αὐτοῦ τὴν ἐξουσίαν (therefore not a test but the management of the whole household, as in St. Matthew; otherwise in St. Luke), ἑκάστῳ τὸ ἔργον αὐτοῦ (to each therefore according to his ability; so also in St. Matthew, otherwise in St. Luke). Thus St. Matthew, in contrast to St. Luke, agrees with St. Mark, who evidently knew of the parable which has been drastically edited by St. Luke. It does not, however, follow that the parable comes from Q, nor—if it comes from Q—that St. Matthew has handed it down to us in its original form. This is indeed improbable. In St. Mark to each servant is assigned his separate function in the household; this idea can indeed be still traced in St. Matthew (and in St. Luke), but it has been thrust into the background by ideas of another kind. The trafficking with money can have had no place in the forms of the parable with which St. Mark was acquainted; for he knows nothing at all of the distribution of money to the servants. Hence the common source of St. Matthew and St. Luke is secondary when compared with St. Mark (whether it was contained in Q we cannot tell). Its form has perhaps arisen from the combination of two parables (C^1: the departing lord delivers his household to the care of his servants; C^2: the departing lord gives his property to his servants that they may develop it).

CHAPTER II

LINGUISTIC AND HISTORICAL INVESTIGATION OF THE NON-MARKAN SECTIONS COMMON TO ST. MATTHEW AND ST. LUKE (Q).

I.—The Text

1. (St. Matt. iii. 5, 7–12; St. Luke iii. 3, 7–9, 16, 17.)

(7) [. . . Πᾶσα ἡ περίχωρος τοῦ Ἰορδάνου . . . ἰδὼν [Ἰωάννης] πολλοὺς [*vel* τοὺς ὄχλους] . . . ἐρχομένους ἐπὶ τὸ βάπτισμα εἶπεν αὐτοῖς·]

Γεννήματα ἐχιδνῶν, τίς ὑπέδειξεν ὑμῖν φυγεῖν ἀπὸ τῆς μελλούσης ὀργῆς; (8) ποιήσατε οὖν καρπὸν ἄξιον τῆς μετανοίας· (9) καὶ μὴ δόξητε [ἄρξησθε?] λέγειν ἐν ἑαυτοῖς· πατέρα ἔχομεν τὸν Ἀβραάμ· λέγω γὰρ ὑμῖν ὅτι δύναται ὁ θεὸς ἐκ τῶν λίθων τούτων ἐγεῖραι τέκνα τῷ Ἀβραάμ·· (10) ἤδη δὲ ἡ ἀξίνη πρὸς τὴν ῥίζαν τῶν δένδρων κεῖται· πᾶν οὖν δένδρον μὴ ποιοῦν καρπὸν καλὸν ἐκκόπτεται καὶ εἰς πῦρ βάλλεται. (11) ἐγὼ μὲν ὑμᾶς βαπτίζω ἐν ὕδατι εἰς μετάνοιαν· ὁ δὲ ὀπίσω μου ἐρχόμενος ἰσχυρότερός μού ἐστιν, οὗ οὐκ εἰμὶ ἱκανὸς τὰ ὑποδήματα βαστάσαι· αὐτὸς ὑμᾶς βαπτίσει ἐν [πνεύματι (ἁγίῳ) καὶ] πυρί, (12) οὗ τὸ πτύον ἐν τῇ χειρὶ αὐτοῦ, καὶ διακαθαριεῖ τὴν ἅλωνα αὐτοῦ, καὶ συνάξει τὸν σῖτον αὐτοῦ εἰς τὴν ἀποθήκην, τὸ δὲ ἄχυρον κατακαύσει πυρὶ ἀσβέστῳ (pp. 40, 41).

2. (St. Matt. iv. 1–11; St. Luke iv. 1–13.)

(1) Ὁ Ἰησοῦς ἀνήχθη εἰς τὴν ἔρημον ὑπὸ τοῦ πνεύματος πειρασθῆναι ὑπὸ τοῦ διαβόλου, (2) καὶ νηστεύσας

ἡμέρας μ' καὶ νύκτας μ' ὕστερον ἐπείνασεν, (3) καὶ ὁ πειράζων εἶπεν αὐτῷ· εἰ υἱὸς εἶ τοῦ θεοῦ, εἰπὲ ἵνα οἱ λίθοι οὗτοι ἄρτοι γένωνται, (4) καὶ ἀπεκρίθη· γέγραπται· οὐκ ἐπ' ἄρτῳ μόνῳ ζήσεται ὁ ἄνθρωπος. (5) παραλαμβάνει δὲ αὐτὸν εἰς Ἱερουσαλὴμ καὶ ἔστησεν αὐτὸν ἐπὶ τὸ πτερύγιον τοῦ ἱεροῦ (6) καὶ λέγει αὐτῷ· εἰ υἱὸς εἶ τοῦ θεοῦ, βάλε σεαυτὸν κάτω· γέγραπται γὰρ ὅτι τοῖς ἀγγέλοις αὐτοῦ ἐντελεῖται περὶ σοῦ καὶ ἐπὶ χειρῶν ἀροῦσίν σε, μή ποτε προσκόψῃς πρὸς λίθον τὸν πόδα σου. (7) ἔφη αὐτῷ ὁ Ἰησοῦς· πάλιν γέγραπται· οὐκ ἐκπειράσεις κύριον τὸν θεόν σου. (8) πάλιν παραλαμβάνει αὐτὸν εἰς ὄρος ὑψηλὸν λίαν καὶ δείκνυσιν αὐτῷ πάσας τὰς βασιλείας τοῦ κόσμου καὶ τὴν δόξαν αὐτῶν, (9) καὶ εἶπεν αὐτῷ· ταῦτά σοι πάντα δώσω, ἐὰν προσκυνήσῃς μοι. (10) καὶ λέγει αὐτῷ ὁ Ἰησοῦς· γέγραπται· κύριον τὸν θεόν σου προσκυνήσεις καὶ αὐτῷ μόνῳ λατρεύσεις. (11) καὶ ἀφίησιν αὐτὸν ὁ διάβολος (pp. 41 ff.).

3. (St. Matt. v. 1–4, 6, 11, 12; St. Luke vi. 17, 20–23.)

(1) (2) [. . . ὄχλοι . . . ἐδίδαξεν τοὺς μαθητὰς λέγων . . .]

(3) Μακάριοι οἱ πτωχοί, ὅτι αὐτῶν ἐστιν ἡ βασιλεία τοῦ θεοῦ,

(4) μακάριοι οἱ πενθοῦντες, ὅτι αὐτοὶ παρακληθήσονται,

(6) μακάριοι οἱ πεινῶντες, ὅτι αὐτοὶ χορτασθήσονται.

(11) μακάριοί ἐστε, ὅταν ὀνειδίσωσιν ὑμᾶς καὶ διώξωσιν καὶ εἴπωσιν πᾶν πονηρὸν καθ' ὑμῶν ψευδόμενοι.

(12) χαίρετε καὶ ἀγαλλιᾶσθε, ὅτι ὁ μισθὸς ὑμῶν

πολὺς ἐν τοῖς οὐρανοῖς· οὕτως γὰρ ἐδίωξαν τοὺς προφήτας τοὺς πρὸ ὑμῶν (p. 48).

4. (St. Matt. v. 39, 40; St. Luke vi. 29.)

(39) Ὅστις σε ῥαπίζει εἰς τὴν [δεξιὰν] σιαγόνα [σου], στρέψον αὐτῷ καὶ τὴν ἄλλην, (40) καὶ τῷ θέλοντί σοι κριθῆναι καὶ τὸν χιτῶνά σου λαβεῖν, ἄφες αὐτῷ καὶ τὸ ἱμάτιον (p. 58).

5. (St. Matt. v. 42; St. Luke vi. 30.)

(42) Τῷ αἰτοῦντί σε δός, καὶ τὸν θέλοντα ἀπὸ σοῦ δανίσασθαι μὴ ἀποστραφῇς (p. 58).

6. (St. Matt. v. 44–48; St. Luke vi. 27, 28, 35[b], 32, 33, 36.)

(44) Ἐγὼ λέγω ὑμῖν· ἀγαπᾶτε τοὺς ἐχθροὺς ὑμῶν καὶ προσεύχεσθε ὑπὲρ τῶν διωκόντων ὑμᾶς, (45) ὅπως γένησθε υἱοὶ τοῦ πατρὸς ὑμῶν, ὅτι τὸν ἥλιον αὐτοῦ ἀνατέλλει ἐπὶ πονηροὺς καὶ ἀγαθοὺς [καὶ βρέχει ἐπὶ δικαίους καὶ ἀδίκους]. (46) ἐὰν γὰρ ἀγαπήσητε τοὺς ἀγαπῶντας ὑμᾶς, τίνα μισθὸν ἔχετε; οὐχὶ καὶ οἱ τελῶναι τὸ αὐτὸ ποιοῦσιν; (47) καὶ ἐὰν ἀσπάσησθε τοὺς ἀδελφοὺς ὑμῶν μόνον, τί περισσὸν ποιεῖτε; οὐχὶ καὶ οἱ ἐθνικοὶ τὸ αὐτὸ ποιοῦσιν; (48) ἔσεσθε οὖν οἰκτίρμονες [? ἐλεήμονες ?] ὡς ὁ πατὴρ ὑμῶν οἰκτίρμων [? ἐλεήμων ?] ἐστίν (p. 59).

7. (St. Matt. vii. 12; St. Luke vi. 31.)

(12) Πάντα ὅσα ἐὰν θέλητε ἵνα ποιῶσιν ὑμῖν οἱ ἄνθρωποι, οὕτως καὶ ὑμεῖς ποιεῖτε αὐτοῖς (p. 9).

8. (St. Matt. vii. 1–5; St. Luke vi. 37, 38, 41, 42.)

(1) Μὴ κρίνετε, ἵνα μὴ κριθῆτε, (2) ἐν ᾧ γὰρ κρίματι κρίνετε κριθήσεσθε, καὶ ἐν ᾧ μέτρῳ μετρεῖτε μετρηθήσεται ὑμῖν. (3) τί δὲ βλέπεις τὸ κάρφος τὸ ἐν τῷ ὀφθαλμῷ τοῦ ἀδελφοῦ σου, τὴν δὲ ἐν τῷ σῷ ὀφθαλμῷ δοκὸν οὐ κατανοεῖς; (4) ἢ πῶς ἐρεῖς τῷ ἀδελφῷ σου· ἄφες ἐκβάλω τὸ κάρφος ἐκ τοῦ ὀφθαλμοῦ σου, καὶ ἡ δοκὸς ἐν τῷ ὀφθαλμῷ σου; (5) ὑποκριτά, ἔκβαλε πρῶτον ἐκ τοῦ ὀφθαλμοῦ σου τὴν δοκόν, καὶ τότε διαβλέψεις ἐκβαλεῖν τὸ κάρφος ἐκ τοῦ ὀφθαλμοῦ τοῦ ἀδελφοῦ σου (p. 8).

9. (St. Matt. xv. 14; St. Luke vi. 39.)

(14) Τυφλὸς τυφλὸν ἐὰν ὁδηγῇ, ἀμφότεροι εἰς βόθυνον πεσοῦνται (p. 28).

10. (St. Matt. x. 24, 25; St. Luke vi. 40.)

(24) Οὐκ ἔστιν μαθητὴς ὑπὲρ τὸν διδάσκαλον οὐδὲ δοῦλος ὑπὲρ τὸν κύριον αὐτοῦ. (25) ἀρκετὸν τῷ μαθητῇ ἵνα γένηται ὡς ὁ διδάσκαλος αὐτοῦ, καὶ ὁ δοῦλος ὡς ὁ κύριος αὐτοῦ (p. 79).

11. (St. Matt. vii. 16–18; xii. 33; St. Luke vi. 43, 44.)

(33) Ἐκ τοῦ καρποῦ τὸ δένδρον γινώσκεται. μήτι συλλέγουσιν ἀπὸ ἀκανθῶν σταφυλὰς ἢ ἀπὸ τριβόλων σῦκα; (17) οὕτως πᾶν δένδρον ἀγαθὸν καρπὸν καλὸν ποιεῖ, τὸ δὲ σαπρὸν δένδρον καρπὸν πονηρὸν ποιεῖ. (18) οὐ δύναται δένδρον ἀγαθὸν καρπὸν πονηρὸν ἐνεγκεῖν οὐδὲ δένδρον σαπρὸν καρπὸν καλὸν ποιεῖν (p. 68).

12. (St. Matt. vii. 21, 24–27; St. Luke vi. 46–49.)

(21) [Οὐ πᾶς ὁ λέγων μοι· κύριε κύριε, εἰσελεύσεται εἰς τὴν βασιλείαν τοῦ θεοῦ, ἀλλ' ὁ ποιῶν τὸ θέλημα τοῦ πατρός μου]. (24) πᾶς οὖν ὅστις ἀκούει μου τοὺς λόγους τούτους καὶ ποιεῖ αὐτούς, ὑποδείξω ὑμῖν τίνι ἐστὶν ὅμοιος· ὅμοιός ἐστιν [or in place of these seven words simply ὁμοιωθήσεται] ἀνδρὶ ὅστις ᾠκοδόμησεν αὐτοῦ τὴν οἰκίαν ἐπὶ τὴν πέτραν. (25) καὶ κατέβη ἡ βροχὴ καὶ ἦλθον οἱ ποταμοὶ καὶ ἔπνευσαν οἱ ἄνεμοι καὶ προσέπεσαν τῇ οἰκίᾳ ἐκείνῃ, καὶ οὐκ ἔπεσεν· τεθεμελίωτο γὰρ ἐπὶ τὴν πέτραν. (26) καὶ πᾶς ὁ ἀκούων μου τοὺς λόγους τούτους καὶ μὴ ποιῶν αὐτοὺς ὁμοιωθήσεται ἀνδρὶ ὅστις ᾠκοδόμησεν αὐτοῦ τὴν οἰκίαν ἐπὶ τὴν ἄμμον. (27) καὶ κατέβη ἡ βροχὴ καὶ ἦλθον οἱ ποταμοὶ καὶ ἔπνευσαν οἱ ἄνεμοι καὶ προσέκοψαν τῇ οἰκίᾳ ἐκείνῃ, καὶ ἔπεσεν, καὶ ἦν ἡ πτῶσις αὐτῆς μεγάλη (p. 70).

13. (St. Matt. vii. 28; viii. 5–10, 13; St. Luke vii. 1–10.)

(28, viii. 5) [After He had spoken these words] εἰσῆλθεν εἰς Καφαρναοὺμ καὶ προσῆλθεν αὐτῷ ἑκατόνταρχος παρακαλῶν αὐτὸν (6) καὶ λέγων· κύριε, ὁ παῖς μου βέβληται ἐν τῇ οἰκίᾳ παραλυτικός, δεινῶς βασανιζόμενος. (7) λέγει αὐτῷ· ἐγὼ ἐλθὼν θεραπεύσω αὐτόν. (8) ἀποκριθεὶς δὲ ὁ ἑκατόνταρχος ἔφη· κύριε, οὐκ εἰμὶ ἱκανὸς ἵνα μου ὑπὸ τὴν στέγην εἰσέλθῃς· ἀλλὰ μόνον εἰπὲ λόγῳ, καὶ ἰαθήσεται ὁ παῖς μου. (9) καὶ γὰρ ἐγὼ ἄνθρωπός εἰμι ὑπὸ ἐξουσίαν, ἔχων ὑπ' ἐμαυτὸν στρατιώτας, καὶ λέγω τούτῳ· πορεύθητι, καὶ πορεύεται, καὶ ἄλλῳ· ἔρχου, καὶ ἔρχεται, καὶ τῷ δούλῳ μου· ποίησον τοῦτο, καὶ ποιεῖ. (10) ἀκούσας δὲ ὁ Ἰησοῦς ἐθαύμασεν καὶ εἶπεν τοῖς ἀκολουθοῦσιν· [ἀμὴν] λέγω ὑμὶν, οὐδὲ ἐν τῷ Ἰσραὴλ τοσαύτην πίστιν εὗρον. [(13) καὶ εἶπεν ὁ Ἰησοῦς τῷ ἑκατοντάρχῃ· [ὕπαγε], ὡς ἐπίστευσας γενηθήτω σοι. καὶ ἰάθη ὁ παῖς ἐν τῇ ὥρᾳ ἐκείνῃ] (pp. 71, 74).

14. (St. Matt. xi. 2–11; St. Luke vii. 18–28.)

(2) Ὁ δὲ Ἰωάννης ἀκούσας ἐν τῷ δεσμωτηρίῳ τὰ ἔργα τοῦ Χριστοῦ, πέμψας διὰ τῶν μαθητῶν αὐτοῦ εἶπεν αὐτῷ· (3) σὺ εἶ ὁ ἐρχόμενος ἢ ἕτερον προσδοκῶμεν; (4) καὶ ἀποκριθεὶς εἶπεν αὐτοῖς· πορευθέντες ἀπαγγείλατε Ἰωάννῃ ἃ ἀκούετε καὶ βλέπετε. (5) τυφλοὶ ἀναβλέπουσιν καὶ χωλοὶ περιπατοῦσιν, λεπροὶ καθαρίζονται καὶ κωφοὶ ἀκούουσιν, καὶ νεκροὶ ἐγείρονται καὶ πτωχοὶ εὐαγγελίζονται· (6) καὶ μακάριός ἐστιν ὃς ἂν μὴ σκανδαλισθῇ ἐν ἐμοί. (7) τούτων δὲ πορευομένων ἤρξατο λέγειν τοῖς ὄχλοις περὶ Ἰωάννου· τί ἐξήλθατε εἰς τὴν ἔρημον θεάσασθαι; κάλαμον ὑπὸ ἀνέμου σαλευόμενον; (8) ἀλλὰ τί ἐξήλθατε ἰδεῖν; ἄνθρωπον ἐν μαλακοῖς ἐμφιεσμένον; ἰδοὺ οἱ τὰ μαλακὰ φοροῦντες ἐν τοῖς οἴκοις τῶν βασιλέων. (9) ἀλλὰ τί ἐξήλθατε; προφήτην ἰδεῖν; ναὶ λέγω ὑμῖν, καὶ περισσότερον προφήτου. (10) οὗτός ἐστιν περὶ οὗ γέγραπται· ἰδοὺ ἐγὼ ἀποστέλλω τὸν ἄγγελόν μου πρὸ προσώπου σου, ὃς κατασκευάσει τὴν ὁδόν σου ἔμπροσθέν σου. (11) [ἀμὴν] λέγω ὑμῖν, οὐκ ἐγήγερται ἐν γεννητοῖς γυναικῶν μείζων Ἰωάννου [τοῦ βαπτιστοῦ]· ὁ δὲ μικρότερος ἐν τῇ βασιλείᾳ τοῦ θεοῦ μείζων αὐτοῦ ἐστιν (pp. 90, 14).

15. (St. Matt. xi. 16–19; St. Luke vii. 31–35.)

(16) Τίνι ὁμοιώσω τὴν γενεὰν ταύτην [καὶ τίνι ἐστὶν ὁμοία]; ὁμοία ἐστὶν παιδίοις καθημένοις ἐν ταῖς ἀγοραῖς ἃ προσφωνοῦντα τοῖς ἑτέροις (17) λέγουσιν· ηὐλήσαμεν ὑμῖν καὶ οὐκ ὠρχήσασθε· ἐθρηνήσαμεν καὶ οὐκ ἐκόψασθε. (18) ἦλθεν γὰρ Ἰωάννης μήτε ἐσθίων μήτε πίνων, καὶ λέγουσιν· δαιμόνιον ἔχει. (19) ἦλθεν ὁ υἱὸς τοῦ ἀνθρώπου ἐσθίων καὶ πίνων, καὶ λέγουσιν· ἰδοὺ ἄνθρωπος φάγος καὶ οἰνοπότης, τελωνῶν φίλος καὶ ἁμαρτωλῶν. καὶ ἐδικαιώθη ἡ σοφία ἀπὸ τῶν τέκνων αὐτῆς (p. 16).

16. (St. Matt. x. 7; St. Luke ix. 2; x. 9, 11.)

(7) Πορευόμενοι κηρύσσετε λέγοντες ὅτι ἤγγικεν ἡ βασιλεία τοῦ θεοῦ (p. 79).

17. (St. Matt. viii. 19–22; St. Luke ix. 57–60.)

(19) [Εἶπέν τις αὐτῷ·] ἀκολουθήσω σοι ὅπου ἐὰν ἀπέρχῃ. (20) καὶ λέγει αὐτῷ ὁ Ἰησοῦς· αἱ ἀλώπεκες φωλεοὺς ἔχουσιν καὶ τὰ πετεινὰ τοῦ οὐρανοῦ κατασκηνώσεις, ὁ δὲ υἱὸς τοῦ ἀνθρώπου οὐκ ἔχει ποῦ τὴν κεφαλὴν κλίνῃ. (21) ἕτερος δὲ εἶπεν αὐτῷ· ἐπίτρεψόν μοι πρῶτον ἀπελθεῖν καὶ θάψαι τὸν πατέρα μου· (22) λέγει δὲ αὐτῷ· ἀκολούθει μοι, καὶ ἄφες τοὺς νεκροὺς θάψαι τοὺς ἑαυτῶν νεκρούς (p. 10).

18. (St. Matt. ix. 37, 38; St. Luke x. 2.)

(37) Λέγει αὐτοῖς [τοῖς μαθηταῖς αὐτοῦ?]· ὁ μὲν θερισμὸς πολύς, οἱ δὲ ἐργάται ὀλίγοι· (38) δεήθητε οὖν τοῦ κυρίου τοῦ θερισμοῦ ὅπως ἐκβάλῃ ἐργάτας εἰς τὸν θερισμὸν αὐτοῦ (p. 12).

19. (St. Matt. x. 16[a]; St. Luke x. 3.)

(16) Ἰδοὺ ἐγὼ ἀποστέλλω ὑμᾶς ὡς πρόβατα ἐν μέσῳ λύκων (p. 13).

20. (St. Matt. x. 12, 13; St. Luke x. 5, 6.)

(12) Εἰσερχόμενοι δὲ εἰς τὴν οἰκίαν ἀσπάσασθε αὐτήν· (13) καὶ ἐὰν ᾖ ἡ οἰκία ἀξία, ἐλθάτω ἡ εἰρήνη ὑμῶν ἐπ' αὐτήν· ἐὰν δὲ μὴ ᾖ ἀξία, ἡ εἰρήνη ὑμῶν πρὸς ὑμᾶς ἐπιστραφήτω. (Preceded by some words which can still be supplied with some degree of certainty from St. Luke x. 4: *μὴ βαστάζετε βαλλάντιον, μὴ πήραν, μὴ ὑποδήματα, καὶ μηδένα κατὰ τὴν ὁδὸν ἀσπάσησθε* [*i.e.* "do not stop"]) (p. 79).

21. (St. Matt. x. 10[b]; St. Luke x. 7[b].)

(10) Ἄξιος γὰρ ὁ ἐργάτης τῆς τροφῆς αὐτοῦ. Preceded by some such words as St. Luke x. 7[a]: *ἐν αὐτῇ τῇ οἰκίᾳ μένετε, ἔσθοντες καὶ πίνοντες τὰ παρ' αὐτῶν* (p. 12).

22. (St. Matt. x. 15; St. Luke x. 12.)

(15) ['Αμὴν] λέγω ὑμῖν· ἀνεκτότερον ἔσται γῇ Σοδόμων καὶ Γομόρρων [or in place of the last four words, Σοδόμοις] ἐν τῇ ἡμέρᾳ [ἐκείνῃ? κρίσεως?] ἢ τῇ πόλει ἐκείνῃ. (Preceded, according to St. Luke x. 8–11, by some such words as follow: *εἰς ἣν ἂν πόλιν εἰσέρχησθε κ. δέχωνται ὑμᾶς, ἐσθίετε τ. παρατιθέμενα ὑμῖν κ. λέγετε αὐτοῖς· ἤγγικεν ἡ βασ. τ. θεοῦ. εἰς ἣν δ' ἂν πόλιν εἰσέλθητε κ. μὴ δέχωνται ὑμᾶς, ἐξελθόντες εἰς τ. πλατείας αὐτῆς εἴπατε· κ. τ. κονιορτὸν τ. κολληθέντα ἡμῖν ἐκ. τ. πόλεως ὑμῶν εἰς τ. πόδας ἀπομασσόμεθα ὑμῖν*) (p. 13).

23. (St. Matt. xi. 21–23; St. Luke x. 13–15.)

(21) Οὐαί σοι, Χοραζείν, οὐαί σοι, Βηθσαϊδάν· ὅτι εἰ ἐν Τύρῳ καὶ Σιδῶνι ἐγένοντο αἱ δυνάμεις αἱ γενόμεναι ἐν ὑμῖν, πάλαι ἂν ἐν σάκκῳ καὶ σποδῷ μετενόησαν. (22) πλὴν [λέγω ὑμῖν] Τύρῳ καὶ Σιδῶνι ἀνεκτότερον ἔσται [ἐν ἡμέρᾳ κρίσεως? ἐν τῇ κρίσει?] ἢ ὑμῖν. (23) καὶ σύ, Καφαρναούμ, μὴ ἕως οὐρανοῦ ὑψωθήσῃ; ἕως ᾅδου καταβήσῃ (p. 17).

[24. (St. Matt. x. 40; St. Luke x. 16.)]

[Ὁ δεχόμενος ὑμᾶς ἐμὲ δέχεται, καὶ ὁ ἐμὲ δεχόμενος δέχεται τὸν ἀποστείλαντά με] (p. 86).

25. (St. Matt. xi. 25–27; St. Luke x. 21, 22.)

(25) Ἐν ἐκείνῳ τῷ καιρῷ εἶπεν· ἐξομολογοῦμαί σοι, πάτερ κύριε τοῦ οὐρανοῦ καὶ τῆς γῆς, ὅτι ἔκρυψας ταῦτα ἀπὸ σοφῶν καὶ συνετῶν καὶ ἀπεκάλυψας αὐτὰ νηπίοις· (26) ναί, ὁ πατήρ, ὅτι οὕτως εὐδοκία ἐγένετο ἔμπροσθέν σου. (27) πάντα μοι παρεδόθη ὑπὸ τοῦ πατρός, καὶ οὐδεὶς ἔγνω [τὸν υἱὸν εἰ μὴ ὁ πατὴρ οὐδὲ] τὸν πατέρα [τις ἔγνω] εἰ μὴ ὁ υἱὸς καὶ ᾧ ἐὰν βούληται ὁ υἱὸς ἀποκαλύψαι (p. 17).

26. (St. Matt. xiii. 16, 17; St. Luke x. 23[b], 24.)

(16) Ὑμῶν μακάριοι οἱ ὀφθαλμοί, ὅτι βλέπουσιν, καὶ τὰ ὦτα [ὑμῶν], ὅτι ἀκούουσιν. (17) [ἀμὴν γὰρ] λέγω ὑμῖν, ὅτι πολλοὶ προφῆται [καὶ βασιλεῖς] ἐπεθύμησαν ἰδεῖν α βλέπετε καὶ οὐκ εἶδαν, καὶ ἀκοῦσαι ἃ ἀκούετε, καὶ οὐκ ἤκουσαν (p. 25).

27. (St. Matt. vi. 9–13; St. Luke xi. 2–4.)

[(9) Πάτερ, (11) τὸν ἄρτον ἡμῶν τὸν ἐπιούσιον δὸς ἡμῖν σήμερον, (12) καὶ ἄφες ἡμῖν τὰ ὀφειλήματα ἡμῶν, ὡς καὶ ἡμεῖς ἀφήκαμεν τοῖς ὀφειλέταις ἡμῶν, (13) καὶ μὴ εἰσενέγκῃς ἡμᾶς εἰς πειρασμόν.] (p. 63).

28. (St. Matt. vii. 7–11; St. Luke xi. 9–13.)

(7) Αἰτεῖτε, καὶ δοθήσεται ὑμῖν· ζητεῖτε, καὶ εὑρήσετε· κρούετε καὶ ἀνοιγήσεται ὑμῖν. (8) πᾶς γὰρ ὁ αἰτῶν λαμβάνει, καὶ ὁ ζητῶν εὑρίσκει, καὶ τῷ κρούοντι ἀνοιγήσεται. (9) ἢ τίς ἐστιν ἐξ ὑμῶν ἄνθρωπος, ὃν αἰτήσει ὁ υἱὸς αὐτοῦ ἄρτον, μὴ λίθον ἐπιδώσει αὐτῷ; (10) ἢ καὶ ἰχθὺν αἰτήσει, μὴ ὄφιν ἐπιδώσει αὐτῷ; (11) εἰ οὖν ὑμεῖς πονηροὶ ὄντες οἴδατε [δόματα] ἀγαθὰ διδόναι τοῖς τέκνοις ὑμῶν, πόσῳ μᾶλλον ὁ πατὴρ ὁ ἐξ οὐρανοῦ δώσει ἀγαθὰ τοῖς αἰτοῦσιν αὐτόν; (p. 8).

29. (St. Matt. xii. 22, 23, 25, 27, 28, 30, 43–45; St. Luke xi. 14, 17, 19, 20, 23–26.)

(22) [ἐθεράπευσεν] δαιμονιζόμενον κωφόν, [ὥστε] τὸν κωφὸν λαλεῖν, (23) καὶ [ἐξίσταντο] [πάντες] οἱ ὄχλοι . . . (25) πᾶσα βασιλεία μερισθεῖσα ἐφ' ἑαυτὴν ἐρημοῦται . . . (27) καὶ εἰ ἐγὼ ἐν Βεελζεβοὺλ ἐκβάλλω τὰ δαιμόνια, οἱ υἱοὶ ὑμῶν ἐν τίνι ἐκβάλλουσιν; διὰ τοῦτο αὐτοὶ κριταὶ ἔσονται ὑμῶν· (28) εἰ δὲ ἐν πνεύματι θεοῦ ἐγὼ ἐκβάλλω τὰ δαιμόνια, ἄρα ἔφθασεν ἐφ' ὑμᾶς ἡ βασιλεία τοῦ θεοῦ. . . . (30) ὁ μὴ ὢν μετ' ἐμοῦ κατ' ἐμοῦ ἐστιν, καὶ ὁ μὴ συνάγων μετ' ἐμοῦ σκορπίζει . . . (43) ὅταν τὸ ἀκάθαρτον πνεῦμα ἐξέλθῃ ἀπὸ τοῦ ἀνθρώπου, διέρχεται δι' ἀνύδρων τόπων

ζητοῦν ἀνάπαυσιν καὶ οὐχ εὑρίσκει, (44) [τότε] λέγει· εἰς τὸν οἰκόν μου ἐπιστρέψω ὅθεν ἐξῆλθον· καὶ ἐλθὸν εὑρίσκει σκολάζοντα [καὶ] σεσαρωμένον καὶ κεκοσμημένον. (45) τότε πορεύεται καὶ παραλαμβάνει μεθ' ἑαυτοῦ ἑπτὰ πνεύματα πονηρότερα ἑαυτοῦ καὶ εἰσελθόντα κατοικεῖ ἐκεῖ, καὶ γίνεται τὰ ἔσχατα τοῦ ἀνθρώπου ἐκείνου χείρονα τῶν πρώτων (pp. 21, 24).

30. (St. Matt. xii. 38, 39, 41, 42; St. Luke xi. 16, 29–32.)

(38) [They said]: θέλομεν ἀπὸ σοῦ σημεῖον ἰδεῖν. (39) ὁ δὲ εἶπεν· γενεὰ πονηρὰ καὶ μοιχαλὶς σημεῖον ἐπιζητεῖ, καὶ σημεῖον οὐ δοθήσεται αὐτῇ εἰ μὴ τὸ σημεῖον Ἰωνᾶ· ὥσπερ γὰρ ἐγένετο Ἰωνᾶς τοῖς Νινευείταις σημεῖον, οὕτως ἔσται καὶ ὁ υἱὸς τοῦ ἀνθρώπου τῇ γενεᾷ ταύτῃ. (41) ἄνδρες Νινευεῖται ἀναστήσονται ἐν τῇ κρίσει μετὰ τῆς γενεᾶς ταύτης καὶ κατακρινοῦσιν αὐτήν, ὅτι μετενόησαν εἰς τὸ κήρυγμα Ἰωνᾶ, καὶ ἰδοὺ πλεῖον Ἰωνᾶ ὧδε. (42) βασίλισσα νότου ἐγερθήσεται ἐν τῇ κρίσει μετὰ τῆς γενεᾶς ταύτης καὶ κατακρινεῖ αὐτήν, ὅτι ἦλθεν ἐκ τῶν περάτων τῆς γῆς ἀκοῦσαι τὴν σοφίαν Σολομῶνος, καὶ ἰδοὺ πλεῖον Σολομῶνος ὧδε (p. 22).

31. (St. Matt. v. 15; St. Luke xi. 33.)

(15) Οὐ καίουσιν λύχνον καὶ τιθέασιν αὐτὸν ὑπὸ τὸν μόδιον, ἀλλ' ἐπὶ τὴν λυχνίαν, καὶ λάμπει πᾶσιν τοῖς ἐν τῇ οἰκίᾳ (p. 53).

32. (St. Matt. vi. 22, 23; St. Luke xi. 34, 35.)

(22) Ὁ λύχνος τοῦ σώματός ἐστιν ὁ ὀφθαλμός [σου]· ἐὰν οὖν ᾖ ὁ ὀφθαλμός σου ἁπλοῦς, ὅλον τὸ

σῶμά σου φωτεινὸν ἔσται· (23) ἐὰν δὲ ὁ ὀφθαλμός σου πονηρὸς ᾖ, ὅλον τὸ σῶμά σου σκοτεινὸν ἔσται. εἰ οὖν τὸ φῶς τὸ ἐν σοὶ σκότος ἐστίν, τὸ σκότος πόσον; (p. 4).

33. (St. Matt. xxiii. 4, 13, 23, 25, 27, 29, 30–32, 34–36; St. Luke xi. 46, 52, 42, 39, 44, 47–52.)

(4) [Perhaps a "Woe"] Δεσμεύουσιν φορτία βαρέα καὶ ἐπιτιθέασιν ἐπὶ τοὺς ὤμους τῶν ἀνθρώπων, καὶ αὐτοὶ τῷ δακτύλῳ αὐτῶν οὐ θέλουσιν κινῆσαι αὐτά.

(13) οὐαὶ ὑμῖν τοῖς Φαρισαίοις, ὅτι κλείετε τὴν βασιλείαν τοῦ θεοῦ ἔμπροσθεν τῶν ἀνθρώπων· ὑμεῖς γὰρ οὐκ εἰσέρχεσθε οὐδὲ τοὺς εἰσερχομένους ἀφίετε εἰσελθεῖν.

(23) οὐαὶ ὑμῖν τοῖς Φαρισαίοις, ὅτι ἀποδεκατοῦτε τὸ ἡδύοσμον καὶ τὸ ἄνηθον καὶ τὸ κύμινον, καὶ ἀφήκατε τὰ βαρύτερα τοῦ νόμου, τὴν κρίσιν καὶ τὸ ἔλεος.

(25) [Perhaps a "Woe"] [νῦν] ὑμεῖς οἱ Φαρισαῖοι, καθαρίζετε τὸ ἔξωθεν τοῦ ποτηρίου καὶ τῆς παροψίδος, ἔσωθεν δὲ γέμουσιν ἐξ ἁρπαγῆς καὶ ἀκρασίας.

(St. Luke xi. 44) οὐαὶ ὑμῖν, ὅτι ἐστὲ ὡς οἱ τάφοι οἱ ἄδηλοι, καὶ οἱ ἄνθρωποι οἱ περιπατοῦντες ἐπάνω οὐκ οἴδασιν.

[(St. Matthew 27) οὐαὶ ὑμῖν τοῖς Φαρισαίοις, ὅτι παρομοιάζετε τάφοις κεκονιαμένοις, οἵτινες ἔξωθεν μὲν φαίνονται ὡραῖοι, ἔσωθεν δὲ γέμουσιν ὀστέων νεκρῶν καὶ πάσης ἀκαθαρσίας.]

(29–32) οὐαὶ ὑμῖν, ὅτι οἰκοδομεῖτε τοὺς τάφους τῶν προφητῶν (30) καὶ λέγετε· εἰ ἤμεθα ἐν ταῖς ἡμέραις τῶν πατέρων ἡμῶν, οὐκ ἂν ἤμεθα αὐτῶν κοινωνοὶ ἐν τῷ αἵματι τῶν προφητῶν. (31) ὥστε μαρτυρεῖτε ἑαυτοῖς, ὅτι υἱοί ἐστε τῶν φονευσάντων τοὺς προφήτας, [(32) καὶ ὑμεῖς πληρώσατε τὸ μέτρον τῶν πατέρων ὑμῶν].

(34–36) διὰ τοῦτο καὶ ἡ Σοφία τοῦ θεοῦ εἶπεν· ἀποστέλλω πρὸς [εἰς] ὑμᾶς προφήτας καὶ σοφοὺς καὶ γραμματεῖς· ἐξ αὐτῶν ἀποκτενεῖτε καὶ διώξετε, (35) ὅπως ἔλθῃ ἐφ' ὑμᾶς πᾶν αἷμα ἐκχυννόμενον ἐπὶ τῆς γῆς ἀπὸ αἵματος Ἄβελ ἕως αἵματος Ζαχαρίου, ὃν ἐφονεύσατε μεταξὺ τοῦ ναοῦ καὶ τοῦ θυσιαστηρίου. (36) ἀμὴν λέγω ὑμῖν, ἥξει ταῦτα πάντα ἐπὶ τὴν γενεὰν ταύτην (p. 96).

34[a]. (St. Matt. x. 26–33; St. Luke xii. 2–9.)

(26) Οὐδέν ἐστιν κεκαλυμμένον ὃ οὐκ ἀποκαλυφθήσεται, καὶ κρυπτὸν ὃ οὐ γνωσθήσεται. (27) ὃ λέγω ὑμῖν ἐν τῇ σκοτίᾳ, εἴπατε ἐν τῷ φωτί· καὶ ὃ εἰς τὸ οὖς ἀκούετε, κηρύξατε ἐπὶ τῶν δωμάτων. (28) καὶ μὴ φοβεῖσθε ἀπὸ τῶν ἀποκτεννόντων τὸ σῶμα, τὴν δὲ ψυχὴν μὴ δυναμένων ἀποκτεῖναι· φοβεῖσθε δὲ μᾶλλον τὸν δυνάμενον καὶ ψυχὴν καὶ σῶμα ἀπολέσαι ἐν γεέννῃ. (29) οὐχὶ δύο [πέντε] στρουθία ἀσσαρίου [ἀσσαρίων β′] πωλεῖται; καὶ ἓν ἐξ αὐτῶν οὐ πεσεῖται ἐπὶ τὴν γῆν ἄνευ τοῦ θεοῦ. (30) ὑμῶν δὲ καὶ αἱ τρίχες τῆς κεφαλῆς πᾶσαι ἠριθμημέναι εἰσίν. (31) μὴ [οὖν] φοβεῖσθε· πολλῷ [yet πολλῶν already stood in Q] στρουθίων διαφέρετε ὑμεῖς. (32) πᾶς οὖν ὅστις ὁμολογήσει ἐν ἐμοὶ ἔμπροσθεν τῶν ἀνθρώπων, ὁμολογήσει καὶ ὁ υἱὸς τοῦ ἀνθρώπου [*vel* ὁμολογήσω κἀγὼ] ἐν αὐτῷ ἔμπροσθεν τῶν ἀγγέλων τοῦ θεοῦ· (33) ὅστις δὲ ἀρνήσηταί με ἔμπροσθεν τῶν ἀνθρώπων, ἀρνήσομαι κἀγὼ αὐτὸν ἔμπροσθεν τῶν ἀγγέλων τοῦ θεοῦ (pp. 14, 82).

34^b. (St. Matt. xii. 32; St. Luke xii. 10.)

(32) καὶ ὃς ἐὰν εἴπῃ λόγον κατὰ τοῦ υἱοῦ τοῦ ἀνθρώπου, ἀφεθήσεται αὐτῷ· ὃς δ' ἂν εἴπῃ κατὰ τοῦ πνεύματος τοῦ ἁγίου, οὐκ ἀφεθήσεται αὐτῷ (p. 21).

35. (St. Matt. vi. 25–33; St. Luke xii. 22–31.)

(25) Διὰ τοῦτο λέγω ὑμῖν, μὴ μεριμνᾶτε τῇ ψυχῇ ὑμῶν τί φάγητε, μηδὲ τῷ σώματι ὑμῶν τί ἐνδύσησθε· οὐχὶ ἡ ψυχὴ πλεῖόν ἐστιν τῆς τροφῆς καὶ τὸ σῶμα τοῦ ἐνδύματος; (26) ἐμβλέψατε εἰς τοὺς κόρακας [τὰ πετεινὰ τοῦ οὐρανοῦ?], ὅτι οὐ σπείρουσιν οὐδὲ θερίζουσιν οὐδὲ συνάγουσιν εἰς ἀποθήκας, καὶ ὁ θεὸς τρέφει αὐτούς· οὐχ ὑμεῖς μᾶλλον διαφέρετε αὐτῶν; (27) τίς δὲ ἐξ ὑμῶν μεριμνῶν δύναται προσθεῖναι ἐπὶ τὴν ἡλικίαν αὐτοῦ πῆχυν ἕνα; (28) καὶ περὶ ἐνδύματος τί μεριμνᾶτε; καταμάθετε τὰ κρίνα πῶς αὐξάνουσιν· οὐ κοπιῶσιν οὐδὲ νήθουσιν· (29) λέγω δὲ ὑμῖν, [ὅτι] οὐδὲ Σολομὼν ἐν πάσῃ τῇ δόξῃ αὐτοῦ περιεβάλετο ὡς ἓν τούτων. (30) εἰ δὲ ἐν ἀγρῷ τὸν χόρτον σήμερον ὄντα καὶ αὔριον εἰς κλίβανον βαλλόμενον ὁ θεὸς οὕτως ἀμφιέννυσιν, οὐ πολλῷ μᾶλλον ὑμᾶς, ὀλιγόπιστοι; (31) μὴ οὖν μεριμνήσητε λέγοντες· τί φάγωμεν; ἢ τί πίωμεν; ἢ τί περιβαλώμεθα; (32) πάντα γὰρ ταῦτα τὰ ἔθνη [τοῦ κόσμου] ἐπιζητοῦσιν· οἶδεν γὰρ ὁ πατὴρ ὑμῶν ὅτι χρῄζετε τούτων ἁπάντων. (33) ζητεῖτε δὲ τὴν βασιλείαν αὐτοῦ, καὶ ταῦτα πάντα προστεθήσεται ὑμῖν (p. 4).

36. (St. Matt. vi. 19–21; St. Luke xii. 33, 34.)

(19) Μὴ θησαυρίζετε ὑμῖν θησαυροὺς ἐπὶ τῆς γῆς, ὅπου σὴς καὶ βρῶσις ἀφανίζει, καὶ ὅπου κλέπται διορύσσουσιν καὶ κλέπτουσιν· (20) θησαυρίζετε δὲ ὑμῖν

θησαυροὺς ἐν οὐρανοῖς, ὅπου οὔτε σὴς οὔτε βρῶσις ἀφανίζει, καὶ ὅπου κλέπται οὐ διορύσσουσιν οὐδὲ κλέπτουσιν· (21) ὅπου γάρ ἐστιν ὁ θησαυρός σου [ὑμῶν], ἐκεῖ ἔσται καὶ ἡ καρδία σου [ὑμῶν] (pp. 66, 4).

37. (St. Matt. xxiv. 43–51; St. Luke xii. 39, 40, 42–46.)

(43) Ἐκεῖνο δὲ γινώσκετε, ὅτι εἰ ᾔδει ὁ οἰκοδεσπότης ποίᾳ φυλακῇ ὁ κλέπτης ἔρχεται, ἐγρηγόρησεν ἂν καὶ οὐκ ἂν εἴασεν διορυχθῆναι τὴν οἰκίαν αὐτοῦ. (44) [διὰ τοῦτο καὶ ὑμεῖς γίνεσθε ἕτοιμοι, ὅτι ᾗ οὐ δοκεῖτε ὥρᾳ ὁ υἱὸς τοῦ ἀνθρώπου ἔρχεται.] (45) τίς ἄρα ἐστὶν ὁ πιστὸς δοῦλος καὶ φρόνιμος, ὃν κατέστησεν ὁ κύριος ἐπὶ τῆς οἰκετείας αὐτοῦ τοῦ δοῦναι αὐτοῖς τὴν τροφὴν ἐν καιρῷ; (46) μακάριος ὁ δοῦλος ἐκεῖνος ὃν ἐλθὼν ὁ κύριος αὐτοῦ εὑρήσει οὕτως ποιοῦντα. (47) ἀμὴν λέγω ὑμῖν ὅτι ἐπὶ πᾶσιν τοῖς ὑπάρχουσιν αὐτοῦ καταστήσει αὐτόν. (48) ἐὰν δὲ εἴπῃ ὁ [κακὸς] δοῦλος ἐκεῖνος ἐν τῇ καρδίᾳ αὐτοῦ· (49) χρονίζει μου ὁ κύριος, καὶ ἄρξηται τύπτειν τοὺς συνδούλους αὐτοῦ, ἐσθίῃ δὲ καὶ πίνῃ μετὰ τῶν μεθυόντων, (50) ἥξει ὁ κύριος τοῦ δούλου ἐκείνου ἐν ἡμέρᾳ ᾗ οὐ προσδοκᾷ καὶ ἐν ὥρᾳ ᾗ οὐ γινώσκει, (51) καὶ διχοτομήσει αὐτὸν καὶ τὸ μέρος αὐτοῦ μετὰ τῶν ὑποκριτῶν θήσει (p. 31).

38. (St. Matt. x. 34, 35, 36; St. Luke xii. 51, 53.)

(34) Δοκεῖτε, ὅτι ἦλθον βαλεῖν εἰρήνην ἐπὶ τὴν γῆν; οὐκ ἦλθον βαλεῖν εἰρήνην ἀλλὰ μάχαιραν. (35) ἦλθον γὰρ διχάσαι ἄνθρωπον κατὰ τοῦ πατρὸς αὐτοῦ καὶ θυγατέρα κατὰ τῆς μητρὸς αὐτῆς καὶ νύμφην κατὰ τῆς πενθερᾶς αὐτῆς. (36) [καὶ ἐχθροὶ τοῦ ἀνθρώπου οἱ οἰκιακοὶ αὐτοῦ] (p. 85).

39. (St. Matt. v. 25, 26; St. Luke xii. 58, 59.)

(25) Ἴσθι εὐνοῶν τῷ ἀντιδίκῳ σου ταχὺ ἕως ὅτου εἶ μετ᾽ αὐτοῦ ἐν τῇ ὁδῷ· μή ποτέ σε παραδῷ ὁ ἀντίδικος τῷ κριτῇ καὶ ὁ κριτὴς τῷ ὑπηρέτῃ, καὶ εἰς φυλακὴν βληθήσῃ· (26) [ἀμὴν] λέγω σοι, οὐ μὴ ἐξέλθῃς ἐκεῖθεν, ἕως ἂν ἀποδῷς τὸν ἔσχατον κοδράντην (p. 54).

40. (St. Matt. xiii. 31–33; St. Luke xiii. 18–21.)

(33) [καὶ πάλιν εἶπεν·] τίνι ὁμοιώσω τὴν βασιλείαν τοῦ θεοῦ; ὁμοία ἐστὶν ζύμῃ, ἣν λαβοῦσα γυνὴ ἐνέκρυψεν εἰς ἀλεύρου σάτα τρία, ἕως οὗ ἐζυμώθη ὅλον. This was most probably preceded by: τίνι ὁμοία ἐστὶν ἡ βασιλεία τοῦ θεοῦ, καὶ τίνι ὁμοιώσω αὐτήν; ὁμοία ἐστὶν κόκκῳ σινάπεως, ὃν λαβὼν ἄνθρωπος ἔσπειρεν ἐν τῷ ἀγρῷ αὐτοῦ, καὶ ηὔξησεν καὶ γίνεται (εἰς) δένδρον καὶ τὰ πετεινὰ τοῦ οὐρανοῦ κατασκηνοῖ ἐν τοῖς κλάδοις αὐτοῦ (p. 26).

41. (St. Matt. vii. 13, 14; St. Luke xiii. 24.)

(13) Εἰσέλθατε διὰ τῆς στενῆς πύλης· ὅτι πλατεῖα [ἡ πύλη] καὶ εὐρύχωρος ἡ ὁδὸς ἡ ἀπάγουσα εἰς τὴν ἀπώλειαν, καὶ πολλοί εἰσιν οἱ εἰσερχόμενοι δι᾽ αὐτῆς. (14) ὅτι στενὴ ἡ πύλη καὶ τεθλιμμένη ἡ ὁδὸς ἡ ἀπάγουσα εἰς τὴν ζωήν, καὶ ὀλίγοι εἰσὶν οἱ εὑρίσκοντες αὐτήν (p. 67).

42. (St. Matt. viii. 11, 12; St. Luke xiii. 28, 29.)

(11) Λέγω ὑμῖν, ὅτι ἀπὸ ἀνατολῶν καὶ δυσμῶν ἥξουσιν καὶ ἀνακλιθήσονται μετὰ Ἀβραὰμ καὶ Ἰσαὰκ καὶ Ἰακὼβ ἐν τῇ βασιλείᾳ τοῦ θεοῦ· (12) οἱ δὲ υἱοὶ τῆς βασιλείας ἐξελεύσονται [ἐκβληθήσονται] ἔξω· ἐκεῖ ἔσται ὁ κλαυθμὸς καὶ ὁ βρυγμὸς τῶν ὀδόντων (p. 77).

43. (St. Matt. xxiii. 37–39; St. Luke xiii. 34, 35.)

(37) Ἱερουσαλήμ, Ἱερουσαλήμ, ἡ ἀποκτείνουσα τοὺς προφήτας καὶ λιθοβολοῦσα τοὺς ἀπεσταλμένους πρὸς αὐτήν, ποσάκις ἠθέλησα ἐπισυναγαγεῖν τὰ τέκνα σου, ὃν τρόπον ὄρνις [ἐπισυνάγει] τὰ νοσσία [αὐτῆς] ὑπὸ τὰς πτέρυγας, καὶ οὐκ ἠθελήσατε· (38) ἰδοὺ ἀφίεται ὑμῖν ὁ οἶκος ὑμῶν ἔρημος. (39) λέγω [γὰρ] ὑμῖν, οὐ μή με ἴδητε ἀπ' ἄρτι ἕως ἂν [ἥξῃ ὅτε] εἴπητε· εὐλογημένος ὁ ἐρχόμενος ἐν ὀνόματι κυρίου (p. 29).

44. (St. Matt. xxiii. 12; St. Luke xiv. 11.)

(12) Ὅστις ὑψώσει ἑαυτὸν ταπεινωθήσεται, καὶ ὅστις ταπεινώσει ἑαυτὸν ὑψωθήσεται (p. 29).

45. (St. Matt. x. 37; St. Luke xiv. 26.)

(37) [Ὁ φιλῶν πατέρα ἢ μητέρα ὑπὲρ ἐμὲ οὐκ ἔστιν μου ἄξιος· καὶ ὁ φιλῶν υἱὸν ἢ θυγατέρα ὑπὲρ ἐμὲ οὐκ ἔστιν μου ἄξιος] (p. 85).

46. (St. Matt. x. 38, St. Luke xiv. 27.)

(38) Ὃς οὐ λαμβάνει τὸν σταυρὸν αὐτοῦ καὶ ἀκολουθεῖ ὀπίσω μου, οὐκ ἔστιν μου ἄξιος (p. 86).

47. (St. Matt. v. 13; St. Luke xiv. 34, 35.)

(13) Ὑμεῖς ἐστε τὸ ἅλας [τῆς γῆς]· ἐὰν δὲ τὸ ἅλας μωρανθῇ, ἐν τίνι ἁλισθήσεται; εἰς οὐδὲν ἰσχύει ἔτι εἰ μὴ βληθὲν ἔξω καταπατεῖσθαι ὑπὸ τῶν ἀνθρώπων (p. 53).

48. (St. Matt. xviii. 12, 13; St. Luke xv. 4–7.)

(12) Τί ὑμῖν δοκεῖ; ἐὰν γένηταί τινι ἀνθρώπῳ ἑκατὸν πρόβατα καὶ πλανηθῇ ἓν ἐξ αὐτῶν, οὐχὶ ἀφήσει τὰ

ἐνενήκοντα ἐννέα ἐπὶ τὰ ὄρη καὶ πορευθεὶς ζητεῖ τὸ πλανώμενον; (13) καὶ ἐὰν γένηται εὑρεῖν αὐτό, [ἀμὴν] λέγω ὑμῖν, ὅτι χαίρει ἐπ' αὐτῷ μᾶλλον ἢ ἐπὶ τοῖς ἐνενήκοντα ἐννέα τοῖς μὴ πεπλανημένοις (p. 91).

49. (St. Matt. vi. 24; St. Luke xvi. 13.)

(24) Οὐδεὶς δύναται δυσὶ κυρίοις δουλεύειν· ἢ γὰρ τὸν ἕνα μισήσει καὶ τὸν ἕτερον ἀγαπήσει, ἢ ἑνὸς ἀνθέξεται καὶ τοῦ ἑτέρου καταφρονήσει· οὐ δύνασθε θεῷ δουλεύειν καὶ μαμωνᾷ (p. 4).

50. (St. Matt. xi. 12, 13; St. Luke xvi. 16.)

(13) Οἱ προφῆται καὶ ὁ νόμος ἕως Ἰωάννου· ἀπὸ τότε ἕως ἄρτι ἡ βασιλεία τοῦ θεοῦ βιάζεται, καὶ βιασταὶ ἁρπάζουσιν αὐτήν [*vel*: Ἀπὸ τῶν ἡμερῶν Ἰωάννου ἕως κτλ. πάντες γὰρ οἱ προφῆται καὶ ὁ νόμος ἕως Ἰωάννου ἐπροφήτευσαν] (p. 15).

51. (St. Matt. v. 18; St. Luke xvi. 17.)

(18) [Ἀμὴν λέγω ὑμῖν], ἕως ἂν παρέλθῃ ὁ οὐρανὸς καὶ ἡ γῆ, ἰῶτα ἓν ἢ μία κεραία οὐ μὴ παρέλθῃ ἀπὸ τοῦ νόμου (p. 53).

52. (St. Matt. v. 32; St. Luke xvi. 18.)

(32) [Ἐγὼ λέγω ὑμῖν·] πᾶς ὁ ἀπολύων τὴν γυναῖκα αὐτοῦ ποιεῖ αὐτὴν μοιχευθῆναι, καὶ ὃς ἐὰν ἀπολελυμένην γαμήσῃ, μοιχᾶται (p. 54).

53. (St. Matt. xviii. 7; St. Luke xvii. 1.)

(7) Ἀνάγκη ἐλθεῖν τὰ σκάνδαλα, πλὴν οὐαὶ τῷ ἀνθρώπῳ, δι' οὗ τὸ σκάνδαλον ἔρχεται (p. 28).

54. (St. Matt. xviii. 15, 21, 22; St. Luke xvii. 3, 4.)

(15) Ἐὰν ἁμαρτήσῃ ὁ ἀδελφός σου, ἔλεγξον αὐτόν· ἐάν σου ἀκούσῃ, ἐκέρδησας τὸν ἀδελφόν σου.—— . . . ποσάκις ἁμαρτήσει εἰς ἐμὲ ὁ ἀδελφός μου καὶ ἀφήσω αὐτῷ; ἕως ἑπτάκις; λέγει αὐτῷ ὁ Ἰησοῦς· οὐ λέγω σοι ἕως ἑπτάκις, ἀλλὰ ἕως ἑβδομήκοντα ἑπτά (p. 93).

55. (St. Matt. xvii. 20[b]; St. Luke xvii. 6.)

(20) Ἐὰν ἔχητε πίστιν ὡς κόκκον σινάπεως, ἐρεῖτε τῷ ὄρει τούτῳ· μετάβα ἔνθεν ἐκεῖ, καὶ μεταβήσεται (p. 91).

56. (St. Matt. xxiv. 26, 27, 28, 37–41; St. Luke xvii. 23, 24, 37, 26, 27, 34, 35.)

(26) Ἐὰν οὖν εἴπωσιν ὑμῖν· ἰδοὺ ἐν τῇ ἐρήμῳ ἐστίν, μὴ ἐξέλθητε· ἰδοὺ ἐν τοῖς ταμείοις, μὴ πιστεύσητε· (27) ὥσπερ γὰρ ἡ ἀστραπὴ ἐξέρχεται ἀπὸ ἀνατολῶν καὶ φαίνεται ἕως δυσμῶν, οὕτως ἔσται ἡ παρουσία τοῦ υἱοῦ τοῦ ἀνθρώπου· (28) ὅπου ἐὰν ᾖ τὸ πτῶμα, ἐκεῖ συναχθήσονται οἱ ἀετοί.

(37) Ὥσπερ αἱ ἡμέραι τοῦ Νῶε, οὕτως ἔσται ἡ παρουσία τοῦ υἱοῦ τοῦ ἀνθρώπου· (38) ὡς γὰρ ἦσαν ἐν ταῖς ἡμέραις [ἐκείναις] ταῖς πρὸ τοῦ κατακλυσμοῦ τρώγοντες καὶ πίνοντες, γαμοῦντες καὶ γαμίζοντες, ἄχρι ἧς ἡμέρας εἰσῆλθεν Νῶε εἰς τὴν κιβωτόν, (39) καὶ οὐκ ἔγνωσαν ἕως ἦλθεν ὁ κατακλυσμὸς καὶ ἦρεν ἅπαντας, οὕτως ἔσται ἡ παρουσία τοῦ υἱοῦ τοῦ ἀνθρώπου.

(40) ἔσονται δύο ἐν τῷ ἀγρῷ, εἷς παραλαμβάνεται καὶ εἷς ἀφίεται· (41) δύο ἀλήθουσαι ἐν τῷ μύλῳ, μία παραλαμβάνεται καὶ μία ἀφίεται (p. 105).

57. (St. Matt. x. 39; St. Luke xvii. 33.)

(39) Ὁ εὑρὼν [ὃς ἐὰν εὕρῃ] τὴν ψυχὴν αὐτοῦ ἀπολέσει αὐτήν, καὶ ὃς ἂν ἀπολέσει [ὁ ἀπολέσας] τὴν ψυχὴν αὐτοῦ εὑρήσει αὐτήν (p. 86).

58. (St. Matt. xxv. 29; St. Luke xix. 26.)

(29) Τῷ ἔχοντι [παντὶ] δοθήσεται καὶ περισσευθήσεται· τοῦ δὲ μὴ ἔχοντος καὶ ὃ ἔχει ἀρθήσεται ἀπ' αὐτοῦ (p. 34).

59. (St. Matt. xix. 28; St. Luke xxii. 28, 30.)

(28) Ὑμεῖς οἱ ἀκολουθήσαντές μοι . . . καθίσεσθε ἐπὶ δώδεκα θρόνους κρίνοντες τοὺς δώδεκα φυλὰς τοῦ Ἰσραήλ (p. 95).

II.—Linguistic Characteristics

Each of the three synoptists (St. Luke most markedly) possesses numerous verbal, stylistic, and grammatical peculiarities,[1] even if the style of each be not distinctly formed and homogeneous. These sections which we have here separated away from their present context do not possess such marked characteristics. It is therefore impossible, or at least unsafe, to uphold their homogeneity upon grounds of vocabulary and style.

[1] The best discussion of these is found in Hawkins, "Horæ Synopticæ" (1899), pp. 1 ff.

A.—*VOCABULARY*

(1) Verbs

Apart from εἶναι, we find in Q about 166 simple verbs (occurring in about 475 places) and about 82 compound verbs (in about 168 places), namely:—

ἀγαλλιᾶσθαι, 3 [1]
ἀγαπᾶν, 6 (ter), 49
αἴρειν, 2, 56, 58
αἰτεῖν, 5, 28 (quinquies)
ἀκολουθεῖν, 13, 17, (bis), 46, 59
ἀκούειν, 12 (bis), 13, 14 (ter), 26 (quater), 30, 34[a], 54
ἀλήθειν, 56
ἁλίζειν, 47
ἁμαρτάνειν, 54 (bis)
ἀριθμεῖν, 34[a]
ἀρκεῖν, 10
ἀρνεῖσθαι 34[a] (bis)
ἁρπάζειν, 50
ἄρχεσθαι (1), 14, 37
ἀσπάζεσθαι, 6, 20 (bis)
αὐλεῖν, 15
αὐξάνειν, 35, 40
ἀφανίζειν, 36 (bis)
βάλλειν, 1, 2, 13, 35, 38 (bis), 39, 47
βαπτίζειν 1 (bis)
βασανίζειν, 13
βαστάζειν, 1, 20
βίαζεσθαι, 50
βλέπειν, 8, 14, 26 (bis)
βούλεσθαι, 25
βρέχειν (6)
γαμεῖν, 52, 56
γαμίζειν, 56
γέμειν, 33 (bis)
γίνεσθαι, 2, 6, 10, 23 (bis), 25, 29, 30, 37, 40, 48 (bis)
γινώσκειν, 11, 25 (bis), 34[a], 37 (bis), 56
γράφειν, 2 (quater), 14
γρηγορεῖν, 37
δαιμονίζεσθαι, 29
δανίζεσθαι, 5
δεικνύειν, 2
δεῖσθαι, 18
δεσμεύειν, 33
δέχεσθαι, 22 (bis), 24 (quater)
διδάσκειν (3)
διδόναι, 2, 5, 27, 28 (ter), 30, 37, 58
δικαιοῦν, 15
διχάζειν, 38
διχοτομεῖν, 37
διώκειν, 3 (bis), 6, 33
δοκεῖν, 1, 37, 38, 48
δουλεύειν, 49 (bis)
δύνασθαι 1, 34[a] (bis), 35, 49 (bis)
ἐάν, 37
ἐγγίζειν, 16, 22
ἐγείρειν, 1, 14 (bis), 30
εἶναι, vv. ll.
εἰπεῖν, 1, 2 (quater), 3, 8, 13 (quater vel ter), 14 (bis), 17 (bis), 22, 25, 30, 33, 34[a] (bis), 34[b] (bis), 37, 40, 43, 55, 56
ἐλέγχειν, 54
ἐρημοῦν, 29

---

[1] The numbers here refer to the sections of the text as given above.

παρέρχεσθαι, 51 (bis)
παρομοιάζειν, 33
περιβάλλειν, 35 (bis)
περιπατεῖν, 14, 33
προσδοκᾶν, 14, 37
προσέρχεσθαι, 13
προσεύχεσθαι, 6
προσκόπτειν, 2, 12
προσκυνεῖν, 2 (bis)
προσπίπτειν, 12
προστιθέναι, 35 (bis)
προσφωνεῖν, 15
συλλέγειν, 11
συνάγειν, 1, 29, 35, 56
ὑπάγειν (13)
ὑπάρχειν (Partic.), 37
ὑποδεικνύναι, 1, 12[1]

The numerical ratio of simple to compound verbs is of interest. They stand in the ratio of 100 : 50—very nearly the same as that which holds in the Gospel of St. John and the Epistle of St. James.[2] In the Epistle of St. John the ratio of simple to compound verbs is actually 100 : 18; in the first Epistle of Peter, on the other hand, as 100 : 63; in the Epistle of St. Jude as 100 : 78, and in the Epistle to the Ephesians as 100 : 79. St. Luke has about 66 per cent. more compounds than St. Matthew, in which gospel the ratio is almost exactly the same as that in St. Mark. The relatively small number of compound verbs in Q (especially if one takes the total number of occurrences: 475 of simple verbs to 168 of compound) may be advanced as evidence of near relationship of this source to the Semitic.[3] The compounds are almost

[1] Of these eighty-two compound verbs, twenty-four are not found elsewhere in St. Matthew, namely: ἀμφιεννύναι, ἀνάγεσθαι, ἀντέχεσθαι, ἀποδεκατοῦν, ἀπομάσσεσθαι, διαβλέπειν, διακαθαρίζειν, διέρχεσθαι, διορύσσειν, εἰσέρχεσθαι, ἐκπειράζειν, ἐξιστάναι, ἐγκρύπτειν, ἐπιδιδόναι, καταμανθάνειν, κατανοεῖν, κατασκευάζειν, παρομοιάζειν, προσδοκᾶν, προσκόπτειν, προσπίπτειν, προστιθέναι, προσφωνεῖν, ὑποδεικνύναι.

[2] In St. John there are about 209 simple verbs to 100 compound; in St. James, 126 simple to 64 compound. In St. John, however, it must be observed that a particular simple verb occurs much more frequently than a particular compound verb.

[3] The rare use of compound verbs in St. John admits of a similar explanation; though here a conscious literary purpose must also be taken into account.

always verbs of the most common description[1]—indeed the majority of them are those in which the preposition has kept its elementary local significance, or those which are no longer felt to be compounds. The only compound verbs that are at all characteristic are διαβλέπειν in 8, διακαθαρίζειν in 1, διορύσσειν in 36 and 37 (*vide* Job xxiv. 16; Exod. xxii. 2; Jer. ii. 34), ἐπιζητεῖν in 30 and 35, ἐμβλέπειν in 35, προσπίπτειν in 12. Compounds with ὑπέρ and πρό are entirely absent. The simple verbs also are practically always verbs in common use; the only exceptions are διχάζειν (38; wanting in the LXX), διχοτομεῖν (37; only here in the New Testament—*cf.* Exod. xxix. 17), κονιᾶσθαι (33, *cf.* Acts xxiii. 3), σαροῦσθαι (29, *cf.* St. Luke xv. 8, a later form of σαίρεσθαι). We can discover scarcely any instances of constant use of, or of prejudice in favour of, particular verbs. Of the eighty-two compounds only twenty-five occur in more than one passage (*viz.* ἀμφιεννύναι, ἀποκαλύπτειν, ἀποκρίνεσθαι, ἀποκτείνειν, ἀπολλύναι, ἀποστέλλειν, ἀφιέναι, διαφέρειν, διορύσσειν, εἰσέρχεσθαι, ἐκβάλλειν, ἐξέρχεσθαι, ἐπιζητεῖν, ἐπιστρέφειν, καθίζεσθαι, καταβαίνειν, μετανοεῖν, παραδιδόναι, παρακαλεῖσθαι, παραλαμβάνειν, περιπατεῖν, προσδοκᾶν, προσκόπτειν, συνάγειν, ὑποδεικνύναι); here the only important trait is the repetition of διαφέρειν, διορύσσειν, but especially of ἀφιέναι. Of the 166 simple verbs only fifty-one are found in more than one passage (*viz.* ἀγαπᾶν, αἴρειν, αἰτεῖν, ἀκολουθεῖν, ἀκούειν, ἄρχεσθαι, ἀσπάζεσθαι, αὐξάνειν, βάλλειν, βαστάζειν, βλέπειν, γαμεῖν, γίνεσθαι,

[1] A double compound is only once found (in 43: ἐπισυνάγειν); *but, as will be shown, in a quotation.*

γινώσκειν, γράφειν, δέχεσθαι, διδόναι, διώκειν, δοκεῖν, δύνασθαι, ἐγγίζειν, ἐγείρειν, εἰπεῖν, ἔρχεσθαι, ἐσθίειν, εὑρίσκειν, ἔχειν, ζητεῖν, ἥκειν, θέλειν, θεραπεύειν, ἰδεῖν, καθαρίζειν, κηρύσσειν, κρίνειν, κρύπτειν, λαμβάνειν, λέγειν, οἶδα, οἰκοδομεῖν, ὁμοιοῦν, πίνειν, πίπτειν [πιστεύειν], ποιεῖν, πορεύεσθαι, σπείρειν, τιθέναι, ὑψοῦν, φαίνεσθαι, χαίρειν); none of these (except perhaps ἐγείρειν in 1, 14, 30, the redundant ἄρχεσθαι in [1] 14, 37, ἀκολουθεῖν, ἀσπάζεσθαι, βάλλειν and δοκεῖν) is characteristic. That our sixty sections form an homogeneous whole does not therefore admit of stringent proof based upon an investigation of the character of the verbs both simple and compound.

(2) Substantives and Adjectives

What has been said of the verbs also holds good for the substantives and adjectives: these also scarcely form a basis for the conclusion that the sections are homogeneous. Remarkable words and phrases are exceedingly rare, and these as a rule occur each only once. Yet attention may perhaps be drawn to the following: Πάσας τὰς βασιλείας τοῦ κόσμου καὶ τὴν δόξαν αὐτῶν (2) and Σολομὼν ἐν πάσῃ τῇ δόξῃ αὐτοῦ (35); τὰς βασιλείας τοῦ κόσμου (2) and τὰ ἔθνη τοῦ κόσμου (35); "loaf" and "stone" in 2 and 28; ἀποθήκη in 1 and 35; ἀνατολή and δυσμοί in 42 and 56; the frequent occurrence of the word βασιλεία; the use of γενεά in 15, 30, 33, of δένδρον in 1, 11, and 40, of δοῦλος in 10 and 37, of ἡ ἔρημος in 2, 14, and 56, of ὁ ἐρχόμενος in 1, 14, and 43, of Ἰσραήλ in 13 and 59, of κλέπτης (together with διορύσσειν) in 36 and 37, of οἱ ὄχλοι in (1) 14 and 29, of περισσόν in 6 and 14, of τὰ πετεινὰ τοῦ οὐρανοῦ in 17, 35, and 40, of πίστις (13, 55: different degrees of faith), of σοφία in 15, 30, and (33), of τελώνης in 6 and 15, of ὑποκριτής in 8 and 37. A noteworthy trait is the great number of adjectives used as substantives. This finds an explanation in the fact that the original was Semitic. Proper names are of very scanty occurrence (Abel, Abraham, Jacob, Jonas, Isaac, Israel, Ninevites, Noah, Solomon, Zacharias, John [the Baptist], Pharisees, Beelzebub, Mammon; Bethsaida, Chorazin, Gomorrha, Jerusalem, Jordan, Capernaum, Sidon, Sodom). *Not one of the disciples of our Lord is mentioned by name, not even St. Peter;* by accident also the name οἱ μαθηταί for them is wanting in the text preserved for us (except in one passage 10; in 14 the word does not refer to disciples of our Lord)—this, however, is only accidental: numerous passages refer to them, *and in 59 we are told of twelve thrones* for the followers of Jesus. The concept "οἱ ἀκολουθοῦντες" (ἀκολουθεῖν) is of great import in Q (13, 17, 46, 59). The term ὁ Χριστός for our Lord is found only once (14). In regard to the title ὁ κύριος as applied to our Lord, it is not quite certain whether St. Matt. vii. 21 (St. Luke vi. 46) stood in Q; but in this context it has no more significance than the κύριε in the mouth of the centurion (in 13); Q itself never calls our Lord "ὁ κύριος," its designation for Him is simply "Jesus" (*vide* 2 [13], 17, and 54). In regard to the adjectives, by far the most noteworthy feature is the use of ἄξιος (1, 20, 21, 45, 46), of μακάριος (3, 14, 26, 37), of ὅλος (32, 40), of πολύς (3, 18, with μισθός and with θερισμός), and of πονηρός (11, 28, 29, 30, 32).

The following is a complete list of the substantives and adjectives :—

ἐρχόμενος, ὁ, 1, 14, 43
ἔσχατα, τά, 29
εὐδοκία, 25
ἐχθροί, οἱ, 6 (38)
ἐχίδνη, 1
Ζαχαρίας, 33
ζύμη, 40
ζωή, 41
ἡδύοσμον, 33
ἡλικία, 35
ἥλιος, 6
ἡμέρα, 2, 22, 23, 33, 37 (50), 56 (ter)
θέλημα, 12
θεός, 1, 2 (bis) 12, 14, 16, 29 (bis), 33 (bis), 34[a] (ter), 35 (bis), 40 (bis?), 42, 49, 50
θερισμός, 18 (ter)
θησαυρός, 36 (ter)
θρίξ, 34[a]
θρόνος, 59
θυγάτηρ, 38 (45)
θυσιαστήριον, 33
Ἰακώβ, 42
ἱερόν, τό, 2
Ἱερουσαλήμ, 2, 43 (bis)
Ἰησοῦς, 2 (ter) (13), 17, 54
ἱμάτιον, 4
Ἰορδάνης, 1
Ἰσαάκ, 42
Ἰσραήλ, 13, 59
ἰχθύς, 28
Ἰωνᾶς, 30 (quater)
Ἰωάννης, 1, 14 (quater), 15, 50
ἰῶτα, 51
καιρός, 25, 37
κάλαμος, 14
καρδία, 36, 37
καρπός, 1 (bis), 11 (quinquies)
κάρφος, 8 (ter)
κατακλυσμός, 56 (bis)
κατασκήνωσις, 17
Καφαρναούμ, 13, 23
κεραία, 51
κεφαλή, 17, 34[a]
κήρυγμα, 30
κιβωτός, 56
κλάδος, 40
κλαυθμός, 42
κλέπτης, 36 (bis), 37
κλίβανος, 35
κοινωνοί, οἱ, 33
κόκκος, 40, 55
κοδράντης, 39
κονιορτός, 22
κόραξ, 35 (?)
κόσμος, 2, 35
κρῖμα, 8
κρίνον, 35
κρίσις, 22, 23, 30 (bis), 33
κριτής, 29, 39 (bis)
κύμινον, 33
κύριος, 2 (bis), 10 (bis), 12 (bis), 13 (bis), 18, 25, 37 (quater), 43, 49
κωφός, ὁ, 14, 29 (bis)
λεπρός, ὁ, 14
λίθος, 1, 2 (bis), 28
λόγος, 12 (bis), 13, 34[b]
λύκος, 19
λυχνία, 31
λύχνος, 31, 32
μαθητής, 10 (bis), 14 (18)
μαλακά, τά, 14 (bis)
μαμωνᾶς, 49
μάχαιρα, 38
μέρος, 37
μέσον (19)
μετάνοια, 1 (bis)
μέτρον, 8, 33
μήτηρ, 38 (45)
μικρότερος, ὁ, 14
μισθός, 3, 6
μόδιος, 31
μῦλον, 56
ναός, 33
νεκρός, ὁ, 14, 17 (bis)
νήπιος, ὁ, 25
Νινευείτης, 30 (bis)
νόμος, 33, 50, 51
νοσσία, τά, 43
νότος, 30
νύμφη, 38
Νῶε, 56 (bis)
ὁδός, 14, 20, 39, 41 (bis)
ὀδούς, 42
οἰκετεία, 37
οἰκία, 12 (quater), 13, 20 (bis), 21, 31, 37
οἰκιακός (38)
οἰκοδεσπότης, 37
οἶκος, 14, 29, 43
οἰνοπότης, 15

Φαρισαῖοι, 33 (quater)
φίλος, ὁ, 15
φορτίον, 33
φυλακή, 37, 39
φυλή, 59
φωλεός, 17
φῶς, 32, 34[a]
χείρ, 1, 2
χιτών, 4
Χοραζείν, 23
χόρτος, 35
Χριστός, 14
χωλός, ὁ, 14
ψυχή, 34[a] (bis), 35 (bis), 57 (bis)
ὦμος, 33
ὥρα (13) (37), 37

ἀγαθός, 11 (bis)
ἅγιος (1), 34[b]
ἄδηλος, 33
ἀκάθαρτος, 29
ἀνεκτός, 22, 23
ἄνυδρος, 29
ἄξιος, 1, 20 (bis), 21 (45) (bis), 46
ἁπλοῦς, 32
ἀρκετός, 10
ἄσβεστος, 1
βαρύς, 33 (bis)
δεινῶς, 13
δεξιός, 4
ἐπιούσιος, 27
ἔρημος, 43
ἔσχατος, 39
ἕτοιμος, 37
εὐρύχωρος, 41
ἱκανός, 1, 13
ἰσχυρός, 1
κακός (37)
καλός, 1, 11 (bis)
κρυπτός, 34[a]
μακάριος, 3 (quater), 14, 26, 37
μέγας, 12, 14 (bis)
μοιχαλίς, 30
νεκρός, 33
οἰκτίρμων, 6 (bis)
ὀλίγος, 18, 41
ὅλος, 32 (bis), 40
ὅμοιος, 12 (bis), 40 (ter ?)
πιστός, 37
πλατύς, 41
πολύς [1], 3, 18, 26, 30 (bis), 34[a], 35 (bis), 41
πονηρός, 11 (bis), 28, 29, 30, 32
σαπρός, 11 (bis)
σκοτεινός, 32
στενός, 41 (bis)
ταχύ, 39
ὑψηλός, 2
φρόνιμος, 37
φωτεινός, 32
χείρων, 29
ὡραῖος, 33

The simplicity and homogeneity of the vocabulary does seem to me to incline the balance in favour of the unity of Q.

(3) Prepositions

Among the prepositions *παρά*, *σύν*, and *ἐνώπιον* are wanting (in place of the latter *ἔμπροσθεν* is used seven times); the prepositions of most frequent occurrence are *ἐν* (about fifty-nine times, and with the most varied significance), then *ἐπί* (about twenty-eight times) and *εἰς* (about twenty-eight times), also *ἀπό* (sixteen times), *ἐκ* (thirteen times).

We observe at once the Semitic original. Of rarer occurrence are διά, ἕως, μετά (only in the sense of "with"), and ὑπό (eight, nine, nine, and ten times respectively).[1] Κατά is found only seven times (always with the genitive in the sense of "against"; the occurrence with the accusative in section 20 is uncertain), πρός and ὑπέρ five times, περί only four times, πρό three times, ἄχρι, μεταξύ, ἄνευ, ὀπίσω each only once.

The absence of παρά and σύν is important; for παρά is found elsewhere in St. Matthew eighteen to twenty times (and indeed with all its three cases), in St. Luke twenty-nine to thirty times; σύν is found elsewhere in St. Matthew two to three times, and in St. Luke twenty-four to twenty-six times. In the absence of the preposition παρά we may clearly recognise a distinct characteristic of Q.[2] — There are a few cases of construction with the article and a preposition in a substantival or adjectival sense.[3]

[1] ἕως also occurs as a conjunction six times (*vide* 39: ἕως ὅτου, 39, 43, 51: ἕως ἄν, 40: ἕως οὗ, 56: ἕως ἦλθεν). Ἀπό is also found with particles—ἀπὸ τότε, 50 [τότε also again in 8 and 29], ἀπ' ἄρτι, 43.

[2] Παρά is found with all three cases in St. Mark; in St. John it frequently occurs with the genitive and dative, but is wanting with the accusative. We should have an instance of occurrence in Q if it were permissible to regard the text of 21 as simply that of Q; but we have not authority for this, seeing that there is no parallel in St. Matthew.

[3] *Cf.* 3: οἱ πρὸ ὑμῶν, 28: ὁ ἐξ οὐρανοῦ, 31: οἱ ἐν τῇ οἰκίᾳ, 32: τὸ ἐν σοί (21: τὰ παρ' αὐτῶν).

B.—*GRAMMAR AND STYLE*

Sentences in Q are most frequently connected by means of καί (as in Semitic languages);[1] δέ, as compared with καί, falls very much into the background—it is indeed found scarcely thirty times (μέν . . . δέ only thrice in 1, 18, and 33). Neither can we speak of γάρ as of frequent occurrence (about twenty times, καὶ γάρ in 13).[2] 'Εάν is twice as frequent as εἰ. The latter is found only about ten times[3] (2 [*bis*]: εἰ υἱὸς εἶ τοῦ θεοῦ, εἰπὲ ἵνα *vel* βάλε. 28: εἰ οἴδατε ἀγαθὰ διδόναι τοῖς τέκνοις, πόσῳ μᾶλλον ὁ πατὴρ δώσει. 29 [*bis*]: εἰ ἐν Βεελζεβοὺλ ἐκβάλλω, οἱ υἱοὶ ἐν τίνι ἐκβάλλουσιν; εἰ ἐν πνεύματι θεοῦ ἐκβάλλω, ἄρα ἔφθασεν. 32: εἰ τὸ φῶς σκότος ἐστίν, τὸ σκότος πόσον; 35: εἰ ἐν ἀγρῷ τὸν χόρτον ὁ θεὸς ἀμφιέννυσιν, οὐ πολλῷ μᾶλλον ὑμᾶς; 23: εἰ ἐν Τύρῳ ἐγένοντο αἱ δυνάμεις, πάλαι ἂν μετενόησαν. 33. εἰ ἤμεθα ἐν ταῖς ἡμέραις τῶν πατέρων, οὐκ ἂν ἤμεθα. 37: εἰ ᾔδει ὁ οἰκοδεσπότης ποίᾳ φυλακῇ ὁ κλέπτης ἔρχεται, ἐγρηγόρησεν ἂν καὶ οὐκ ἂν εἴασεν). Besides the four instances just quoted, ἄν occurs again in sections 14, 34[b], 52, 57 (ὃς ἄν), 25 (ᾧ ἄν), 39, 43, 51 (ἕως ἄν), 56 (ὅπου ἄν).[4] *The*

[1] *Cf. e.g.* sections 12 and 13. Also καί with the apodosis is not rare—*vide e.g.* sections 13, 35.

[2] Οὖν is found about a dozen times—*cf.* 1 (with imperative), 1, 6 (with the imperative future), 12, 18, 28, 32 [*bis*], 34[a] [*bis*, but one of these is doubtful], 35 (with imperative), 56. Διὰ τοῦτο occurs in sections 29, 33, 35 (37).

[3] Also ἐι μή (=except) three times (*vide* 25, 30, 47); and πλήν (23, 53).

[4] Section 22 is doubtful: εἰς ἣν ἄν. Ὅταν is found only twice (3 and 29), ὅτε never (for in 43 it is very doubtful).

particle τε *is never found*, nor in consequence τε . . . καί, while they occur both in St. Matthew and St. Luke. Οὐδέ occurs about ten times, οὔτε . . . οὔτε once (36), μηδέ once (35), μήτε . . . μήτε once (15), once also the interrogative μήτι (11), οὐ μή thrice (39, 43, 51), ἤ . . . ἤ once (49).

Temporal clauses with ὡς *are entirely absent*;[1] in their place we have simple participial clauses; *the genitive absolute is found only once* (14), not in a saying of our Lord but in a descriptive passage (τούτων πορευομένων). Participial constructions, both with a temporal significance and as a substitute for relative clauses, are extraordinarily frequent—moreover, several participles (co-ordinated or subordinated) are found in conjunction. *However, the construction of* εἶναι *with the participle*, so common with St. Luke, *is very rare*; I have only found it in section 56.

So far as I see, the accusative with infinitive occurs only once (53).

Final clauses are often expressed by the simple infinitive (*vide*, 2, 14 [*ter*], 37 [here with the genitive of the article], 38 [*ter*], 47); ἵνα and ὅπως are not frequent. The former is only found in the following combinations: εἰπὲ ἵνα οἱ λίθοι ἄρτοι γένωνται (2),

[1] Ὡς throughout = "just as," *vide* 6, 10 (13), 27 (ὡς καί), 33, 35, 56; *cf.* ὥσπερ in 30 and 56 [*bis*]; καθώς is wanting. Ὃν τρόπον is found once (43). Οὕτως is used in the apodosis, *vide* 7 (πάντα ὅσα ἐὰν θέλητε . . . οὕτως ποιεῖτε), 30, 56 [*ter*] in the connection ὥσπερ (ὡς) . . . οὕτως, also in the principal sentence in 3, 11, 37.—Ὅστις is also found a few times (4, 12 [*bis*], 33, 34 [*bis*], 44 [*bis*]).—Ὅπου also occurs a few times (also in the sense of "whither"), *vide* 17, 36, 56 (followed by ἐκεῖ in 36 and 56; ἐκεῖ also occurs in 55).

ὅσα ἐὰν θέλητε ἵνα ποιῶσιν ὑμῖν οἱ ἄνθρωποι (7), μὴ κρίνετε ἵνα μὴ κριθῆτε (8), ἀρκετὸν τῷ μαθητῇ ἵνα γένηται ὡς ὁ διδάσκαλος (10), οὐκ εἰμὶ ἱκανὸς ἵνα μου ὑπὸ τὴν στέγην εἰσέλθῃς (13; but in section 1 ἱκανός is combined with the infinitive). The third passage alone answers to the classical use. Ὅπως occurs only three times (6: ὅπως γένησθε υἱοὶ τοῦ πατρός, 18: δεήθητε τοῦ κυρίου ὅπως ἐκβάλῃ ἐργάτας, 33: ὅπως ἔλθῃ ἐφ' ὑμᾶς πᾶν αἷμα). Μή, in the sense of "*ne*," is found only in a quotation from the LXX (2) and in section 39 (and, moreover, in both cases in the combination μή ποτε).[1]

Clauses introduced by ὅτι (in the sense of "that," "for," and "because") are frequent; they are found about thirty-three times, and present no remarkable feature. Ὥστε, in the sense of "*itaque*," is found once (33); on the other hand, ὥστε consecutive is probably altogether wanting, for its occurrence in section 29 is doubtful. *The various constructions with γίνομαι, which are so usual in St. Luke and are also found in St. Matthew, are likewise entirely absent. This is of importance.* A redundant γίνεσθαι occurs only once (48: ἐὰν γένηται εὑρεῖν).

One characteristic of these sections is the copious use that is made of interrogative sentences[2] (with or without interrogative particles)[3]; *cf.* 1, 6, 8, 11 (12),

[1] Otherwise the use of particles presents no point of special interest. We find ἀλλά (12, 13, 14 [*bis*], 31, 38, 54; here the use in 14 is alone noteworthy), ἀμήν (14, 26, 33, 37, 39, 48), ἄρα (29, 37), ἤδη (1), ναί (14, 25), νῦν (33), &c.

[2] The frequent use of the future with a significance of continuity is also to be noticed.

[3] *Vide* πῶς, 8, 35; πόσῳ μᾶλλον, 28; οὐ πολλῷ μᾶλλον, 35 [μᾶλλον also again in 34ᵃ, 35, 48]; ποσάκις, 43, 54; ἤ, 28, 35, &c.

14, 15 (17), 23, 28, 29, 32, 34[a], 35, 37, 38, 40 (43), 47, 48, 54. These interrogative sentences give the discourses a certain individuality, to which the not unfrequent employment of parataxis and of *parallelismus membrorum* lends a further distinctive trait. Not a few of the sayings are conceived in this simple artistic form. Taken together, the stylistic expedients which are employed impress upon the sayings a stamp of homogeneity. Use is not often made of the historic present (*vide* 2, 13, 17, 18, 40, 55). The imperfect is practically never found (yet see 29, 30); the optative is absolutely wanting. The frequent use of the redundant personal pronoun and of the superfluous αὐτός in its oblique cases (more than 100 times) is characteristic. Both traits are Semitic. Lastly, we might adduce a by no means small number of unclassical constructions occurring in the majority of the sections, some of which may likewise be due to the influence of Semitic idiom, such as those we have already noticed above in the case of ἵνα, but to mention them in detail would lead us too far (*vide* εἰπὲ λόγῳ and similar phrases).

All these characteristics taken together, and especially the negative characteristics, give to the sections, or at least to the great majority of them, a certain individuality, and distinguish them from the style of St. Mark, of St. Matthew, and of St. Luke. We cannot give a convincing proof of their unity from the results of investigation into their vocabulary and style; and yet—especially if it is considered how different and various is the content of these sections—it must be acknowledged that there is in them a certain unity of grammatical and stylistic character and colouring.

III.—The Formal Characteristics of the Subject-matter

The sixty sections (34 is a double section) which we have obtained as the result of our analysis consist of seven narratives, eleven (twelve) parables (and similes), thirteen groups of sayings, and twenty-nine single sayings of smaller or greater length.

The seven narratives comprise the Temptation story (2), the narrative concerning the centurion at Capernaum (13), the question sent by St. John from his prison and the answer of our Lord (14), the story of one who declared himself ready to follow Jesus, and of one who desired first to bury his father (17), the cure of a demoniac and the Beelzebub controversy (29), the demand for a sign, together with our Lord's answer (30), and the question how often one ought to forgive, together with our Lord's command (54). There are thus only two stories of miracles (and these miracles of healing) in Q—one a very notable miracle, a cure wrought at a distance. The introduction to some of these stories may have been longer in Q, but we have no means of settling this point. Nor can we at once discover any motive for the choice of just these seven stories; they have nothing in common with one another. It is important that (in 23) the towns Chorazin, Bethsaida, and especially Capernaum, appear as the chief scenes of our Lord's ministry (concerning Jerusalem in 43 *vide infra*). An equally important point is the strong emphasis laid upon the significance of St. John the Baptist. The discourse concerning him, which was suggested by his doubting question and which is continued in 15, is preceded by an account of his preaching of a baptism of repentance (1), and is followed by the testimony (50) that with him closes the epoch of the Law and the Prophets. No mention is made of the disciples of our Lord in these stories.

Q includes the following parables and similitudes: the Blind leaders of the blind (9), the Good and corrupt tree (11), the House on the rock and on the sand (12), the Querulous children at play (15), the Sheep and the wolves (19), the Light under the bushel (31), the Thief by night and the Faithful and unfaithful steward (37), Concerning the correct behaviour to the adversary (39), the Leaven and the Mustard seed (40), the Strait gate and the narrow way (41), the Lost sheep (48). Eight of these parables have an individual address without any closer definition—only two refer to the Kingdom of God, one to the present generation (15), and one to the disciples (19). This preponderance of the individual address is noteworthy, and it is also noteworthy that the two parables concerning the Kingdom of God are not eschatological, and are closely connected together (*vide infra*). The parables in sections 12, 37, 39 (41) close with an outlook towards the end. Without anticipating a closer critical examination, a cursory glance suffices to inform us that the parables bear the impress of genuineness in a high degree.

The thirteen collections of sayings (discourses)[1] may be grouped in regard to subject-matter as follows: The discourse of the Baptist, together with the reference to the Coming One (1); the Beatitudes (3); Love for enemies (6); against Judging, mote and beam (8); the Lord's Prayer and the power of Prayer (27, 28); Fear not, be not anxious, lay not up treasure (34[a], 35, 36); The great thanksgiving to the Father (25); The great denunciation of the scribes and Pharisees (33); Not peace but a sword (38); False Messiahs, the Parousia of the Son of Man (56).—In judging of Q it is specially important to note that this source also contains a sermon of the Baptist, and further, that formal teaching concerning the better righteousness, and that exact directions concerning prayer, fasting, and almsgiving, are wanting, although an ethical code is imparted in sections 3, 6, 8, 27, 28, 34[a], 35, 36. In the discourses concerning our Lord's relationship to the Father, concerning His attitude towards the scribes and Pharisees and towards the world, and in the discourse concerning the Parousia, the most important relationships *ad extra* are dealt with, except the relationship to the Baptist, which has been explained in the narrative section 14 (and also beforehand in section 1).

The twenty-nine shorter or longer sayings are less varied in content, as appears at the first glance; many of them may be regarded with more or less probability as parts of discourses in Q, the restoration of which must however remain problematical; in

[1] Besides these, it is very probable that sections 16 and 18–24 belong to one discourse.

the case of others, it is possible at once to recognise that they are either related to one another or depend upon the larger groups of sayings. Nine of the sayings in subject-matter, and perhaps also in form, belong to the ethical code—namely, sections 4 (The blow upon the cheek, non-resistance when the coat is taken away), 5 (Give to him that asketh), 7 (The Golden Rule), 32 (The light of the body is the eye), 44 (He that exalteth himself), 49 (No man can serve two masters), 57 (He that findeth his life), 58 (Whosoever hath to him shall be given), 52 (Against divorce).—Fifteen sayings belong together as special directions and promises to the disciples—namely, 10 (The disciple is not above his master), 16 (Proclaim that the Kingdom of God is at hand), 18 (The harvest is great, the labourers few), 19 (I send you forth as sheep), 20, 21 (Conduct of the mission from house to house), 22, 23 (The mission in the cities, sayings concerning the Galilean cities), 24 (He that receiveth you receiveth me), 26 (Blessed are your eyes and your ears), 55 (The faith which removes mountains), 45 (He that loveth father or mother), 46 (The bearing of the Cross), 47 (Ye are the salt of the earth), 59 (Ye will sit upon twelve thrones). Of the still remaining sayings, section 50 (The Law and the Prophets until John) connects with the narrative of section 14; the saying concerning Jerusalem (43), as well as the saying that the children of the kingdom would be cast out while the Gentiles would enter in (42), in their purport belong together, and can be connected with the Great Denunciation (33). Quite by themselves stand the sayings concerning the Son of Man and the Holy Spirit (34^b), concerning offences (53) and the permanence of the Law (51).

The first impression that one receives when one surveys the content of Q is twofold. For the most part, the subject-matter seems to fall asunder into disconnected parts, and this impression cannot be quite overcome; but as soon as one calls to mind the content of the three gospels and compares Q with it, *then Q appears to be undoubtedly more homogeneous than any of the three.* What varied material stands in peaceful juxtaposition in St. Matthew and St. Luke, and even in St. Mark! Even if one neglects the stories of the Infancy, what a multitude of varied interests, indeed of discrepancies, cross one another in those gospels! Who would ever have believed that all that St. Matthew or St. Luke or St. Mark narrate stood in one book, if in each case the book itself had not been handed down to us as a single complete whole? Compared with these gospels, the content which we have assigned to Q is simply *homogeneous.* Here a great number of points of view and tendencies which prevail in those gospels are absolutely wanting.

It is characteristic of St. Mark that he emphasises the supernatural in our Lord, the Son of God; of St. Matthew, that he treats a great part of the gospel material from the point of view of the primitive community, giving to his whole narrative a Jewish and yet anti-Judaistic tone in the interests of apologetics; and of St. Luke, that with the large-heartedness of a Greek he thrusts those traits, which display Jesus as the Great Healer, into the foreground. But in Q all these tendencies are absent. Here we receive rather the impression that the author is simply concerned with the commandments of our Lord, and aims at giving a description of His message, in which description he appears to be influenced by no special and particular bias. Perhaps we may not be mistaken in supposing that his selection was also determined by his desire to illustrate our Lord's message and His witness to Himself, in their main and characteristic features, by specially striking examples. The Messiahship (Divine Sonship) having been established in the introduction, is in the body of the work presupposed as a fact that admits of no further controversy.

The geographical horizon of Q is bounded by Galilee, and indeed much more strictly so than that of the synoptists. It is indeed a question whether Q ever looks beyond Galilee. Reference is made to section 43, but I regard it as being very improbable (with Schmiedel, "Das viertes Evang. gegenüber den drei ersten" [1906], s. 45 ff.) that this utterance concerning Jerusalem stood in Q as a saying of our Lord. It has been shown above that in section 33 the words (St. Matt. xxiii. 34–36 = St. Luke xi. 49–51) form a quotation from an apocryphal Jewish writing, wherein they were spoken by the *Wisdom of God;* for so St. Luke (therefore Q) describes the author; nor could Jesus have said that *He* was sending forth prophets and *wise men* and *scribes.* Moreover, in St. Matthew this passage is followed immediately, and without a fresh introduction, by the words concerning Jerusalem (St. Matt. xxiii. 37–38; St. Luke does not give them until xiii. 34). It is therefore in itself very probable that these words also belong to the quotation, and that it is accordingly *Wisdom* which says: *ποσάκις ἠθέλησα ἐπισυναγαγεῖν τὰ τέκνα σου.* It is Wisdom herself who, by sending forth prophets, wise men, and scribes who had been slain by Jerusalem, had in vain essayed this gathering together of the children of Jerusalem (while if ascribed to our Lord this *ποσάκις*, together with the lament over the murdered prophets, wise men, and scribes whom He is supposed to have sent, hangs in the air—is indeed impossible).[1] Thus, according to the intention of Q, our Lord's own words first begin with *λέγω* [*γὰρ*] *ὑμῖν, οὐ μή με ἴδητε κτλ.* (St. Matt. xxiii. 39; St. Luke xiii. 35).[2] Hence from section 43 we can draw no conclusion

[1] The style also is somewhat different from that of the sayings of our Lord in Q. Ὃν τρόπον does not occur elsewhere in Q (ὡς is the only word used); verbs compounded with two prepositions are wanting elsewhere. Yet I do not wish to lay much stress upon these points.

[2] The history of this passage is accordingly as follows: In Q, St. Matt. xxiii. 34–38 was given as a quotation used by our Lord to give force to what He was saying, to which verse 39 was appended as a real utterance of our Lord Himself. This caused some uncertainty in regard to the limits of the quotation. The result was that St. Matthew did not treat it as a quotation at all, but transformed the whole passage into an original discourse of our Lord (and yet with the help of St. Luke we can still detect in διὰ τοῦτο a trace of what has been obliterated), while St. Luke has broken off the quotation directly before the appeal to Jerusalem, and omitting the latter here, has given it in a different place as a saying of our Lord Himself. If this explanation is correct, then it further follows that St. Luke has torn asunder verses which stood together in Q. This is important; for we see that it is not always the case that St. Matthew has arbitrarily combined passages from Q which did not stand together in that source, but that on the contrary St. Luke also has separated passages which were in juxtaposition.

concerning any close connection of our Lord's mission with Jerusalem—nevertheless there is a strong balance of probability that sections 33 and 43 were spoken in Jerusalem, where it is more natural that they should have been delivered than in Galilee.[1]

Together with Jerusalem—which is thus never mentioned in Q except in the Woe against the Pharisees—the Passion and all references to the Passion are absent from Q. The single isolated saying concerning the taking up of one's own cross (46) would at the best, if it really stood in Q, only afford an indirect reference to the Passion, and the sign of the prophet Jonah (30), according to the account in Q, had absolutely nothing to do with the Passion. *So far therefore as we can judge, all that after the precedent of St. Mark goes to form the main theme of the Synoptic Gospels—the Passion and the narratives and discourses leading up to the Passion—was completely wanting in Q. Herein lies the fundamental difference between the gospels and Q. The latter, in fact, was not a gospel at all in the sense that the Synoptics are.* The narrative of this source must therefore have been wanting in historical climax—no thread of historical continuity could have run through it, binding the end to the beginning; for what climax or what thread of continuity could have existed where the Passion, and the thoughts connected with the Passion, were left out of consideration? Thus Q in the main could only have been a compilation of sayings and discourses of varied content. There is

[1] Still one must remember that we are told in St. Mark vii. 1 that "There came together to Him the Pharisees, and certain of the scribes, which came from Jerusalem"—*cf.* vii. 5, &c.

no force in the objection that St. Matthew and St. Luke may have omitted the parts of Q which dealt with the Passion. If from St. Luke xvii. 34 to the end only two isolated verses can be proved to be derived from Q, or if from St. Matthew xv. 15 to the end only a very few isolated verses in chaps. xvii., xviii., xix., xxv., and a couple or so of longer passages in chaps. xxiii. and xxiv. belong to Q, this cannot be merely accidental. A source which afforded the evangelists such ample and excellent material for the first half of their works would have been used by them elsewhere if it had contained further material. But may it not be that one of the two evangelists for some reason or other departed from the source while the other still followed it, so that the matter peculiar to him in the concluding third part of his work was derived from the source? This is possible, and it will therefore be necessary to examine the matter which is peculiar to each of the two gospels, keeping this contingency in view. Until this is done, the only verdict which the facts before us allow us to give is that *Q is a compilation of discourses and sayings of our Lord, the arrangement of which has no reference to the Passion, with an horizon which is as good as absolutely bounded by Galilee, without any clearly discernible bias, whether apologetic, didactic, ecclesiastical, national, or anti-national.* So far as any purpose at all—beyond that of imparting catechetical instruction—can be discovered in the compilation, it consisted perhaps in an endeavour to give, with a certain degree of completeness, a representation of the main features of our Lord's relationship with

His environment. Perhaps an investigation of the order of the sections will help us further.

IV.—The Order of the Sections

Since we may regard St. Matthew as independent of St. Luke and *vice versâ*, it follows that if they agree in the order in which they present sections which do not occur in St. Mark, that order is thereby proved to be the order of the source. This point has been rightly emphasised by the critics, and has lately been investigated by Wernle and Wellhausen ("Einleitung," s. 65 ff.).

In the first place, the first thirteen sections show an astonishing coincidence in order:—

	St. Luke.		St. Matthew.
(1)	iii. 7–9, 16, 17	=	iii. 7–12 (The Baptist).
(2)	iv. 1–13	=	iv. 1–11 (The Temptation).
(3)	vi. 20, 21–23	=	v. 2–4, 6, 11, 12 (Introduction to Sermon; the Beatitudes).
(4)	vi. 29	=	v. 39, 40 (Blow upon the cheek, robbery of garment).
(5)	vi. 30	=	v. 42 (Give to him that asketh).
(6)	vi. 27, 28, 35b, 32, 33, 36	=	v. 44–48 (Love your enemies).
(7)	vi. 31	=	vii. 12 (Golden Rule).
(8)	vi. 37, 38, 41, 42	=	vii. 1–5 (Judge not; Mote and Beam).

[(9) vi. 39 = xv. 14 (Leaders of the Blind).]
[(10) vi. 40 = x. 24, 25 (The disciple not above his master).]
(11) vi. 43, 44 = vii. 16–18; xii. 33 (The good and corrupt tree).
(12) vi. 46–49 = vii. 21, 24–27 (The house upon the rock and upon the sand).
(13) vii. 1–10 = vii. 28; viii. 5–10, 13 (Conclusion of sermon; the centurion at Capernaum).

We must accordingly judge that Q began with the preaching of the Baptist, that then there followed the story of the Temptation, then important parts of the so-called Sermon on the Mount,[1] which concluded with the notice: "After Jesus had spoken these words he entered into Capernaum," and was immediately succeeded by the narrative of the centurion at Capernaum. The subject-matter in question in St. Luke, chaps. iii., iv., vi., vii., is found in its entirety (with the exception of St. Luke vi. 39, 40) in St. Matt., chaps. iii., iv., v., vii., and viii. with very few changes in order.

St. Luke now introduces in vii. 18–35 (sections 14 and 15) the discourse concerning the Baptist; St. Matthew does not give this discourse until

[1] St. Luke and St. Matthew differ concerning the site. The former says (v. 1) *ἀνέβη εἰς τὸ ὄρος*, the latter (vi. 17) *καταβὰς ἔστη ἐπὶ τόπου πεδινοῦ.* But both agree in stating that a great multitude (*ὄχλος*) was present, and that the sermon was nevertheless addressed to the disciples. These statements must have occurred in the source.

chap. xi., and he inserts beforehand the sections concerning discipleship and the charge to the disciples; in this gospel they occur in viii. 19–22; ix. 37, 38, and x.; in St. Luke these sections (16–22, 24, 34, 38, 45, 46, 57) are found dispersed throughout chaps. ix. (2), 57–60; x. 2 (3), 5, 6 (7[b]), 9, 11, 12, (16); xii. 2–9, 51, 53; xiv. 26, 27; xvii. 33.

At first glance it seems impossible to throw light upon this chaos and to discover the order of the source, but as soon as one sets down the related sections side by side in lists the chaos falls into order in an astonishing fashion, as is seen from the following table:—

(16)	(St. Luke	ix. 2	and St. Matt.	x. 7).
(17)	„	ix. 57–60	„ „	viii. 19–22.
(18)	„	x. 2	„ „	ix. 37, 38.
(19)	(„	x. 3	„ „	x. 16[a]).
(20)	„	x. 5, 6	„ „	x. 12, 13.
(21)	(„	x. 7[b]	„ „	x. 10[b]).
(22)	„	x. 12	„ „	x. 15.
(24)	(„	x. 16	„ „	x. 40).
(34[a])	„	xii. 2–9	„ „	x. 26–33.
(38)	„	xii. 51, 53	„ „	x. 34–36.
(45)	„	xiv. 26	„ „	x. 37.
(46)	„	xiv. 27	„ „	x. 38.
(57)	„	xvii. 33	„ „	x. 39.

As we see, the bracketed passages alone present difficulty and disturb the otherwise absolutely identical order. But in our previous critical investigation we have already noted that these four passages rouse suspicion as to their belonging to

Q. It is now still more uncertain whether as a whole they belong here;[1] *for when they are omitted there is absolutely no disturbance in order*, the remaining nine sections follow one another in exactly the same succession both in St. Matthew and St. Luke. *It is at the same time shown that these sections, which are indeed closely allied in subject-matter, were not first brought together by St. Matthew, but that in Q they stood in the same order of succession as that of the first gospel;* for it is clear that St. Luke also found them in this order. It is noteworthy that this evangelist has distributed them throughout the chaps. ix., x., xii., xiv., xvii., *without altering their order of succession.*[2]

Seeing then that the sections (16), (19), (24) are to be left on one side, and are perhaps to be altogether excluded from Q, the only question which remains open in connection with the order of the sections (1)–(8), (11)–(15), (17), (18), (20)–(22), (34ª), (38), (45), (46), (57), is whether the material belonging to Q in St. Matt. viii.–x. originally stood before or after the discourse concerning the Baptist. As it is proved that St. Matthew (and not St. Luke) has reproduced the arrangement of the source in chapters viii.–x., it is accordingly probable that we must also follow him here, and conclude that in Q the discourse concerning the Baptist came after the discourse to the disciples.

Now follow, in St. Matt. xi. 21–23 and xi. 25–27

[1] Nevertheless internal reasons demand that at least section 21 be assigned to Q.

[2] In an important passage we thus gain insight into St. Luke's method of composition (*vide supra*, p. 169, note 2).

as in St. Luke x. 13–15 and x. 21–22, the Woe denounced against the Galilean cities (section 23), and the great thanksgiving to the Father (section 25).

But just as in the case of sections 9 and 10, we cannot form any judgment as to their original position in Q, so is it also with all those passages of the Sermon on the Mount which we have not already given in the above list. If we take them in the order of St. Matthew, we have the following table:—

St. Matt.	v. 13	=(section	47)[1]
"	v. 15	=("	31)
"	v. 18	=("	51)
"	v. 25, 26	=("	39)
"	v. 32	=("	52)
"	vi. 9–13	=("	27)
"	vi. 19–21	=("	36)
"	vi. 22, 23	=("	32)
"	vi. 24	=("	49)
"	vi. 25–33	=("	35)
"	vii. 7–11	=("	28)
"	vii. 13, 14	=("	41)

This is hopeless; for it is simply impossible to trace any sign of correspondence in the order of the parallel passages; we are therefore left at first quite in the dark as to the order of these sections in Q—indeed one of sceptical mind might doubt whether they belong to Q at all.

The remaining seventeen sections give more favour-

[1] Let it be remembered that the numbers of the sections express their order in the text of St. Luke.

able results, if we only neglect the eight short sayings (sections 26, 34[b], 42, 44, 50, 53, 55, 59) and the short parables (40 and 48); then we find in the following order:—

Beelzebub (section 29). St. Matt. xii. 22, 23, 27, 28, 30, 43, 45; St. Luke xi. 14, 19, 20, 23–26.
Sign of Jonah (section 30). St. Matt. xii. 38, 39, 41, 42; St. Luke xi. 16, 29, 30, 31.
Woe against the Pharisees (section 33). St. Matt. xxiii. 4, 13, 23, 25, 27, 29, 30–32, 34–36; St. Luke xi. 46, 52, 42, 39, 44, 47, 49–51.
The coming of the Lord as a thief; the trustworthy and the untrustworthy steward (section 37). St. Matt. xxiv. 43–51; St. Luke xii. 39, 40, 42–46.
Jerusalem, Jerusalem (section 43). St. Matt. xxiii. 37–39; St. Luke xiii. 34, 35.
How oft shall I forgive? (section 54). St. Matt. xviii. 15, 21, 22; St. Luke xvii. 3, 4.
The Parousia (section 56). St. Matt. xxiv. 26, 27, 28, 37–41; St. Luke xvii. 23, 24, 37, 26, 27, 34, 35.
To him that hath shall be given (section 58). St. Matt. xxv. 29; St. Luke xix. 26.

Since we have already seen above that St. Luke has arbitrarily separated the section concerning Jerusalem from the Woe against the Pharisees, it is evident that the correspondence in order in this list is only disturbed by the question concerning forgiveness and by the splitting up of the discourse, St. Matt. xxiv. 26–51 (St. Luke has divided it and placed the second half before the first); otherwise the order is identical. It is of importance for our knowledge of Q to notice that discourses which had the end of the world in view evidently stood at the conclusion of this source, such discourses, namely, as the Woe against the Pharisees, the prophecy of judgment upon Jerusalem, the coming of the Lord as a thief in the night, the faithful and unfaithful steward, the warning against false Christs with the announcement of the Parousia, lastly, the saying, "To him that hath shall be given" (with its converse).

From this investigation, which has been carried somewhat further than that of Wernle and Wellhausen, we derive the following results:—

(1) The sections distinguished above by the numbers 1–8, 11–15, 17, 18, 20, 21, 22, 23, 25, 29, 30, 33, 34[a], 37, 38, 43, 45, 46, 56, 57, 58, permit of being arranged in an order which is practically identical in St. Matthew and St. Luke; they therefore certainly belong to a single source.[1]

(2) *This source had an order which in essential points is natural and intelligible.*[2] It proceeded as follows:—

The preaching of the Baptist.

The story of the Temptation (probably preceded by the Baptism of our Lord with the voice from heaven, *vide infra*).

[1] I have long adopted an extremely sceptical attitude towards the hypothesis which assumes a single definite source for the material (not in St. Mark) which is common to St. Matthew and St. Luke; but the facts which are here disclosed seem to me to be conclusive (against Hilgenfeld, Zahn, Godet, and others). It is, moreover, astonishing how superficially and cursorily Zahn passes over this question in his voluminous "Einleitung" (II^2, s. 410 ff.).

[2] *Cf.* Wernle, "Synopt. Frage," s. 226 ff.

The most important parts of the Sermon on the Mount.

The charge to the disciples concerning their mission.

The discourse concerning the Baptist.

The Woes against the cities.

The great Thanksgiving to the Father.

The Beelzebub section, and (bound up with it)—

The sign of Jonah.

The Woes against the Pharisees, together with the pronouncement of judgment against Jerusalem.

The warning against false Christs; the discourse concerning the Parousia.

The coming of the Son of Man as a thief in the night; the faithful and unfaithful steward.

The saying that to him that hath shall be given, and the other saying that the disciples should govern the twelve tribes of Israel.[1]

The sections 9, 10, 16, 19, 24, 26–28, 31, 32, 34^{b}, 35, 36, 39–42, 44, 47–55 do not admit of being arranged in a definite order. *It is therefore only more or less probable that they belong to Q*, and therefore in an investigation into the characteristics of Q they ought to be regarded as of only secondary authority (St. Matthew and St. Luke can well have depended upon more than one source for their common matter which is not found in St. Mark; still the difference in order is no proof in favour of such an hypothesis).

[1] St. Luke gives this saying (59) at the end, St. Matthew at a very much earlier point (in chap. xix.); perhaps St. Luke is in the right here.

In this connection the following points must also be noted:—

These twenty-seven sections are almost all of them short, indeed very short.[1] Eighteen of them have been already included above among the very short sayings, and seven of them are short parables or only similitudes (9, 19, 31, 39, 40, 41, 48) which could easily change their place; only five sections (27, 28, 35, 36, 54) are of greater extent. So far as their content is concerned, the majority of these sayings admirably suit the character of Q and give no occasion for postulating another source.

(3) From the discourse to the disciples (*i.e.* the subject-matter in St. Matt. x.), and from the fact that in the first gospel the sections 33 and 43, as well as sections 56 and 37, are correctly given in juxtaposition, we conclude that St. Matthew has preserved the order of the source more faithfully than St. Luke.[2] It therefore follows with no slight probability that those parts of the Sermon on the Mount which are common to St. Matthew and St. Luke, and yet do not stand in the same order in the two gospels (sections 27, 28, 31, 32, 35, 36, 39, 41, 47, 49, 51, 52), occurred in Q in the order of St. Matthew, and that St. Luke has separated and distributed them throughout his work for reasons which can no longer be discovered (in the belief that he could trace a better τάξις). We shall be justified in deciding similarly concerning other sections which

[1] Together they form scarcely a quarter of the whole contents of Q.

[2] We now recognise that the great composite discourses of St. Matthew had their outline already given in Q.

occur in different positions in St. Matthew and St. Luke, and in regarding St. Luke in this matter as capricious in the extreme.

(4) Q was no gospel like St. Matthew, St. Mark, and St. Luke, and yet it was not a merely formless compilation of sayings and discourses of our Lord without any thread of connection. Rather we learn from the beginning and the conclusion (eschatological discourses) that it possessed a certain definite arrangement of subject-matter and the outlines of a chronological order. It was, however, in no sense a biographical narrative, but essentially a collection of discourses.[1] This is the very reason that it makes no mention of the Passion. Nor need we be surprised at the composition of a work which confined itself to the discourses and sayings of our Lord; indeed, if one keeps in mind the contemporary Jewish fashion, the composition of such a work is *a priori* probable, and, moreover, finds support in Christian terminology, which from the first distinguished between the acts

[1] The seven narratives (*vide supra*, p. 163), which at least were included in Q, do not alter this character; for in five of these the important feature is clearly a saying of our Lord, and the story is cursorily narrated only in order to give the occasion of the utterance. It is otherwise with the story of the Temptation, and, as it seems, with the narrative concerning the centurion. But the inclusion of the former becomes at once intelligible if the story of the Baptism was also included; in this case we must conceive of Q as a compilation of sayings which received its necessary determination, and thereby an historical character, in that it was prefaced by an account of the consecration of Jesus as the Messiah. This hypothesis is corroborated by the strongly Messianic character of the story of the Temptation in Q (*vide* the following note). Accordingly, only the story of the Centurion seems to fall outside the framework of Q. Yet *vide infra*.

and the sayings of Jesus (*vide* St. Paul's Epistles; Acts i. 1: περὶ πάντων ὧν ἤρξατο Ἰησοῦς ποιεῖν τε καὶ διδάσκειν—Is St. Luke here thinking of his two main sources, St. Mark and Q?—*cf.* St. Luke xxiv. 19, &c.).

V.—Can we Discover any Trace of Q in the Matter that is Peculiar to St. Matthew or to St. Luke, or in Indirect Evangelic Tradition?

Seeing that Q is so neutral in linguistic characteristics, we can scarcely use arguments based upon phenomena of style and vocabulary in order to prove that passages in question belong to Q. Nor does an analysis based upon phenomena of subject-matter promise much success. But one thing is at all events possible: we can distinguish numerous passages in both gospels which certainly could *not* have stood in Q.

Let us begin with St. Matthew and with the Sermon on the Mount.[1] Of the passages that stand in St. Matt. v.–vii. and are wanting in St. Luke, it is possible that v. 14, 16 (Light of the world, City upon a hill), v. 41 (If one constrain

[1] Wellhausen ("Einl.," s. 74) judges that the Baptism of our Lord by St. John could not well have been absent from Q. There is by no means little to be said in favour of this theory (*vide supra*, and note that both "ἀνήχθη" and "ὑπὸ τοῦ πνεύματος" in the story of the Temptation can only be understood in the light of the story of the Baptism)—and in this case there is much that is attractive in the hypothesis that the original form of the voice from heaven in St. Luke is to be derived from Q (*vide* Excurs. II.). But Wellhausen's combination of the temptation by the devil with the temptation by St. Peter (St. Mark viii. 32, 33), and his confident

thee to go one mile, then go two), vi. 34 (which finishes off the verses 25–33 belonging to Q), and vii. 22, 23 (Many will say to me in that day, &c.) stood in Q; all else, namely, v. 17, 19, 20–24, 27–31, 33–38, 43; vi. 1–8 (14, 15), 16–18; vii. 6–15, must have been wanting in that source, because these passages are strongly marked by the peculiar characteristics of St. Matthew (better righteousness, formal directions concerning almsgiving, prayer, and fasting, &c., *vide supra*, p. 167) and because St. Luke offers absolutely no parallel to them. The by no means slight degree of homogeneity which is discernible in the passages in question (while nothing similar is found in the passages which certainly belong to Q) is in itself a strong proof that they are alien to Q. They indeed all partake of that controversial attitude towards Judaism which is a peculiar characteristic of St. Matthew.

The same may be said of the sayings concerning the Sabbath in xii. 5 ff., 11 f. Of the parables peculiar to St. Matthew in chap. xiii. the Buried Treasure and the Pearl (verses 44–46) may have stood in Q, because they are similar to the Mustard Seed and the Leaven;[1] but we have no certainty that this was so, especially as they are

assertion that the ὕπαγε Σατανᾶ of St. Matthew is derived from the record of our Lord's repulse of St. Peter, are rash. Wellhausen's other conjecture that a trait in the story of the Baptism, in which St. Matthew differs from St. Mark, namely, St. John's objection to baptize our Lord, had its origin in Q, is destitute of all foundation and is, according to Q, section 14, improbable.

[1] So Wernle, "Synopt. Frage," s. 187.

separated from the latter parables by the interpretation of the parable of the Tares and seem like an appendix added by St. Matthew. No one is likely to claim the parables of the Tares and of the Draw-net for Q, any more than the concluding passage (xiii. 51 f.) of the collection of parables in chapter xiii.

The story of St. Peter's walking on the sea (xiv. 28–31) is a narrative of entirely secondary character, likewise the words addressed to St. Peter concerning the Rock upon which the Church would be built (xvi. 17–19), perhaps also the story of the coin in the fish's mouth (xvii. 24–27), certainly the discourse on discipline in the Church (xviii. 16–18). Possibly xviii. 10 (The angels of the little ones) stood in Q; that the parables of the Great Supper (xxii. 1–11) and the parable of the Talents belong to Q is not impossible, as we have seen (pp. 119 ff.); but we can arrive at no certainty on this point—above all, we can no longer restore the form in which they stood in Q.[1] All that remains—the parables and discourses that occur in the last chapter of St. Matthew preceding the Passion—must probably be kept distinct from Q, for they present no indication of relationship to that source.[2] As for the narratives peculiar to

[1] The order in which the parable of the Talents occurs in the two gospels is in favour of its belonging to Q; for it is found in St. Matt. xxv. and in St. Luke xix., thus in both cases it follows the discourse concerning the Parousia, St. Matt. xxiv. and St. Luke xvii. This is not so in the case of the Great Supper (St. Matt. xxii. and St. Luke xiv.).

[2] Naturally, in the case of many parables and discourses, the "possibility" of such relationship cannot be disputed.

the account of the Passion in St. Matthew, it would be a most arbitrary proceeding to assign these to Q, seeing that even the prophecies of the Passion are wanting in this source and that these passages of St. Matthew are secondary or even tertiary in character.

In St. Luke the situation is not different; we can state with considerable probability that such and such passages that are peculiar to St. Luke did *not* stand in Q—all the narratives, discourses, and parables which specially emphasise the contrast between the poor and the rich and our Lord's love for sinners, and are so characteristic of St. Luke's peculiar genius. Apart from these, there is much that is peculiar to this gospel which may possibly have belonged to Q; but I have sought in vain for any clear principles upon which a probable proof of such relationship could be based.

We must content ourselves with this. It is *a priori* probable, indeed quite certain, that much which occurs only in St. Matthew or in St. Luke is derived from Q, but except the parable of the Mustard Seed which grows into a great tree—and this has been by us already assigned to Q, though it also occurs in St. Mark—I believe that there is no part of the subject-matter peculiar to any one of the two gospels which we are justified in definitely assigning to Q.[1]

Any one that adopts the standpoint of Resch and assumes that the "apostolic source" existed for

[1] We must therefore be more discreet in this connection than Wernle and many other scholars.

centuries side by side with our gospels, and with them exercised influence upon the evangelic tradition, will attempt to discover passages of Q in the gospel sayings found in the Fathers. He, however, who cannot convince himself that there is any proof, or possibility of proof, that the later tradition has been influenced by the sources of our gospels, will hope for very little from the examination of the "Agrapha" and related material. Nevertheless, I have investigated afresh the material which Resch has collected ("Texte und Unters.," Bd. 5, 10, and 30). The appearance of light at the Baptism (Bd. 30, Heft 3–4, s. 36), which is a very early tradition and is found in Codd. Vercell. and Sangerm. at St. Matt. iii. 15; the saying found in Syr. Cur. at St. Matt. xx. 28 (*cf.* also the same passage in Cod. D) ὑμεῖς δὲ ζητεῖτε ἐκ μικροῦ αὐξῆσαι καὶ μὴ ἐκ μείζονος ἔλαττον εἶναι (*l.c.* s. 39); the Logia in 1 Clem. ii. 13, 46 and Polycarp. ii., and in Acts xx. 35; the ἐν οἷς ἂν ὑμᾶς καταλάβω, ἐν τούτοις καὶ κρινῶ of Justin Martyr and others (*l.c.* s. 102); the saying strongly attested from Clement of Alexandria onwards: αἰτεῖσθε, φησί, τὰ μεγάλα, καὶ τὰ μικρὰ ὑμῖν προστεθήσεται (*l.c.* s. 111); the yet more constantly quoted saying: γίνεσθε δόκιμοι τραπεζῖται (s. 112 ff.); the saying attested by Origen: διὰ τοὺς ἀσθενοῦντας ἠσθένουν καὶ διὰ τοὺς πεινῶντας ἐπείνων καὶ διὰ τοὺς διψῶντας ἐδίψων (s. 132); the saying: σῴζου σὺ καὶ ἡ ψυχή σου (s. 180); the saying in Clement of Alexandria and Tertullian: εἶδες τὸν ἀδελφόν σου, εἶδες τὸν θεόν σου (s. 182); the saying in Origen: ὁ ἐγγύς μου ἐγγὺς τοῦ πατρός (MS. πυρός), ὁ δὲ μακρὰν ἀπ' ἐμοῦ μακρὰν ἀπὸ τῆς βασιλείας (s. 185)—these are passages which could be offered for consideration here.

It is indeed most improbable that the interpolations found in some manuscripts of the gospels, of which two examples have been given at the beginning of the above list, are derived from Q. Seeing that they can scarcely have belonged to the original text either of St. Matthew or St. Luke (*cf.* especially the interpolations in D)—in which case only could there be any real question concerning their origin from Q—they must therefore have been derived either from other written gospels or from oral tradition. To suppose that they were derived directly from Q, the source of St. Matthew and St. Luke, would be to assume a remarkable accident without any justification, seeing that these passages show no relationship in subject-matter with Q.

The quotations in the Acts of the Apostles and in the epistles of Clement of Rome and of Polycarp perhaps afford more promising material; for these writings date from a time at which Q may still have been known and when the canonical gospels had not yet reached all parts of the Church, or at least were not everywhere recognised as canonical. It is therefore remarkable that the five sayings which are quoted in these writings have introductions of essentially the same character as is here seen:—

Acts xx. 35: . . . μνημονεύειν τε τῶν λόγων τοῦ κυρίου Ἰησοῦ, ὅτι αὐτὸς εἶπεν· Μακάριόν ἐστιν μᾶλλον διδόναι ἢ λαμβάνειν.

1 Clem. xiii.: *μάλιστα μεμνημένοι τῶν λόγων τοῦ κυρίου Ἰησοῦ, οὓς ἐλάλησεν διδάσκων ἐπιείκειαν καὶ μακροθυμίαν· οὕτως γὰρ εἶπεν· Ἐλεᾶτε ἵνα ἐλεηθῆτε, ἀφίετε ἵνα ἀφεθῇ ὑμῖν· ὡς ποιεῖτε, οὕτω ποιηθήσεται ὑμῖν· ὡς δίδοτε, οὕτως δοθήσεται ὑμῖν· ὡς κρίνετε, οὕτως κριθήσεσθε· ὡς χρηστεύεσθε, οὕτως χρηστευθήσεται ὑμῖν· ᾧ μέτρῳ μετρεῖτε, ἐν αὐτῷ μετρηθήσεται ὑμῖν.*

1 Clem. xlvi.: *μνήσθητε τῶν λόγων τοῦ Ἰησοῦ τοῦ κυρίου ἡμῶν· εἶπεν γάρ· Οὐαὶ τῷ ἀνθρώπῳ ἐκείνῳ· καλὸν ἦν αὐτῷ εἰ μὴ ἐγεννήθη ἢ ἕνα τῶν ἐκλεκτῶν μου σκανδαλίσαι. κρεῖττον ἦν αὐτῷ περιτεθῆναι μύλον καὶ καταποντισθῆναι εἰς τὴν θάλασσαν, ἢ ἕνα τῶν ἐκλεκτῶν μου διαστρέψαι.*

Polyc. c. ii.: *μνημονεύοντες ὧν εἶπεν ὁ κύριος διδάσκων· μὴ κρίνετε, ἵνα μὴ κριθῆτε· ἀφίετε, καὶ ἀφεθήσεται ὑμῖν· ἐλεᾶτε, ἵνα ἐλεηθῆτε· ᾧ μέτρῳ μετρεῖτε, ἀντιμετρηθήσεται ὑμῖν· καὶ ὅτι· μακάριοι οἱ πτωχοὶ καὶ οἱ διωκόμενοι ἕνεκεν δικαιοσύνης, ὅτι αὐτῶν ἐστιν ἡ βασιλεία τοῦ θεοῦ.*

1 Clem. ii.: *πάντες ἐταπεινοφρονεῖτε . . . ὑποτασσόμενοι μᾶλλον ἢ ὑποτάσσοντες, ἥδιον διδόντες ἢ λαμβάνοντες τοῖς ἐφοδίοις τοῦ Χριστοῦ ἀρκούμενοι καὶ προσέχοντες, τοὺς λόγους οὐτοῦ ἐπιμελῶς ἐνεστερνισμένοι ἦτε τοῖς σπλάγγνοις.*

There is no doubt that in all these passages the sayings of our Lord are referred to as a compilation, and the form of the quotations suggests that this compilation was crystallised in a written document which bore the title, "Λόγοι τοῦ κυρίου Ἰησοῦ," and was regarded as giving the authoritative teaching of our Lord.[1] In such a case identity with Q would be practically proved. But, in the first place, we can here only arrive at a certain degree of probability; in the second place, close examination of the subject-matter of these sayings is not favourable to the hypothesis; for (*a*) if the saying, "It is more blessed to give than to receive" stood in Q, why has St. Luke not taken it up into his gospel? (yet this is not a very weighty objection); (*b*) in Polycarp the formula of quotation and the quotation itself (the latter only partly and freely reproduced) are most probably derived from 1 Clem. xiii.; for Polycarp has made constant use of the epistle of Clement ("Clement. Alex. Strom.," ii. 18, is also dependent upon the same passage); (*c*) the first saying quoted by Clement of Rome in the parts which have no direct parallel in St. Matthew and St. Luke (*ἐλεᾶτε ἵνα ἐλεηθῆτε, ἀφίετε ἵνα ἀφεθῇ ὑμῖν· ὡς ποιεῖτε, οὕτω ποιηθήσεται ὑμῖν· ὡς δίδοτε, οὕτως δοθήσεται ὑμῖν· ὡς χρηστεύεσθε, οὕτως χρηστευθήσεται ὑμῖν*) may very well have stood in Q; but the part in which it coincides in subject-matter with Q, as we have given this source above, has a different wording. In place of *μὴ κρίνετε, ἵνα μὴ κριθῆτε, ἐν ᾧ γὰρ κρίματι κρίνετε, κριθήσεσθε* we have *ὡς κρίνετε, οὕτως κριθήσεσθε*. It may, however, be objected that Clement here has simply omitted a phrase or so, and for the rest has followed another translation of Q; but *μὴ κρίνετε, ἵνα κτλ.* does not at all suit his context. The

[1] After having written this I see from "Theol. Jahresbericht" for 1905 (iii. Abt. s. 246), that Harris, and lately Lake (in "Hibb. Journ." iii. 332 ff.), have preceded me in commending this hypothesis.

dependence upon Q remains therefore uncertain. (*d*) The second passage of Clement (I neglect "Clem. Alex. Strom.," iii. 18, because it depends upon "Clem. Rom.") reproduces sayings which are found in all three evangelists—they may, nevertheless, have also stood in Q; indeed, we have shown that the allied words: *ἀνάγκη ἐλθεῖν τὰ σκάνδαλα, πλὴν οὐαὶ τῷ ἀνθρώπῳ δι' οὗ τὸ σκάνδαλον ἔρχεται*, probably stood in Q (*vide* section 53).

St. Mark xiv.	St. Matt. xxvi.	St. Luke xxii.	Clem. Rom.
21: οὐαὶ τῷ ἀνθρώπῳ ἐκείνῳ δι' οὗ ὁ υἱὸς τοῦ ἀνθρώπου παραδίδοται· καλὸν αὐτῷ εἰ οὐκ ἐγεννήθη ὁ ἄνθρωπος ἐκεῖνος.	24: as St. Mark (except that ἦν is added after καλὸν).	22: οὐαὶ τῷ ἀνθρώπῳ ἐκείνῳ δι' οὗ παραδίδοται [scil. ὁ υἱὸς τ. ἀνθ.].	οὐαὶ τῷ ἀνθρώπῳ ἐκείνῳ· καλὸν ἦν αὐτῷ εἰ μὴ ἐγεννήθη ἢ ἕνα τῶν ἐκλεκτῶν μου σκανδαλίσαι.
St. Mark ix. 42: ὃς ἂν σκανδαλίσῃ ἕνα τῶν μικρῶν τούτων τῶν πιστευόντων, καλόν ἐστιν αὐτῷ μᾶλλον εἰ περίκειται μύλος ὀνικὸς περὶ τὸν τράχηλον αὐτοῦ καὶ βέβληται εἰς τὴν θάλασσαν.	St. Matt. xviii. 6, 7: first as in St. Mark, then πιστευόντων εἰς ἐμέ· συμφέρει αὐτῷ ἵνα κρεμασθῇ μύλος ὀνικὸς περὶ τὸν τράχηλον αὐτοῦ καὶ καταποντισθῇ ἐν τῷ πελάγει τῆς θαλάσσης. οὐαὶ τῷ κόσμῳ ἀπὸ τῶν σκανδάλων· ἀνάγκη γὰρ ἐλθεῖν τὰ σκάνδαλα, πλὴν οὐαὶ τῷ ἀνθρώπῳ δι' οὗ τὸ σκάνδαλον ἔρχεται.	St. Luke xvii. 1, 2: ἀνένδεκτόν ἐστιν τοῦ τὰ σκάνδαλα μὴ ἐλθεῖν, πλὴν οὐαὶ δι' οὗ ἔρχεται· λυσιτελεῖ αὐτῷ εἰ λίθος μυλικὸς περίκειται περὶ τὸν τράχηλον αὐτοῦ καὶ ἔρριπται εἰς τὴν θάλασσαν, ἢ ἵνα σκανδαλίσῃ τῶν μικρῶν τούτων ἕνα.	κρεῖττον ἦν αὐτῷ περιτεθῆναι μύλον καὶ καταποντισθῆναι, ἢ ἕνα τῶν ἐκλεκτῶν μου διαστρέψαι.

The interpretation of the phenomena presented in the above table is difficult. It is possible that Clement erroneously understood the saying concerning Judas in a general sense and combined it wrongly with the saying concerning offending the little ones, freely reproduced by him as "elect"; it is, however, also possible that not only the general clause, ἀνάγκη ἐλθεῖν τὰ σκάνδαλα, πλὴν οὐαὶ τῷ ἀνθρώπῳ δι' οὗ τὸ σκάνδαλον ἔρχεται, stood in Q, but also something concerning offending the elect in just that double form in which Clement gives it (this would then be the more ancient form, while St. Mark has introduced the special reference to Judas); St. Matthew and St. Luke had St. Mark and Q before them, and have on the whole followed the former in that they have reproduced from Q only the general saying concerning offences. Yet this second explanation is far less probable than the first; for (1) it is strange that they have both hit upon the same solution of the problem (yet in St. Luke xvii. 1, 2, the order is different from that in St. Matt. xviii. 6, 7); (2) we can form no definite conception of the wording of this hypothetical text of Q (according to Clement); in its two halves it is extremely tautologous, and accordingly gives the impression that these two halves were originally separate from one another and came from different sources (just as it is in the three gospels). Lastly, we have the ἐκείνῳ at the beginning, which tells a tale. There is therefore at least no surety that we have Q before us here, however attractive the hypothesis may be and though it may claim the support of what seem to be translation-variants. (*e*) Neither can we well claim for Q that it is the source of the second half of the quotation in Polycarp; for though "μακάριοι οἱ πτωχοί" (without τῷ πνεύματι) answers to the wording of Q (and of St. Luke), yet διωκόμενοι ἕνεκεν δικαιοσύνης, which is found in St. Matthew, cannot be proved to have stood in Q.

Accordingly we must reluctantly abandon the hope of recovering from these quotations, which seem to presuppose our gospels, anything which certainly belongs to Q; there is, in fact, no sufficient basis of probability for the hypothesis that these "λόγοι τοῦ κυρίου Ἰησοῦ" are identical with Q. The case is here one of very moderate possibility, and it is permissible only with considerable reservation to claim the quotations in 1 Clem. xiii., xlvi. for Q.[1]

If, however, our investigation of these passages leads to such unsure results, the uncertainty is very much greater in regard to the "Agrapha" which are found in writers from Justin downwards. In all these cases it is more probable that these sayings have been derived from the gospel of the Egyptians, the gospel of St. Peter, or other sources, than that they were directly taken from Q. This specially holds good of the sayings discovered by Grenfell and Hunt, and likewise of those in the Clementine

[1] If it is thought certain that "λόγοι κτλ." in Clement signifies the title of a book, which must therefore be identical with Q, it will then be necessary to assume a separate recension of Q, which was afterwards amplified from the canonical gospels. It is in favour of this hypothesis that in St. Matthew (and so also probably in Q) the Sermon on the Mount is introduced with the words: ἐδίδασκεν αὐτοὺς λέγων.

Homilies, though it is possible that elements of great antiquity are preserved therein. We know that the gospels mentioned were still read in the second and third centuries, while we have no such knowledge concerning Q. Therefore in each particular case the burden of proof rests with him who advances the claims of Q; but with Resch and others of his way of thinking one seeks in vain for real proofs.[1]

VI.—The Essential Characteristics of the Contents of Q. A Comparison of Q with the Gospel of St. Mark.

In the comprehensive chapter of his "Einleitung in die drei ersten Evangelien," ss. 73–89, Wellhausen has made a complete comparison of Q and St. Mark. Since, according to him, mutual independence is "not to be thought of," he discusses the question of priority and decides in favour of St. Mark. Compared with St. Mark the content of Q is everywhere, or almost

[1] Let me bring forward yet another instance. In 2 Clem. v. we read: *λέγει ὁ κύριος· Ἔσεσθε ὡς ἀρνία ἐν μέσῳ λύκων.* This form of the saying seems to be more ancient than the form which we have ascertained for Q in section 19: *ἰδοὺ ἐγὼ ἀποστέλλω ὑμᾶς ὡς πρόβατα ἐν μέσῳ λύκων.* But without regard to the fact that 2 Clem. has probably used an uncanonical gospel which was certainly not Q (probably the gospel of the Egyptians), we have already seen above, pp. 13, 174 f., that the saying is perhaps not to be assigned to Q, but that its presence in St. Matthew and St. Luke is to be attributed to another source. The gospel of the Egyptians (the gospel, that is, which is used by 2 Clem.) is on the whole certainly secondary to Q, indeed to the Synoptic Gospels; yet, like the gospel of the Hebrews, it has preserved some very ancient elements.

everywhere, secondary, and presents the traditions concerning Jesus in a form which had already advanced in the direction of definite Christian dogma and of ecclesiasticism. I, on the contrary, believe that I can show in the following pages that Wellhausen in his characteristic of Q has unconsciously allowed himself to be influenced by the tendencies of St. Matthew and St. Luke, that he has attributed to Q what belongs to these gospels, and that in not a few passages he has preferred St. Mark on insufficient grounds. The conclusions at which I have arrived stand therefore in strong opposition to the results of his criticism.

In comparing Q with St. Mark we must base our investigation on those passages which certainly belong to Q—the probable constituents of Q must be marshalled in the second line for our review.

St. Mark begins with the preaching of the Baptist, the baptism of our Lord, and a summary account of a forty days' temptation of our Lord in the wilderness; Q, with the preaching of the Baptist (the baptism of our Lord) and a detailed account of a temptation of our Lord to disbelief in His Messianic vocation, which took place after a forty days' abode in the wilderness. Even if, as is probable, the baptism of our Lord stood in Q, it does not necessarily follow that St. Mark and Q are dependent upon one another; for it may very well have happened that at a particular epoch these sections were the regular passages with which the catechetical tradition of the sayings of Jesus the Messiah began

(St. Luke i. 4). Here, however, the subject-matter of Q is clearly the more original, for St. Mark only introduces the Baptist in order that he may point forward to the "Mightier One," while Q first describes the preaching of the Baptist concerning repentance and judgment, and then only attaches the reference to the "Mightier One" that was coming. Besides, St. Mark is guilty of hysteron-proteron in his description of the Coming One as one that would baptize with the Holy Ghost, while Q speaks of Him as of one who would appear with the fire of judgment and would thoroughly purge His floor.[1] Similarly, in regard to the story of the Temptation, it can neither be proved that Q is dependent upon St. Mark, nor can it be asserted that in St. Mark the Temptation is conceived as being non-Messianic in character,[2] nor can the narrative in Q be claimed as a later legend. If the story of the Temptation, with the voice from heaven in the form, "Thou art my Son, to-day have I begotten Thee," stood in Q, it is then natural that the devil should address himself to Jesus as the Son of God, and should wish to upset His faith in His Divine Sonship. There is no need to suppose that this must have been a later tradition than the shorter account of St. Mark, which always arouses the suspicion that St. Mark here knew more than he has

[1] The priority of Q is here recognised by Wellhausen (s. 74).

[2] Wellhausen (*l.c.*) makes this assertion; but if the *Spirit* which descended upon Jesus drives Him *into the wilderness*, where He is tempted for forty days of Satan, surrounded by the uncanny creatures of the desert, while the *angels* supply Him with food, this can then be no ordinary temptation but is the period *par excellence* of Messianic temptation.

told us,[1] for legend is not accustomed to work by a method so concise and allusive.[2]

The Sermon on the Mount now follows in Q. St. Mark here affords us only four parallel sayings.[3] He writes (iv. 24): ἐν ᾧ μέτρῳ μετρεῖτε μετρηθήσεται ὑμῖν (just as in Q, section 8). Again, in ix. 50—out of connection with his context—: καλὸν τὸ ἅλας· ἐὰν δὲ

[1] The circumstances may be conjectured to have been as follows:—St. Mark was obliged to touch upon the fact of the Messianic temptation by Satan, since it belonged to the stereotyped material of catechetical instruction (St. Luke i. 4: περὶ ὧν κατηχήθης λόγων); it was, however, known to him, not in the narrative of Q but in another form. If the narrative of Q had been known to him, the trait of fasting could not have been omitted by him, nor could he have mentioned the wild beasts and the angels in his short summary. St. Mark presupposes a legend where there was no mention of our Lord's fasting in the wilderness, where, on the contrary, it was recorded that He was fed by angels, so that there could scarcely have been a place therein for a temptation by means of hunger. Nothing is said of the nature of the temptation of Satan—that the wild beasts played a rôle therein is uncertain—but that St. Mark knew something about them is more than probable. The "Gospel of Jesus Christ," according to him, first begins with verse 14; in a double introduction, verses 1-8 and 9-13, he simply says what is absolutely necessary concerning the Baptist and his testimony, and concerning the Divine Sonship of Jesus. The wondrous "φαντασία" (Theodore of Mopsuestia) of the story of the Temptation in Q is independent of St. Mark, and may have arisen at any time after the year A.D. 30—*i.e.* it possibly belongs to the primitive tradition.

[2] It is quite another question whether the story of the Baptism (Spirit and voice from heaven) was the oldest form of the tradition. I am with Wellhausen of the conviction that it was not, rather that it has taken the place of the more ancient story of the Transfiguration. But this question cannot be discussed here, as it belongs rather to the period of development that lies behind Q and St. Mark.

[3] And in the case of three of these it is only probable that they stood in Q.

τὸ ἅλας ἄναλον γένηται, ἐν τίνι αὐτὸ ἀρτύσετε; while Q, section 47, reads: ὑμεῖς ἐστε τὸ ἅλας [τῆς γῆς]· ἐὰν δὲ τὸ ἅλας μωρανθῇ, ἐν τίνι ἁλισθήσεται. Here, in the first place, we notice a genuine translation-variant, and next, that Q interprets the "salt" as referring to the disciples. This is probably the original reference, as Wellhausen also recognises ("Mark," s. 82).—In St. Mark iv. 21 we read—again out of connection with his context—: μήτι ἔρχεται ὁ λύχνος ἵνα ὑπὸ τὸν μόδιον τεθῇ . . . οὐχ ἵνα ἐπὶ τὴν λυχνίαν τεθῇ; In Q, section 31, we find: οὐ καίουσιν λύχνον καὶ τιθέασιν αὐτὸν ὑπὸ τὸν μόδιον ἀλλ' ἐπὶ τὴν λυχνίαν, καὶ λάμπει πᾶσιν τοῖς ἐν τῇ οἰκίᾳ. In St. Mark the "light" represents the teaching of our Lord, in St. Matthew the good conduct of the disciples (this is secondary) —but this is only the interpretation of St. Matthew. St. Luke, who gives the saying twice, gives it first (viii. 16) with the same significance and in the same connection as St. Mark, and a second time (xi. 13), according to Q, without reference to the disciples. *Thus in Q the reference to the disciples was unexpressed, and Q was therefore not secondary when compared with St. Mark.* Here also note the translation-variants.—St. Mark writes (x. 11 f.): ὃς ἂν ἀπολύσῃ τὴν γυναῖκα αὐτοῦ καὶ γαμήσῃ ἄλλην, μοιχᾶται ἐπ' αὐτήν· καὶ ἐὰν αὐτὴ ἀπολύσασα τὸν ἄνδρα αὐτῆς γαμήσῃ ἄλλον [or probably more correctly, καὶ ἐὰν γυνὴ ἐξέλθῃ ἀπὸ τοῦ ἀνδρὸς αὐτῆς καὶ ἄλλον γαμήσῃ], μοιχᾶται. Here we have ascertained for the text of Q in section 52: [ἐγὼ λέγω ὑμῖν]· πᾶς ὁ ἀπολύων τὴν γυναῖκα αὐτοῦ ποιεῖ αὐτὴν μοιχευθῆναι, καὶ ὃς ἐὰν ἀπολελυμένην γαμήσῃ, μοιχᾶται. Wellhausen's judgment on this verse depends upon the supposition that the words immediately preceding it in St. Luke (εὐκοπώτερον δέ ἐστιν τὸν οὐρανὸν καὶ τὴν γῆν παρελθεῖν ἢ τοῦ νόμου μίαν κεραίαν πεσεῖν, xvi. 17) are to be regarded as explaining, or rather confirming, the statement of the verse concerning divorce. But verse 17 belongs, as is shown by the δέ, to verse 16, and is intended to correct the seeming Antinomianism of the words: ὁ νόμος καὶ οἱ προφῆται μέχρι Ἰωάννου, while the saying concerning divorce then follows without any connection. We have therefore no surety that even St. Luke intended that verses 17 and 18 should be taken together. As for Q, it is inconceivable that they stood together in that source, for St. Matthew presents them in complete separation in v. 18 and 32. Then again, it is more than questionable that St. Mark x. forms the starting-point for the version of the saying in Q. St. Mark says: "He who divorces his wife and marries another commits adultery against her, and likewise she that is divorced and marries again commits adultery." Q says: "He who divorces his wife makes her an adulteress [because she will marry again], and the new husband also commits adultery." That there is a difference here is clear, but it is not to be sought where Wellhausen sees it. According to Wellhausen, in St. Mark's form the adultery lies not in the divorce but only in the marrying again; but this is quite improbable, for (1) it is opposed to the context in St. Mark (verses 1–9), and (2) it is artificially read into the words of St. Mark. And besides, especially in an Oriental environment, a second marriage was sure to follow a divorce. Therefore the difference between St. Mark and Q does not lie in this point, but rather in the circumstance that St. Mark declares the husband and the wife, if she marries again, to be guilty of adultery, while Q condemns the wife who marries again and her new husband. Yet this difference is only in appearance; Q has only left unexpressed what was self-evident; according to my opinion, this writer intended to say: "He who divorces his wife (not only makes himself guilty of adultery, but besides) calls a twofold adultery into being: she that is divorced together with her new husband are guilty of adultery." The saying is then one of pregnant conciseness and force;[1] while the saying in St. Mark is feeble in comparison. Thus Q, section 52, is certainly not derived from St. Mark x. 11 f. It follows, therefore, that neither is Q 52 founded upon St. Mark x. 1–9, but in the most favourable case it must be assumed that there was in Q an account parallel to that of St. Mark, of which Q 52 formed the conclusion. Nevertheless, the verse requires no other context than that given in St. Matthew: Ἐρρέθη· ὃς ἀπολύσῃ τὴν γυναῖκα αὐτοῦ, δότω αὐτῇ ἀποστάσιον. Yet the context in Q could scarcely have been quite like this.

These are the only passages in which St. Mark affords a parallel to those parts of St. Matt. v.–vii. which belong to Q; for the theory that St. Mark

[1] St. Matthew alone has preserved it so; St. Luke has already modified the first half of the saying in accordance with the form in St. Mark. St. Matthew, however, has also offended in that he has inserted παρεκτὸς λόγου πορνείας—an interpolation which is self-evident, and yet, as it stands, quite out of place in the context.

xi. 25 is the germ of the Lord's Prayer may be left on one side.[1]

If we now investigate the contents of the passages of the Sermon on the Mount which stood in Q (of the first-class sections 3–8, of the second-class sections 9, 10, 27, 28, 31, 32, 35, 36, 39, 41, 47, 49, 51, 52), we notice scarcely anything which might not pass as *primary* tradition. But Wellhausen is of another opinion (*vide* his note on St. Matt. v. 1 ff.). He finds that just as Q runs parallel to St. Mark in the preaching of the Baptist (the Baptism) and the Temptation, so is it also with the Sermon on the Mount, for both documents now proceed to give a programme of the preaching of our Lord, Q a manifesto which is evidently an artificial fabrication, St. Mark (i. 15) a short and unassuming general summary of the ever-recurring subject of our Lord's preaching. "And the difference which exists between the two is not simply formal but extends also to the subject-matter. In St. Mark our Lord's theme is the same as that of the Baptist, namely, μετάνοια—men are warned to repent by the rousing proclamation of the near approach of the Kingdom of God. In Q, on the other hand, our Lord, unlike St. John,

[1] The Lord's Prayer does not belong to those passages which can almost certainly be claimed for Q; if, however, in a shorter form (*vide* section 27) it belonged to Q, it cannot have taken its origin from the single clause of St. Mark xi. 25, which corresponds to the so-called fifth petition. This clause says absolutely nothing about the *content* of the prayer, and is thus related in *form* not to St. Matt. vi. 12, but to the saying in St. Matt. v. 23, 24 (which, however, is more ancient in form). Yet it of course confirms the genuine character of the so-called fifth petition as it is found in St. Matthew (*vide infra* for a more detailed discussion).

shows not the reverse but, even in the very beginning of His ministry, the obverse of the Kingdom of God; with it He entices men, He proclaims it as good tidings of great joy. He begins not with a stern warning to the whole Jewish nation but with blessing to His disciples."

Here we must first object that St. Matthew at all events did not regard the Sermon on the Mount as a detailed substitute for St. Mark i. 15, seeing that he himself has given us in a passage preceding the Sermon on the Mount the words (iv. 17): *ἀπὸ τότε ἤρξατο ὁ Ἰησοῦς κηρύσσειν καὶ λέγειν· μετανοεῖτε· ἤγγικεν γὰρ ἡ βασιλεία τῶν οὐρανῶν.* Still less can we speak of such an interpretation of Q by St. Luke, seeing that he has assigned these passages of Q to a much later position in his gospel, indeed has distributed them throughout his work. And next, even according to Wellhausen, St. Mark i. 15 contains a flagrant hysteron-proteron from which St. Matthew and St. Luke, and therefore Q, are free; for St. Mark writes: "Jesus came into Galilee and *preached the Gospel of God*, saying, the time is fulfilled and the Kingdom of God is at hand; repent ye, and *believe the Gospel.*" When estimating the full meaning of this saying it does not do to pass by the mention of the "Gospel." But if we take this into consideration, then the whole question presents a quite different appearance from that given it by Wellhausen in his representation of the contents of the verse in St. Mark. St. Mark also has from the very beginning taken up the "message of joy" into the theme of our Lord's message; he also shows at the very first the "obverse" of this message, and indeed in a much more secondary form than is ever found in Q,[1] where the word "Gospel" never occurs. But it seems to me a most extraordinary proceeding to set the whole Sermon on the Mount, as Q has given it, side by side with the short sentence of St. Mark i. 15. The "gospel" in Q signifies the Beatitudes[2]—in fact, it is the proclamation which appears in Q, section 14: "Tell John what ye *hear* and see: The blind receive their sight, the lame walk . . . the poor receive good tidings." Why should not Q be justified in setting this message of good tidings in the forefront in contrast to the message of the Baptist? seeing, moreover, that its historical character cannot be disputed. And even if this preaching of good tidings was in reality more deeply set in the framework of the stern summons to repentance than appears in Q, why need we therefore regard the attractive side of the message as something especially secondary? Again, is not the whole Sermon on the Mount together with the Beatitudes also a most powerful summons to repentance? How indeed are we to conceive of our Lord's preaching of repentance? It could not have consisted simply in the repetition of the word "repent," it must have pictured in glowing colours the blessedness of conversion and

[1] Wellhausen's discussion of the significance of the word "Gospel" in St. Mark seems to me correct. St. Mark means by the word much the same as St. Paul.

[2] Here, therefore, the difference from St. Mark is as great as it possibly can be.

of the new life! And this is just what we find in the Sermon on the Mount.[1]

But a second fault is detected in this sermon: it must be regarded as a sermon addressed to the Christian community—*i.e.* it presupposes the union of Christians in a distinct and compact society. This is, in my opinion, true of St. Matthew but not of Q. According to St. Matthew and St. Luke the Sermon on the Mount was spoken to the disciples (in the presence of the people); it was therefore so given in Q. Now it is true that, if we stretch Q upon the Procrustes' bed of chronology, a discourse to the disciples occupies a strange position here at the beginning; but, in the first place, we do not know whether in Q something may not have preceded the Sermon on the Mount, and secondly, chronological tests ought not to be applied to Q. Q of course did not begin with the end but with the beginning, nor did it conclude with the beginning but with the discourses on the Second Coming; apart from this, however, chronology has no further influence upon Q, which is simply a heterogeneous collection of discourses and sayings, for the most part bound together in groups. If Q was a compilation of the sayings of our Lord, made with the aim of giving authoritative teaching (and that principally ethical), it is not strange that this great discourse to the disciples was set in the forefront as being *the most important of all.* Certainly the Christian reader was intended to say to

[1] There is no want of sternness either in the Sermon on the Mount or elsewhere in Q; the "μακάριος" stands in contrast to fearful warnings.

himself: "All the promises and commandments here addressed to the disciples apply to thyself," but it does not necessarily follow that the compiler has coloured his reproduction of the sayings of our Lord with a view to contemporary readers. Taking first only the sections of Q that are certainly genuine, where is such colouring to be found in the Beatitudes (section 3) in the saying concerning the blow upon the cheek and the cloak that is taken (4), in the direction to give to him that asks (5), in the command to love one's enemies (6), in the Golden Rule (7), in the prohibition of judging and the similitudes of the Mote and the Beam (8), the Good and Corrupt Tree (11), and the House upon the Rock and upon the Sand (12)? But, object Wellhausen and others, in the last Beatitude mention is made of persecutions which are also implied in the saying concerning love to one's enemies. Here we come to a question of principle. In modern criticism of the Gospel narrative, it constantly happens that everything which can possibly be a hysteron-proteron is at once pronounced to be such with absolute certainty. This seems to me to be a form of critical conscientiousness which leads to critical narrow-mindedness. Of course there are numbers of instances of hysteron-proteron in the gospels—the merest suggestion of practical aim or purpose leads to a hysteron-proteron, and the gospels follow practical aims—yet it by no means follows therefrom that saying after saying must have been coloured and corrected in accordance with the circumstances of later times. Very often the saying receives its desired practical significance from the very context in which it is set without any change from the hand of the editor. Must it be that Jesus could not have said to His disciples, "Blessed are ye, when men revile you, and persecute you, and say all manner of evil against you falsely"? Surely even in the lifetime of Jesus the disciples must have experienced such treatment again and again, and in the most varied forms; and it seems quite impossible that He should not have spoken about it. I confess that I cannot understand the objections that are usually made to such sayings, and in their removal, as a matter of principle, from the genuine sayings of our Lord, I discern a most serious error.[1] By this method of destructive analysis we are left at last with only the critic himself; for, considering the likeness which naturally existed between the circumstances of the first disciples and of the later community, it is possible with very little trouble to object to everything as hysteron-proteron. Again, in reference to the persecutions which the Sermon on the Mount has in view, it is to be noticed that we do not read, "So also have they persecuted me," but "So persecuted they the prophets which were before you."

In Q, sections 3–8, 11, 12, nothing is to be found which must be assigned to secondary tradition. How does it stand with those sections of the Sermon on the Mount which can only with probability be assigned to Q? The direction, "Ask, and it shall

[1] It is another question whether these sayings *in certain cases* are not coloured by the circumstances of later times—this seems to me, of course, certain.

be given you," together with the similitudes of the Bread and the Fish (section 28), the Light and the Bushel (31), the saying concerning the eye as the light of the body (32), the great discourse concerning anxiety (35), the warning against laying up treasure on earth (36), the Adversary and the Judge (39),[1] the Strait gate and the Narrow way (41), the Salt that had lost its savour (47), the warning against serving two masters (49), the word concerning the permanent obligation of the Law (51), the saying concerning divorce (52), and lastly, the Lord's Prayer (27), still remain to be considered.[2] In section 28 there is nothing that can be objected to as secondary; it is, however, well worth noticing that the disciples also are reckoned among the *πονηροί*. We have already discussed (pp. 196 ff.) sections 31, 47, and 52. In sections 32, 35, 36, 39, 49, even the sharpest eye will discover nothing that Jesus could not have said. But on section 41 Wellhausen remarks: "The eschatological colouring in St. Luke disappears in St. Matthew here, just as it does in vi. 19. The strait gate is presupposed as something known, for it is the needle's eye of St. Mark x. 25, as we shall see in St. Luke. At a still later time Jesus Himself has become the Door (St. John x.). From the 'one gate' St. Matthew passes on to the 'two ways,' leaving,

[1] Note the threat with which it concludes.

[2] Perhaps also the word concerning the leaders of the blind (section 9), and the saying that the disciple is not above his master (10). St. Luke has both sayings in his Sermon on the Plain; St. Matthew has the first in chap. xv., the second in the charge to the disciples in chap. x. (this may have been its original position).

however, the 'gate' in the singular and reserving it for the 'narrow way'—if Lachmann's reading of vii. 13, which I have followed in my translation, is correct. The favourite Jewish metaphor of the 'two ways' is not derived from some such foreign source as the Greek legend of Hercules, but from Ps. i. 6, and originally from Jer. xxi. 8." I gladly agree with the last remark, and am only sorry that there is in these days need to make it; but I cannot follow Wellhausen in what precedes. I can neither hold the text of St. Luke for the more original (*vide supra*, pp. 67 f.), nor does it seem to me permissible to bring in the "needle's eye" here. The "gate" and the "way" need, in my opinion, no interpretation: every one must at once understand what they mean, seeing especially that they are sufficiently explained by "the many" and "the few." The eschatological colouring is, moreover, clear enough in the version of Q (St. Matthew), and nothing secondary can be found in the simile that is used.

In the saying of section 51 concerning the permanent obligation of the Law, Q has given expression to our Lord's attitude towards the Law. We may not interpret this saying as pointing to an ultimate abolition of the Law, for the emphasis does not lie upon this point—on the contrary, the meaning is that the Law abides as long as heaven and earth abide. There is no ground for disputing that this was really what our Lord meant; and yet in St. Mark no such saying is to be found—on the contrary, it is written in St. Mark xiii. 30: "Heaven and earth shall pass away, but My words shall not pass away." If it is proposed to bring this saying into comparison with the saying in Q—and it is almost impossible to avoid doing so—there can then be no doubt where the secondary traits are to be found.

There still remains the Lord's Prayer.[1] Whether it ever stood in Q is, as we have already shown, questionable, and its original form is a matter of controversy. If we follow the short form which we have given above, the character of a common prayer, and in a certain sense of a stereotyped prayer, still remains. But it is far too hasty a proceeding because of this to regard the tradition as secondary. Even according to St. Mark our Lord directs His disciples to pray, and I doubt whether in the East a prophet or teacher has ever given directions concerning prayer without giving a pattern prayer. Wellhausen remarks: "Jesus could not give to His disciples a stereotyped form for congregational prayer, because they did not yet form a congregation" ("Einl.," s. 87). But does it follow that the Lord's Prayer is a congregational prayer because it is a common prayer? and did there not exist among the companions of our Lord a close bond of discipleship which even during his lifetime united them in a common life? Our knowledge of the nature of the common fellowship that existed in this circle of disciples must be far more

[1] The sayings concerning the leaders of the blind, and that the disciple is not above his master and must expect no other fortune than he (sections 9, 10), arouse no justifiable suspicion. A sceptic will suspect a hysteron-proteron in the second saying—on the presupposition that our Lord could have said nothing which might also refer to the circumstances of a later time.

detailed before we can have the least justification for asserting the impossibility of a prayer being given them by our Lord. It may, of course, be admitted that the Lord's Prayer in the form given in St. Matthew, and indeed even in St. Luke, is liturgical in character, and is accordingly a congregational prayer; but this does not hold good of the short form. This form, in my opinion, presents nothing that can be objected to in point of genuineness.

Judged in detail and as a whole, all that is presented as teaching of our Lord in the Sermon on the Mount bears the stamp of unalloyed genuineness. It is astonishing that at a time when St. Paul was actively engaged in his mission, and when the problem of apologetics and the controversy concerning the Law were burning questions, the teaching of our Lord should have been still so clearly and distinctly preserved in the memory of Christians in the simple force of its essentially ethical character.

The didascalia given in the Sermon on the Mount were immediately followed in Q by the story of the Centurion at Capernaum (section 13). How little the compiler of Q cared for chronology is seen from the words in which our Lord here looks back upon a fairly long period of ministry. Wellhausen ("Matt.," s. 36) is of opinion that Q here, in strong contrast to St. Mark, lays the greatest emphasis upon the miracle wrought simply by a word and at a distance, and, moreover, he thinks that the centurion may be a duplicate of Jairus. In regard to the latter point, the stories seem to me far too different to allow of the experiment of deriving one from the other; but Wellhausen's first assertion demands detailed examination.[1]

(1) When we consider the import of this section in the context of Q, we cannot but wonder that it stands in Q at all if its point lies in the miracle. On this supposition it falls out of the sphere of Q, which is elsewhere a compilation of discourses.[2]

(2) If one looks more closely one sees that the point of the narrative does not lie in the miracle of healing, but in the great faith of the heathen centurion (just as in the story of the Canaanitish woman) in the unlimited power of our Lord; for it is the word of our Lord testifying to this faith, not the word of healing, which forms the climax of the narrative. *The word of healing comes in haltingly at the close in St. Matthew, and is not even mentioned in St. Luke.*

(3) This in itself is decisive enough, but we may perhaps proceed a step further. We have above (p. 77) left the question open as to the conclusion of this section in Q. St. Matthew concludes it much in the same way as the story of the Canaanitish woman: *καὶ εἶπεν ὁ Ἰησοῦς τῷ ἑκατοντάρχῃ· [ὕπαγε], ὡς ἐπίστευσας γενηθήτω σοι· καὶ ἰάθη ὁ παῖς ἐν τῇ ὥρᾳ ἐκείνῃ.* St. Luke writes quite summarily (and with three participles, thus in his own style): *καὶ ὑποστρέψαντες εἰς τὸν οἶκον οἱ πεμφθέντες εὗρον*

[1] We may at the same time question whether St. Mark really would have rejected a miracle wrought at a distance (*vide* the Canaanitish woman).

[2] In the Beelzebub section the miracle only gives the occasion of a long and most significant discourse of our Lord.

τὸν δοῦλον ὑγιαίνοντα. *Not a single word in these two conclusions is identical.* This is very strange. What then may we suppose was the conclusion of Q? We cannot tell. Since this is so, it seems to me to be not too bold an hypothesis to assume that in Q either nothing at all was said about the cure, or that in this source there stood something quite different from what we read in St. Matthew and St. Luke. Either alternative is possible, and not improbable;[1] it is at all events certain that the concluding verse, both in St. Matthew and also in St. Luke, is suspicious. Neither is it surprising that they have both independently of one another given the story the conclusion which we now read.

If the point of this passage lies in a short saying of our Lord, in which He testifies to the receptivity of a Gentile, and if the miraculous cure takes a secondary place, having been either not narrated at all or described in some other form, then there is nothing strange in the fact that the narrative occurs in Q,[2] nor can it be described as containing tradition which is secondary to that of St. Mark. The Baptist had already proclaimed in warning tones that God could raise up from the stones children to Abraham, and the story of the Canaanitish woman (St. Mark) affords an important parallel to our section.

[1] In the case of the Canaanitish woman, our Lord also shows reluctance in performing the cure.

[2] Wernle ("Synoptische Frage," s. 232) thinks that we are forced to conclude that the section was interpolated in Q at a later time, seeing that it conflicts with the Judaistic tendency of Q; but Q does not bear the traces of a Judaism which would not allow the expression of such appreciation of faith in a Gentile.

The passages in the gospels referring to the sending forth of the disciples contain much tradition of a secondary character, but it does not therefore follow that the event itself is impossible or improbable however certain it is that we have here an intermixture of later elements. Wellhausen says ("Mark.," s. 46, on St. Mark vi. 7 ff.): "The twelve only make an experiment, and afterwards are just as dependent and passive as before, although the experiment is a success. In fact, Jesus did not institute experimental missions as an exercise for His seminary." But the fact of the sending forth of the disciples itself is too strongly attested by the twofold tradition in St. Mark and Q to allow of its being summarily rejected, nor is it in itself improbable that our Lord thought that, in the short space of time allowed Him, He must provide for the widest possible circulation of His message of the near approach of the Kingdom. Yet we are not here concerned with the fact itself; the question for us is only the relationship of the account in Q to the account in St. Mark. They are, partly in subject-matter, partly almost verbally, identical, and are combined together in St. Matthew, but in St. Luke (chaps. ix. and x.) they are kept apart from one another. In the parallel sections where the text of Q can no longer be ascertained with certainty (therefore they are included in brackets in our construction of the text), the chief difference is that St. Mark allows a staff and sandals, while Q does not. The version of St. Mark seems to me to reflect a relaxation which had arisen in actual practice. In Q the missionary charge to the disciples was preceded by the story of two men, of whom one offered himself as a disciple and the other wished first to bury his father (section 17). It is related for the sake of the two sayings of our Lord that it contains, in the former of which the expression "Son of Man" is found for the first time in Q. The sayings bear the stamp of perfect genuineness. Then followed (section 18) the saying concerning the greatness of the harvest and the paucity of labourers. Wellhausen ("Matt.," s. 44) remarks: "The harvest elsewhere is the end of the world, and the reapers are the angels. If by the lord of the harvest we must understand that God is signified, then the prayer does not quite correspond with the active intervention of Jesus who, in what follows, Himself sends forth the reapers." This objection has some weight—however, it does not seem to me to be decisive against the originality of the tradition: the simile of the harvest can well have been variously applied by our Lord Himself.—In the missionary charge to the disciples there would be a most important difference between St. Mark and Q if it were true that the former speaks only of the private mission in houses, while Q speaks also of the mission in cities. Wellhausen ("Luk.," s. 49) says: "The public mission in the cities is later than the secret mission in the house, just as the reception into the city is later than that into the house. Accordingly St. Mark, who speaks only of the house, has the priority over Q; for it is not doubtful, and is indeed correctly recognised by St. Matthew, that St. Mark vi. 7 ff. and St. Luke x. 1 ff. are variants which must be compared together." But in Q the mission to the cities did not stand in the place of the mission in the house, both stood together side by side. This is not redundant, nor is it in the strictest sense tautologous. The horizon of our Lord's missionary outlook included cities as well as households, *vide* the Woe against Chorazin, Bethsaida, and Capernaum. We cannot therefore see why directions concerning the mission in cities should be later in date than those concerning the mission in the houses; in practice, as is shown by the most ancient records, both phases of the mission coincided in point of time. But the whole presupposition that the mission in the cities is wanting in St. Mark is to me very questionable. According to Wellhausen there is in St. Mark vi. 10, 11, no difference between οἰκία and τόπος, this however is not, in my opinion, the interpretation that first suggests itself, rather τόπος, as usual, signifies "city," but the mission in the city and in the house are conceived as one and the same; and thus no real difference can be discovered here between St. Mark and Q.—The warning in Q, that it would be more tolerable for Sodom in the Judgment than for the perverse cities (section 22), presents no difficulty.—I pass by section 24 (*vide supra*).—In section 34^b Q proclaims that words spoken against the Son of Man will be forgiven; this is wanting in St. Mark. This fact is in favour of the priority of Q; Wellhausen's argument to the contrary ("Matt.," s. 62 f.) is not convincing. In section 34^a, which otherwise shows all the signs of the earliest tradition, it is possible that the duty of confession of the person of Jesus may be a secondary trait; but it is not necessary to suppose this, and the promise: "I will acknowledge Him in the presence of the angels of God" (thus at the Judgment), sounds very primitive. The same must be said of section 38: it is possible to regard it as a *vaticinium ex eventu*; but why might not our Lord foretell the result of His preaching, seeing that other prophets have made similar predictions? He must have seen how that even in His lifetime His preaching had brought division into families and had separated those who were nearest to one another. I pass by the closely related section 45, because it is not quite certain that it belongs to Q.—In section 46 (Bearing the cross) we have probably a hysteron-proteron,[1] but certainly a primitive one. The saying concerning the finding and losing of the soul (section 47) presents no difficulty.

These passages which we have here discussed briefly have some other parallels in our second gospel, apart from St. Mark vi. 7–11. St. Mark also writes, parallel to section 34[a] (iv. 22): *οὐ γάρ ἐστιν κρυπτόν, ἐὰν μὴ ἵνα φανερωθῇ· οὐδὲ ἐγένετο ἀπόκρυφον, ἀλλ' ἵνα ἔλθῃ εἰς φανερόν* (this looks like a translation-variant of an identical Semitic text), again parallel to section 46 (viii. 34): *εἴ τις θέλει ὀπίσω μου ἐλθεῖν, ἀπαρνησάσθω ἑαυτὸν καὶ ἀράτω τὸν σταυρὸν αὐτοῦ καὶ ἀκολουθείτω μοι*, again parallel to section 57 (viii. 35): *ὃς ἐὰν θέλῃ τὴν ψυχὴν σῶσαι, ἀπολέσει αὐτήν· ὃς δ' ἂν*

[1] The hypothesis of a reference to the custom that one condemned to be crucified was compelled to bear the transverse beam of his cross is, of course, not satisfactory. On the other hand, we may perhaps conjecture, as Reinach has lately pointed out again, that the crucifixion of the righteous man, in accordance with the well-known passage in Plato and Ps. xxii., had become a typical and widely spread conception. Yet much is still wanting to establish this hypothesis.

ἀπολέσει τὴν ψυχὴν αὐτοῦ ἕνεκεν ἐμοῦ καὶ τοῦ εὐαγγελίου, σώσει αὐτήν, lastly, parallel to section 24—yet this saying did not perhaps occur in Q at all —(ix. 37): ὃς ἂν ἐμὲ δέχηται, οὐκ ἐμὲ δέχεται ἀλλὰ τὸν ἀποστείλαντά με. Nowhere here does Q show itself secondary to St. Mark, indeed the contrary is the case; for the anachronistic addition, ἕνεκεν ἐμοῦ καὶ τοῦ εὐαγγελίου, is foreign to Q.—Hence in these commandments to the disciples Q is neither dependent upon St. Mark nor secondary when compared with that gospel. It is not surprising that identical sayings should be found here and in St. Mark; for these directions of our Lord certainly stood in the forefront of tradition, and could not but be received into every compilation thereof.

There now follows the great discourse concerning the Baptist (sections 14, 15), occasioned by the question brought by a deputation of St. John's disciples; to this there is no parallel in St. Mark. The story, together with the discourse, is so important, and bears at the same time so clearly the stamp of genuineness—in the first place because of the candid admission of the doubt of St. John; then because our Lord's ministry of healing appears as His characteristic work [1] (thus involving the near approach of the Kingdom of God); and lastly, because, together with a most valuable account of the Baptist, we have here from the mouth of our Lord an appreciation of his person and mission. Only the words, ὁ δὲ μικρότερος

[1] The considerations which Wellhausen advances in order to prove the probability that the words are to be understood allegorically, do not seem to me to have much force.

ἐν τῇ βασιλείᾳ τοῦ θεοῦ μείζων αὐτοῦ ἐστιν, look like a hysteron-proteron (from the standpoint of the Christian community); whether they are really so cannot be ascertained, for we do not know how far our Lord went in this direction. In St. Matthew it is indeed very probable that βασιλεία τοῦ θεοῦ has much the same significance as ἐκκλησία, but can we say the same of Q? Now follows the passage with the wonderful comparison between children at play and the nation which advanced such peevish claims upon its leaders. Wellhausen presses the double ἦλθεν in section 15, and argues: "The tenses for John and Jesus are exactly the same. If then John here belongs to the past, so also does Jesus." If this kind of argument is intended to prove that the discourse belongs to a later time than that of our Lord, I do not understand it. Our Lord's ministry had already lasted a considerable time, and His life (in contrast to that of St. John) was in the full view of the public eye. Why then could He not have spoken as He speaks here? or, rather, in what other way would Wellhausen have Him speak? This discourse also, in my opinion, bears both as a whole and in detail the stamp of originality. There is nothing that can be said against it, except that it *may possibly* be a hysteron-proteron, but that is no objection at all; the less so seeing that the words "ἰδοὺ ἄνθρωπος φάγος καὶ οἰνοπότης" do not exactly suggest the prevalence here of later tradition. It is also a good sign that nothing is recorded concerning the result of the question of St. John, so that the Baptist is, as it were, left in a state of doubt.

It is possible that section 23 (the Woe against the cities) now followed in Q. The "δυνάμεις αἱ γενόμεναι ἐν ὑμῖν" are what make the cities so inexcusable. It is the same idea upon which emphasis is laid in the answer to St. John in the preceding section (the acts of our Lord compel faith; if in spite of these He is rejected, the reason can only be hardness of heart); also the statement that Tyre and Sidon would have repented is to be compared with section 30. We thus perceive that these sections are closely bound together, so far as their subject-matter is concerned, by one and the same idea.

The following section (25), the great thanksgiving to the Father, is at present regarded by many critics as altogether secondary, indeed as a Christian hymn. I cannot bring myself to agree with them, and I am glad to see that Schmiedel also judges otherwise ("Das vierte Evangelium," 1906, s. 48 ff.). As to whether the section is genuine word for word, who is there that can assert this and who can prove it? But it can be shown that it contains conceptions which fit in with our Lord's genuine sphere of thought. We do not know when it was that these words of exulting joy were uttered. They stand in sharp contrast to the preceding section. Our Lord here thanks the Father that He has nevertheless met with success—success for His message and in His teaching (for "ταῦτα" can only mean this)—and that among the simple folk. The rejection on the part of the wise and prudent, and the rejection of these prudent ones by our Lord, are traits which are certainly neither unhistorical nor abnormal (they find their echo in St. Paul's first epistle to the Corinthians). If, however, "*ταῦτα*" signifies "knowledge" or "doctrine," the meaning also of "*πάντα*" is thus fixed—it signifies, as indeed we see from what follows, "the knowledge of God." Wellhausen is correct in saying: "In this context there is no reference made to power but to knowledge, to insight into divine things, to the true nature of religion. All doctrine and all knowledge is with the Jews '*παράδοσις*,' the *παράδοσις*, however, of Jesus proceeds directly from God, not from men." Our Lord here uses the word "*Πατήρ*"—most probably not "*πατήρ μου*"—just as in the introduction "*πάτερ κύριε τοῦ οὐρανοῦ καὶ τῆς γῆς*." The absolute use of "the Father, the Son" is likewise found in St. Mark (xiii. 32) and is accordingly no sign of the secondary character of Q as compared with St. Mark. The conclusion: "No man hath knowledge of the Father except the Son, and to whomsoever the Son will reveal Him," says nothing about an "eternal" relationship between the Father and the Son, but simply expresses an historical fact. It does not lie beyond the line which is drawn in St. Matt. xiii. 16, 17 (*ὑμῶν μακάριοι οἱ ὀφθαλμοί, ὅτι βλέπουσιν κτλ.*), in St. Matt. xi. 9–11 (concerning the Baptist), and in St. Matt. xii. 38 ff. (a greater than Jonah and Solomon). The union in this exultant thanksgiving of elements of ecstatic elevation, of which individual examples can be found elsewhere, is no sign of secondariness—or is Jesus the only one to whom we may not ascribe ecstatic utterance such as one expects from every great prophet? The saying thus contains nothing that can be objected to, and may therefore be used as one of the most important sources of our knowledge of the personality of our Lord. In St. Mark we find parallels to separate traits of the saying, but no parallel to the whole; this evangelist with his restless and hasty temperament was incapable of reproducing such an utterance.[1]

The Beelzebub section (29), which is given not for the sake of the miracle of healing but of the discourse, has a parallel in St. Mark; in St. Matthew and St. Luke the Markan text is so intermingled with Q that one can only make certain of remnants of the latter source.[2] There is an inclination to discover secondary traits in Q in the clause: *ἄρα ἔφθασεν ἐφ' ὑμᾶς ἡ βασιλεία τοῦ θεοῦ*, and in the saying: *ὁ μὴ ὢν μετ' ἐμοῦ κατ' ἐμοῦ ἐστιν, καὶ ὁ μὴ συνάγων μετ' ἐμοῦ σκορπίζει*, for in the former the Kingdom is described as already present; and in the latter there is a proclamation of the dogma "extra ecclesiam nulla salus," so that it is less original than St. Mark ix. 40 ("He who is not

[1] For further detail *vide* Excursus I.—The continuation of this saying in St. Matt. (xi. 28–30) is regarded by many critics as its real continuation. But if it is so, and if it stood in Q, why has St. Luke omitted it? It was just what would have appealed to him. Besides, its connection with verses 25–27 is rather superficial than essential. The question of its genuineness is not affected by the decision that it is independent of the preceding verses.

[2] This is especially so at the beginning.

against you is for you"[1]). But St. Mark also says, if indeed only indirectly (iii. 27), that the kingdom of Satan is drawing to its close, because the "strong man" is now bound; the direct statement ought not to be treated in contrast as a later development of the thought. In regard to the following saying, no one has yet thoroughly ascertained its connection with its context in St. Matthew and St. Luke; it is therefore still less possible to say what was intended by the saying in Q. I do not see why we must suppose that the saying implies "extra ecclesiam nulla salus." Even if, as is probable, συνάγειν and σκορπίζειν are to be interpreted in accordance with the metaphor of a flock (συνάγειν is also used of grain [section 1] in the discourse of the Baptist), yet these are well-known prophetic *termini technici* for the leading of Israel to God and their alienation from Him, into which we have no right without special reasons to read an ecclesiastical significance, even if St. Matthew thus understood them. Moreover, our Lord certainly more than once spoke of His own συνάγειν. We had better neglect altogether a comparison of this saying with the seemingly contradictory saying of St. Mark ix. 40 (St. Luke has both sayings); for these sayings occur in different contexts and could both of them have been quite well spoken by our Lord. If, however, it is thought that we must not desert the principle of the critical school, which in such cases aims at unification, then we may well ask whether the more original saying is not the one which is exclusive

[1] According to D. The Greek codices have the first person.

and which does not transfer to the disciples the prerogative of Jesus. Arguments at least can be brought forward on either side, hence: "non liquet"! Lastly, in the passage which is appended in Q, the ironical criticism of the results of exorcisms is so paradoxical, so singular, and without all "Gospel" significance, that no one will dispute its originality.

The section concerning the sign of Jonah (30), if we only remove the artful interpolation in St. Matthew, is of peculiar simplicity and force. This evil and adulterous generation must repent, and if in frivolity it seeks for signs, it receives only the preacher of repentance, as did the Ninevites—yet a greater than Jonah; nevertheless it abides unrepentant. What objection can one wish to make against the genuineness of this discourse?[1]

The sections which now follow, 33, 43 (the Woe against the Pharisees and the announcement of judgment upon Jerusalem), 56 (the warning against false Messiahs; the discourse concerning the Parousia), 58 (Whosoever hath, to him shall be given), 37 (The coming of the Son of Man as a thief in the night; the faithful and unfaithful steward), and 59 (The disciples will judge the twelve tribes), so far as we can judge, formed the conclusion of Q.[2] Section 58

[1] The story of the refusal of the demand for a sign also stands in St. Mark (viii. 11 f.), but in an entirely independent form, which cannot have been the source of Q. St. Mark says nothing of the sign of Jonah in the reply with which the demand was dismissed —a trait which with its bitter irony cannot have been invented. In St. Matthew it is transformed, because in its summary plainness it seemed to the evangelist insufficient and unsuitable.

[2] And also the two parables of the Great Supper and of the Talents, if they really stood in Q (*vide supra*, pp. 119 ff.).

is also found in St. Mark (iv. 25). Sections 33, 34, have been discussed above (pp. 103 ff., 168 ff.). The flagrant anachronism, which Wellhausen thinks must be accepted in the case of Zacharias, is in all probability not to be laid to the charge of Q. Sections 33, 43, are already eschatological in character; the same is true of 56, 37, 58, 59. The warning against false Messiahs in section 56 *may be* an anachronism; but this does not mean that it *is* one. Otherwise they all bear the stamp of genuineness, *and stand in brilliant contrast to the detailed eschatological discourses in St. Mark.* The promise to the Twelve that they would rule Israel after the Parousia, most clearly shows the Jewish horizon. Q has transmitted no discourses concerning the Passion.

There now remain only the isolated sayings—26, 40, 42, 44, 48, 50, 53, 54, 55. We can no longer discover their position in Q. If in St. Matthew section 26 stands in place of St. Mark iv. 13 (reproach of the disciples), this implies nothing for Q, seeing that St. Luke has the saying in a quite different place (x. 23ᵇ, 24). The saying itself shows no trace of later colouring, neither do the three parables of the Mustard Seed, the Leaven, and the Lost Sheep in sections 40 and 48; they give rather the impression of exquisite originality.[1]—The saying that the Gentiles would sit at meat with the Patriarchs in the Kingdom

[1] *Vide* Jülicher "Gleichnisse II." s. 569 ff., 314 ff.—The parable of the Mustard Seed, which also stands in St. Mark (iv. 30–32), is somewhat shorter and more concise in Q than in the second gospel.

of God, while the sons of the Kingdom would be cast out (section 42), presents a thought similar to that of the Baptist's warning. The sympathy with the Gentiles does not pass beyond the bounds which the prophets of the Old Testament had already reached; the figure of the feast is genuinely Jewish.—The saying concerning pride (section 44) is also found in St. Mark.—The statement concerning the position of the Law and the Prophets in the history of religion (section 50), and the saying combined with it wherein the epoch "from John until now" is marked off, arouse the suspicion of later composition; but the three stages, "Prophets, John, Jesus," are also distinguished in section 14, and there the genuineness of the distinction can scarcely be disputed. Here again we have no means of judging with certainty what our Lord could say and could not say, strange though this marking off of a period "from the days of John until now" may seem (the saying must have been spoken after the death of the Baptist, and also stands in St. Luke at a very much later point than section 14). Besides, it is difficult to ascertain the wording and the significance of the saying. Does it mean that the Prophets and the Law lasted until John, or that they prophesied until John? Has "they lasted" the same signification as "they were in force," or as "no more new prophets appeared"? What is meant by "The Kingdom of God is taken by storm"? and who are those "who take it by storm"? The original character of the expression is a strong guarantee for the genuineness of the saying itself. No more can be said.—The short saying, "It is necessary that offences come, but woe unto the man through whom they come," is wanting in clearness, because we do not know in what context it stood in Q. Is Judas referred to (scarcely so), or has the saying a general significance?—The twofold command in section 54, in which each half is quite independent of the other, is an excellent example of the way in which St. Matthew has made Q serve ends which are foreign to that source. Q said: (1) One ought *to correct* the sinning brother—by this means one may be able to save a brother; again, Q taught (2) that one ought without limitation *to forgive* personal injuries at the hand of a brother. St. Matthew has here introduced the community, and has established a rule of ecclesiastical discipline. Cases of sin, injury, and wrong were certainly not of rare occurrence in the circle of the disciples, and there is no reason why our Lord should not have expressed Himself concerning their treatment. Besides, we have instances of the kind in St. Mark.—The last saying which remains is section 55. St. Mark has also transmitted it (xi. 22, 23): *ἔχετε πίστιν θεοῦ. ἀμὴν λέγω ὑμῖν, ὅτι ὃς ἂν εἴπῃ τῷ ὄρει τούτῳ· ἄρθητι καὶ βλήθητι εἰς τὴν θάλασσαν, καὶ μὴ διακριθῇ ἐν τῇ καρδίᾳ αὐτοῦ, ἀλλὰ πιστεύῃ, ὅτι ὃ λαλεῖ γίνεται, ἔσται αὐτῷ*). No one can ever prove that this version of the saying is preferable to that of Q (*ἐὰν ἔχητε πίστιν ὡς κόκκον σινάπεως, ἐρεῖτε τῷ ὄρει τούτῳ· μετάβα ἔνθεν ἐκεῖ, καὶ μεταβήσεται*).

This comparison of Q and St. Mark, as well as our examination of the subject-matter of Q, have in no instance led us to conclude that Q is dependent upon St. Mark, and scarcely ever to acknowledge that Q, from the historical point of view, is inferior to St. Mark; in several instances, indeed, they have convinced us of the superiority of the former to the latter. There exists, of course, a relationship between Q and St. Mark, even a literary relationship, but it is confined to only a few sections and is evidently *indirect*—*i.e.* both have received and delivered some tradition in the same fixed form, but as a rule in a different translation. The dependence of St. Mark upon Q—for if there exists a relationship of direct dependence between the two this would be the only possible hypothesis—is also difficult to establish; for this assumption is nowhere demanded, and the attitude of St. Mark towards Q would in this case be almost unintelligible. Whether St. Mark had knowledge of much that has been taken up into Q, whether, moreover, he betrays this knowledge in some passages of his work, whether behind St. Mark (and known to him) there did not lie compilations of sayings of our Lord that had strong points of similarity with Q, are different questions which might well be answered in the affirmative; but that this evangelist made use of Q, no one will be able to prove. The most striking instance of relationship between the two—the similarity in the order in the opening sections of each—need not be in any way a literary relationship, as we have already remarked, but is explained from the customary order of catechetical instruction in the apostolic epoch. The Galilean horizon, within which Q seems to move more exclusively than

St. Mark, must be simply accepted as an historical fact.[1]

[1] This definition of the relationship between Q and St. Mark agrees essentially with that of Holtzmann, Wernle, Bousset (in a review of Wellhausen's Einleitung in the "Theol. Rundschau"), and of Jülicher; but Jülicher (Einleitung[5], s. 320 ff.) believes that he is compelled to make some important concessions to Wellhausen's criticism. He finds that this scholar has shown that it is *extremely probable* that the edition of Q used by St. Matthew and St. Luke was posterior in time to St. Mark. In support of this theory, he adduces the story of the Temptation, of the centurion at Capernaum (healing at a distance, which it is implied presupposes a more developed craving for the miraculous than the simple stories of healing in St. Mark), the "undoubtedly later" version in Q of the saying: "Whosoever is not with Me, &c.," also of the saying concerning blasphemy, and of the saying concerning light. In these cases, however, he assumes no literary dependence. There is, of course, nothing against St. Mark's having sometimes given a tradition in a more original form than Q, but among the instances given—they have been already discussed above—I can recognise scarcely one of which this is true. The saying concerning blasphemy in Q, when compared with St. Mark, does not seem secondary; the "light" in Q had no reference to the disciples (this reference was first introduced by St. Matthew); whether the two sayings, "He that is not with Me is against Me," and "He that is not against you is for you," ought to be confronted with one another at all is doubtful, and even if they are so confronted, the decision as regards priority is uncertain; in other places, at all events, the latter trait counts as the more original. The pericope concerning the centurion has its point not in the healing at a distance but in the faith of the Gentile, and the story of the Temptation in St. Mark most probably presupposes a fuller description and one which differed from that of Q. Jülicher then (s. 321 f.) proceeds to sketch a conjectural history of the origin of Q, in which he holds a development by successive steps as probable; at a distinct moment in the history of this development the plan of St. Mark is supposed to have influenced Q; on the other hand, it seems natural, indeed quite necessary, to explain St. Mark's neglect of so many important discourses of our Lord from the circumstance that a compilation of discourses was already in the hands of the faithful. "Accordingly Q would be both older

Chronological arrangement in detail should not be looked for in Q. Except in the introduction and in the collection of eschatological discourses at the close, the prevailing arrangement is an arrangement according to subject-matter, and probably even this does not hold good everywhere. The choice of material and its arrangement were determined by the needs of Christian teaching—more especially of ethical teaching—though by no means exclusively, for in these sayings and discourses the relation of Jesus to all powers in heaven and earth comes to expression. They are Λόγοι Ἰησοῦ,[1] which give a clear impression of His message in all its manifold aspects. The "δυνάμεις" are presupposed, but not narrated. Q in character occupies the mean position between an amorphous collection of sayings of our Lord and the definite literary form of the written gospels, and so prepared the way for the latter. Q could not have

and younger than St. Mark; however, the common elements of St. Mark and Q are so slight in extent and in importance, that it is simply not worth while to take up again and again the hopeless task of knitting together a linen and a silken texture—both of which indeed are something far more than mere collections of separate threads." I entirely agree with the last remark, also with the premise that Q grew by separate stages; but I consider it unnecessary to assume that St. Mark influenced Q at a definite moment in its development. Absolutely the only evidence for this hypothesis is found at the beginning of Q, and this is not sufficient.

[1] To characterise Q as a mixture of discourses and narratives would be incorrect. Apart from the story of the Temptation, which serves as a prelude, in the other six narratives the story serves only as an introduction to the discourse. This is especially obvious in the story of the centurion, in the Testimony of our Lord concerning the Baptist, and in the Beelzebub section. Nor is it otherwise with the other three narratives (sections 17, 30, 54).

first come into existence after the time that the gospel-type—sayings, miracles, and Passion, proof of Messiahship—had been created by St. Mark; for Q cannot possibly be regarded as a completion of St. Mark's gospel, and the gospel-type, after it had once arisen, established itself with sovereign authority (compare the apocryphal with the canonical gospels).

An inquiry into the character of the subject-matter of Q will confirm this verdict. I shall attempt in what follows to summarise the main characteristics of the contents of Q.

The great sermons, which take up so much of the space and form the principal part of Q (corresponding to St. Matt. v.–vii., x.), comprise directions to the disciples (first in presence of the people, then privately). Everywhere where the interests of Christological apology did not as yet preponderate, the interest in the *commandments* of Jesus stood in the foreground. We can see that this is so from the time of St. Paul to Justin, but we can trace it still further. Naturally the Christians set themselves in the place of the disciples, and applied to themselves what was once said to these. And yet we find in Q very few traces of conscious or unconscious modification of the sayings. Ecclesiastical organisation and the Church, as St. Matthew knows them, do not appear in Q. The sayings apply to the individual even when they are addressed to a multitude. The controversy of Christianity with Judaism as between two distinct religious principles, the opposition of the old and new precepts, are wanting; only in reference to divorce does Jesus go beyond the Law. Elsewhere it is said that the

Law abides so long as heaven and earth remain.[1] The Jewish horizon and Jewish sentiment are also shown in the fact that the bliss of the Kingdom of God is pictured as a sitting at meat with Abraham, Isaac, and Jacob, and in the promise to the apostles that they should rule the twelve tribes of Israel. But the opposition to the present generation in Israel, to the "evil and adulterous generation," which would bend the men of God to its will, and the conflict against its spiritual rulers the Pharisees, are nowhere more sharply brought out than in this source. The children of the Kingdom will be cast out; weeping and gnashing of teeth await them; it will be more tolerable for Sodom and Gomorrha than for Chorazin, Bethsaida, and Capernaum, and a fearful Woe is launched against the Pharisees. The expression of friendliness towards the Gentiles—who in place of the children of the Kingdom will feast with Abraham—fits without difficulty into the picture, or rather offers no greater difficulty than earlier utterances of a similar purport found in the Prophets. The same remarks apply to the emphasis laid upon the faith of the Gentile centurion. The commandments in detail, though they are so different and so manifold, nevertheless breathe one and the same spirit—a spirit one in its austere assertion of the unique claim of goodness, in its recognition of the absolute sovereignty of Good—that is, of God—in the heart, a spirit which declares itself in humility, in trustful prayer, in love

[1] The Law and the *Prophets*. The latter stand in the foreground. Their lot to suffer persecution is the point upon which our Lord lays special stress, *vide* sections 3, 33, 43.

and placability, in the renunciation of earthly rights, earthly goods, and earthly cares, and lastly, in the readiness to suffer. Neither is there lacking a sense of the necessity of repentance; for this is implicit in all these commandments (*vide supra*, pp. 201 f.), and is, moreover, strongly emphasised in section 30 (*cf.* 23). Taken as a whole, we have here our Lord's own rule of life and all His promises—a summary of genuine ordinances transforming the life, such as is not to be found elsewhere in the Gospel. Their noblest characteristic is their implicit assumption of the self-evidence of their claim, because man belongs to God; in this lies the force of their appeal.

It is not otherwise in the sections belonging to the great charge at the sending forth of the disciples. The words are austere and stern in tone; scarcely ever is the terrifying prospect lightened otherwise than by reference to the "World to come," or by the comfort that the foe cannot kill the soul. On earth nothing but the fate of the Prophets is to be expected. God's good and gracious will, and His *providentia circa minimum*, is recognisable only when all is over; until then He never makes up His account; yet He gives "good things" to those who ask Him for them, and He knows the needs of His children.

In these discourses and sayings the term "the Kingdom of God" is of frequent occurrence.[1] It is regarded as belonging to the future in section 12 (Not all that say Lord, Lord, shall enter into the Kingdom of God), in section 16 (Proclaim that the

[1] Q and St. Mark agree in this characteristic.

Kingdom of God is nigh at hand), in section 42 (Gentiles will sit down with Abraham in the Kingdom of God; but the children of the Kingdom will be cast out), also in section 33 (Ye shut the Kingdom of God: ye yourselves enter not in, and ye prevent others from entering),[1] and in 35 (Seek ye after the Kingdom of God, and all these things will be [there] given to you). But in the four remaining passages it is otherwise. In section 29 it is said that the deliverance from the power of the evil spirits implies that the Kingdom of God had already come among the people. In the parables of the Mustard Seed and the Leaven (section 40) it is represented as a growing power, an influence gradually leavening mankind, and this conception makes it possible to regard the new epoch which dawned with the active ministry of our Lord, succeeding the mission of the Baptist, as already the epoch of the Kingdom (as if present; sections 14, 50). This conception has nothing to do with that of the "Church." Whatever the words: ἡ βασιλεία τοῦ θεοῦ βιάζεται, καὶ οἱ βιασταὶ ἁρπάζουσιν αὐτήν may mean, they certainly do not sound ecclesiastical. If, however, any one finds it impossible to accept the antinomy "the Kingdom is future and yet present," argument with him is useless. The sovereignty of the eschatological point of view is not impaired by this antinomy—only this sovereignty must not be sought for exclusively in that dramatic eschatology to which Q also bears testimony, with the result that the message of Jesus

[1] The eschatological sense is not certain here.

is stunted in the interest of a meagre and inferior unity. Behind and above the dramatic eschatology stands the "eschatology" that God is guided by justice in His rewards and punishments, and that His will is expressed in the moral law, to which man must offer himself a living sacrifice.

The proof that Q is essentially a *homogeneous* and an *ancient* source, is ultimately based upon the nature of its description of the personality of our Lord. Here the following observations may be made:—

(1) As has already been noticed above (pp. 170 f.) Q omits any reference to the Passion. Even if the probable object of the compilation—namely, to record the "Λόγοι τοῦ κυρίου Ἰησοῦ, οὓς ἐλάλησεν διδάσκων"—be kept well in view, this is still an extraordinary circumstance. However, this extraordinary circumstance is a fact from which we cannot escape, and it proves at all events that we have to do with a very ancient compilation.[1]

[1] A sceptic acquainted with the comparative history of religions will perhaps find even more here. He will argue as follows: The most ancient source which we possess for the life of Jesus knows nothing of His death upon the cross. This is the more strange in that we have here no amorphous collection of sayings, but one which begins with stories telling us of a consecration to Messiahship and of a Messianic temptation successfully withstood. If this source had an historical introduction, it must also have possessed an historical conclusion—*i.e.* it must have given a narrative of the Passion—if this really happened. Seeing that no such narrative is given, the Passion did not really take place. This doubt receives confirmation when it is once considered that the Passion (and that indeed as a death upon the cross) is bound up closely with the Resurrection, *and together with it formed in certain circles a constant element in the history of the Christ* (long

(2) In close connection with what has just been said comes the observation that Q has no interest in Christological apologetics such as would explain the choice, the arrangement, and the colouring of the discourses and sayings it contains. In this Q shows itself absolutely different from St. Mark, St. Matthew, and St. John. St. Luke here stands nearest to Q; but this gospel cannot well be compared with Q, because its chief interest, the description of the supernatural mission of healing, is quite wanting in Q (though it evidently forms the background here). All that is Christological in Q, after the Messiahship (Divine Sonship) of

before the time of Jesus); and when it is further considered that the Resurrection and all that is connected with it is absolutely untrustworthy, and is simply the result of the projection of dogma into the realm of history, and when, lastly, it is remembered how uncertain, how mysterious and questionable are all the announcements of the Passion in the gospels, and how uncertain and full of discrepancies is the narrative of the Passion itself. If all these circumstances are taken into account, we only adopt half measures in claiming from the ideal story of the Christ only the element of the Passion for the historical Jesus, while rejecting the rest. We must rather make a clean sweep of everything, obliterating also the clause "crucified under Pontius Pilate." The proof that our most ancient source knows nothing of the Passion, imprints the seal of truth upon our critical operation. From Q we can only conclude that Jesus suddenly vanished in a more or less mysterious way. This indeed is hinted at by the words of Q (St. Matt. xxiii. 39), "*Ye shall not see Me henceforth* until ye shall say, Blessed is He that cometh in the name of the Lord." I regard it as quite possible that we shall very soon have to listen to this or to similar absurdities. The beginning is already made. In fact, there are far too many possible explanations of this remarkable limitation of Q, and above all, our knowledge of Q and of its conclusion is far too uncertain to allow of the building up a critical theory upon such a foundation.

our Lord has been established in the introduction (the stories of [the Baptism and] the Temptation), is only implicit, receiving its determination from the introduction (with the exception of section 25 and the Announcement of the Second Coming). This of itself is a proof that *the compilation in Q was intended solely for the Christian community and was addressed to those who did not require the assurance that their Teacher was also the Son of God.* Of course the apologetic epoch of Christian doctrinal tradition dated from the first origin of the Christian community, but there is no need to assume that apologetical interests affected the details of that tradition from the very beginning. This indeed is just what is shown in Q.

(3) But although Q was not compiled in the interests of Christological apologetics, it is nevertheless rich in discourses and sayings in which special prominence is given and special attention is drawn to the personality of Jesus. The following sections are to the point: 1, 2, 12, 13–15, 17, 18, (19), 22–26, 29, 30, 31, 34^{a}, 34^{b}, 37, 38, 43, 45, 46, 50, 56, 59. What do we learn from these?

After St. John had drawn attention to the One coming after him who was greater than he, and had described him as one who would appear with the fire of judgment (in complete agreement with the eschatological phase of the Messianic expectation), Q then probably proceeded to narrate the baptism of our Lord, together with the descent of the Spirit and the voice from heaven, by which He was marked off as the Son of God (the Messiah) in the sense of Ps. ii. 7. The use here made of the word from the Psalm excludes all ideas of pre-existence and of a miraculous birth. Q then goes on to describe how the Son of God (the Messiah) at once approved Himself as such by standing the test of temptation by Satan. The temptations are Messianic—*i.e.* our Lord is tempted to use His miraculous power to break through the limitations imposed upon Him, the Messiah, to test Him; to win for Himself acceptance by working a miracle of display in reliance upon the angelic help that had been promised Him; to submit Himself to Satan in order that at one stroke He might become Lord of the earth. He resists all these temptations. Now begin the Λόγοι Ἰησοῦ, the question of Christological apologetics is answered and done with.

In the Sermon on the Mount, which as a whole lies above the level of a prophetic manifesto, the personality of our Lord comes into prominence at two points. He describes His teaching as the light which ought to be set on the candlestick that it may give light to all (section 31), and it is by the obedience to His commandments, *which is treated as the same thing as doing the will of the Father*,[1] that

[1] In section 6 we read, "That ye may be children of *your* Father," and "Be ye merciful as *your* Father"; in section 25, God is four times called simply *the Father*, or "Father, Lord of heaven and earth" (as compared with "the Son"), in section 27 the disciples are instructed to address God in prayer as "Father"; in 28 we read, "How much more will the Father (ὁ ἐξ οὐρανοῦ) give good things," and in 35, "Your Father knoweth that ye have need of all these things." "My Father" is thus only found in the above passage (12), but it must be remembered that the text is doubtful here.

it is decided whether a man is building his house on a rock or on sand; the mere saying "Lord, Lord," is worthless (12).

The story of the Centurion which now follows (13) is intended to give an instance not so much of the miraculous power of our Lord as of the faith of the Gentile; it only shows us implicitly that wondrous forces stood at His command. Jesus claims absolute faith and finds it—not in Israel, but among the Gentiles. If this story, and this story alone, broke the context of the sayings which stand in St. Matt. v.–vii. and viii.–x., it accordingly gains extraordinary significance, but this significance is not Christological.

In the charge to the disciples, and in the two sections which precede it (17 and 18), the special significance of the personality of our Lord is stated again only indirectly but the more impressively. *Now* is the field ripe unto harvest (18), but the labourers are few; to be a labourer means to follow Jesus wherever He goes, even to the extreme point of destitution,[1] and to follow Him renouncing all earlier relationships, even that to one's own father (17); for "I am come not to bring peace, but the sword, and to set nearest relations at variance with

[1] Notice that the saying: "Foxes have holes, &c.," says *nothing* of the following even unto death, but only unto the bitterest poverty. What a sign of genuineness! In section 46 however it is otherwise; there the bearing of the cross is demanded as the necessary form of discipleship. It is, as already noticed, the only passage in which the death upon the cross is referred to in Q. As has been shown, it is not certain whether "I send you as sheep into the midst of wolves," and "He that receiveth you, receiveth Me, &c.," stood in Q.

another" (38 and 45). Jesus must be confessed before men; for only those that make such a confession will be acknowledged by Him at the Judgment before the Angels (34[a]). Capernaum is "lifted up to Heaven" by our Lord's ministry in that city, Chorazin and Bethsaida have seen mighty works such as had been wrought in no other city—with the result that the judgment upon their unbelief would be only the more terrible. With Jesus begins a new epoch—He is the touchstone, the sign of final decision and judgment for all.

In these sayings, besides the mention of the Messianic acknowledgment at the Judgment, we find the expression "Son of Man" used three times (17, 34[a, b]);[1] while it occurs four times elsewhere in Q (15, 30, 37, 56)—"The Son of Man hath not where to lay His head," "The Son of Man will acknowledge those who confess Him," "A word said against the Son of Man will be forgiven," "The Son of Man came eating and drinking," "As Jonah was to the Ninevites, so is the Son of Man become a sign to this generation," "The Son of Man cometh at an hour when ye expect Him not," "As the days of Noah, so also will be the coming of the Son of Man." Three of these sayings are eschatological in character; but the four others seem to deprive this circumstance of its significance. We must acknowledge that in Q the phrase has become simply a term which our Lord ordinarily used when speaking of Himself. Seeing that Q pays no regard to chronology, this

[1] Yet it is doubtful in section 34.

source is not suitable as an authority upon which to base investigations as to the period at which our Lord began so to describe Himself. Such investigations can only be based upon the Gospel of St. Mark. Q, however, gives some help in that we learn from this source how completely and quickly the consciousness, that there was once a time when our Lord did not so name Himself, had vanished from tradition. There can scarcely be any doubt as to the sense of the expression in Q. If in Q the only historical passages—historical, that is, in the narrower sense of the word—are the narratives of the testimony of the Baptist to the coming Messiah (of the Baptism), and of the Messianic temptation, and if then abruptly and repeatedly the expression "the Son of Man" crops up in the collection of sayings, it necessarily follows that in Q the term can mean nothing else than "the Messiah."[1]

The compiler of Q, when he himself speaks, never uses the term; he speaks simply of Jesus (not ὁ κύριος) or of "ὁ Χριστός." The latter term is used in the introduction to the sections concerning the Baptist (14, 15, 50). The references to the personality of our Lord in this discourse, and in the great thanksgiving to the Father, are the most important in the whole collection of sayings. Our Lord here

[1] I am still of the opinion that it is very probable that also in the mouth of Jesus it never had any other meaning.—Of course one cannot be sure that Jesus always called Himself Son of Man in those passages where Q makes Him thus speak of Himself. It is, for example, more than doubtful that Jesus used the expression in section 15, when before in the same discourse (section 14) He had plainly enough avoided any Messianic self-designation.

appeals to His *works* (as in section 23 to His δυνάμεις). These are the works of Messiah; but the open declaration "I am the Messiah" is avoided. To these works belong also the "πτωχοὶ εὐαγγελίζονται," and it is this which is either exclusively or principally referred to in the Beatitude "μακάριός ἐστιν ὃς ἂν μὴ σκανδαλισθῇ ἐν ἐμοί," which in Q must naturally be understood in a Messianic sense. In the following passage the high appreciation of the Baptist, who is represented as surpassing all the prophets, is ultimately based not upon the real greatness of the man himself but upon his office as forerunner; this again gives *indirect* expression to the Messiahship of Jesus, which is fully disclosed in the sentence that the least in the Kingdom of God is greater than John. Accordingly, the simple contrasting phrases: "The Baptist came"—"The Son of Man came," cannot be understood as implying equality in the contrasted subjects in a passage whose genuineness is guaranteed by the unique information it affords us: "The Son of Man came eating and drinking, and they say, Behold a man gluttonous and a winebibber, a friend of publicans and sinners!" This definition of the significance of the Baptist, in contrast to the prophets on the one hand, and to our Lord on the other hand, removes all cause for hesitation in accepting the genuineness of the saying that the Prophets and the Law lasted until John.

It is said—I return yet again to the historical question (*vide supra*, pp. 216 f.)—that this whole discourse is the product of a later time. Who indeed would defend the exact verbal accuracy of such a discourse! But, on the other hand, we must bear in mind that in Q it stands in the midst of a context whose interest is purely ethical, and that Q's aims are not those of apologetical Christology. We must further remember that it is purely a *petitio principii* to assume that our Lord could not Himself have spoken concerning matters which also in after times claimed men's attention and were the subject of their discussion. Why could He not have given expression to His views concerning the Baptist just as we read in Q, seeing that the context (St. Matt. xi. 4–6 and xi. 16–19) is as trustworthy as it is possible to imagine it to be? Must we not, indeed, confess that He was simply compelled to express Himself concerning the Baptist, and that there is nothing extraordinary in the fact that He on the one hand subordinated St. John to Himself, and on the other ranked him above the Prophets? Nothing else, however, nothing more of essential importance, is said about him, with the exception of the scarcely genuine ἀπὸ τότε ἕως ἄρτι. That in the background of the whole discourse there lies the presupposition "I am He," affords no ground for suspicion; if so, one must draw the pen through the whole content of the gospels.

The following pericope (section 25), to which section 26 perhaps belongs, has been already discussed above from the Christological standpoint (pp. 218 ff.). It forms the climax of our Lord's self-revelation, and yet it does not assert more than that He had been permitted to bring to the simple ones the knowledge of God—that knowledge which He alone as the Son (the Messiah) was the first to receive, and which He was now revealing to whomsoever He willed. The saying in which the disciples are pronounced blessed because they see and hear what all the Prophets (and kings) had desired in vain to see and hear, once again brings to light the final and absolute character of this knowledge of God, and at the same time testifies to the fact that our Lord (*vide* the preceding paragraph) really did reflect upon the relationship of the past and the present—not only in reference to the Law but also to the Prophets.

This also appears in the Beelzebub section (29); for if in our Lord's exorcism of devils through the power of the Spirit of God, the Kingdom of God had already appeared upon earth, then it followed that a new epoch had dawned, the epoch, namely, of Messiah. He needs not to give Himself this name, nor does He assume it—the facts speak for themselves. Here again He is proclaimed to be the sign of decision and of judgment for all (*vide supra*, p. 238) in the words: "He that is not with Me is against Me." It is the same thought which is expressed in the next section (30) in the words: "As Jonah was to the Ninevites, so am I also to this generation"[1]—the preacher of repentance—but the preacher who is greater than Jonah, and the king who is wiser than Solomon. The thought of the Second Coming is first touched upon in the concluding sections, and with it is combined the revelation of the Messiahship; this is found in

[1] The seeming discrepancy that also in Q our Lord points to His δυνάμεις and ἔργα, and yet declares that no sign should be given to this generation, is no discrepancy at all. He will not have wonders and signs wrung from Him by this generation any more than by Satan.

section 43: *οὐ μή με ἴδητε ἀπ' ἄρτι ἕως ἂν (ἥξῃ ὅτε) εἴπητε· εὐλογημένος ὁ ἐρχόμενος ἐν ὀνόματι κυρίου*, in section 37 where it lies at the foundation of the whole section, and in section 56 where it likewise dominates every sentence. In the first section the destruction of Jerusalem (of the Temple?) is also foretold, but only in words quoted from a more ancient prophecy. In the second section the thought of the Second Coming is employed to enforce the need of watchfulness, of preparedness, of conscientious faithfulness; in the third section a description is given of the state of the world at the Second Coming—just as it was in the days of Noah—and of the awful suddenness and unexpectedness of that coming; a warning is also given against false Messiahs. Perhaps the last saying that stood in Q is section 59: "Ye, that follow Me, shall sit upon twelve thrones, judging the twelve tribes of Israel." This saying affords us the strongest imaginable testimony that Q is dominated by the belief in the Messiahship of Jesus; the fact of the Messiahship is proved in the introduction, it is presupposed as self-evident from beginning to end of the work, and in the eschatological discourses it is revealed by Jesus Himself.

The "Christology" of the source, *as the compiler understood it*, presents a perfectly simple and consistent picture.[1] The compiler of Q could not

[1] Only in section 10 does our Lord describe Himself (indirectly) as teacher and His disciples as pupils; nevertheless this relationship is implicitly presupposed also in other places. The existence of this relationship, side by side with that of the Messiah to His subjects, presented no problem to the compiler, who simply subordinated one to the other. The Messiah who brought the revelation of the knowledge of God could only reveal by *teaching*.

imagine otherwise than that Jesus was the Messiah, consecrated as Son of God at the Baptism; all the sayings of his compilation, therefore, stand out against this background. *If, however, we think away the introduction, the resultant picture is essentially different.* We now have before us a compilation of sayings in which the speaker is a teacher, a prophet, one who is more than a prophet—*the final decisive Messenger of God;* but so surely as He demands unconditional *obedience* to His commands, in which the Will of God is expressed, and calls upon men *to follow Him,* so little does He do this with the expressed self-witness: "I am the Messiah." Rather He points simply to His miracles and His works (in so far as He does not count upon the self-evidence of His commands in their appeal to the hearts of His hearers). If one therefore neglects the term "Son of Man"—which was certainly used by our Lord, though we cannot be sure that it is genuine in any particular saying—Jesus first asserts His claim to the Messiahship in the sayings at the close of the source, *but only in connection with and under the imagery of the Second Coming;* He who already in His present state of existence is more than a prophet and greater than John, He who is the *Son,* will be the coming King and Judge.

Critical investigation of the accounts in St. Mark seems to compel us to the conclusion that our Lord during the first and longest period of His ministry did not speak of Himself as the Messiah (because He at first neither regarded Himself as Messiah, nor indeed could so regard Himself) and even rejected the title of Messiahship when it was applied to

Himself, but that, on the other hand, He was possessed by the strongest conviction that as a messenger of God He was entrusted with a mission of decisive import, and that He knew God as none other knew Him—a conviction to which He again and again gave expression; and that at a later period after He had accepted at Cæsarea Philippi the confession of the disciples: "Thou art the Messiah"—*i.e.* "Thou wilt be He"[1]—He from henceforth (though indeed still with reserve until the entry into Jerusalem) called Himself the Son of Man, and with growing confidence proclaimed His Parousia, *i.e.* His Messiahship. There is nothing in the compilation of discourses in Q, if only we neglect the introduction, which can be alleged to be discrepant with this picture of gradual development. We cannot, it must also be acknowledged, derive from Q certain testimony to the detailed accuracy of this picture, because Q pays such slight regard to chronology; nevertheless Q also bears witness to the main position, in that in the sayings collected in Q the Messiahship is only clearly expressed under the form of the Parousia,[2] and in that in

[1] The absence of this important passage in Q suggests that we should not exaggerate its importance. Besides, the question of St. John, together with the answer of our Lord in Q, can be regarded as a parallel to the passage in question.

[2] The great thanksgiving to the Father could be in point of time posterior to St. Mark viii. 27 ff., but this hypothesis is not necessary. With the most careful and reverent application of psychological methods, it is obvious that our Lord's consciousness of Sonship must have preceded in time His consciousness of Messiahship, must indeed have formed a stepping-stone to the latter. In spite of all that has been deduced from the apocalyptic and dogmatic Messianic conceptions of the times, we must assert that the consciousness of Divine Sonship and of Messiahship could

these sayings our Lord claims faith not because He is the present Messiah—this is unthinkable—but because He works the works of God and proclaims His commandments.

VII.—CONCLUSION

THE ORIGIN AND THE HISTORICAL VALUE OF Q

If we consider Q apart from its introduction (sections 1 and 2), we see at once that we are dealing with a document of the highest antiquity—there is here no need of proof; but even if we take into our view Q together with the introduction, there is little difference in the final verdict. The idea that Jesus was endowed with the Messiahship at the Baptism had, as St. Mark shows, already taken form in the apostolic age and in the circle of the immediate disciples—how early we do not know. An idea so impressive and so incapable of proof or of disproof could have taken form and have established itself in the Christian community at a very early date. The view indeed which preceded it, according to which Jesus was declared by God to be the Messiah by means of an act of glorification, is an idea which had already completely lost its significance for St. Mark, while St. Matthew and

not have existed together from the beginning; for the consciousness of Messiahship never meant anything else for our Lord than a consciousness of *what He was about to become.* In His soul the consciousness of what *He was* must have come first, and only when this had attained to the height of consciousness of Sonship could the tremendous leap be taken to the consciousness of Messiahship.

St. Luke knew no more of it than what they read in St. Mark. Further, the fact that our Lord throughout the principal part of His ministry had not represented Himself as being the future, and still less the present, Messiah, was afterwards found to be no difficulty at all. The disciples needed only to say to themselves: "We did not understand Him," and this is just what they did say. The cases of discrepancy and confusion which we find in their own and their disciples' reproduction of particular stories and discourses, and which have led to the adoption of such strange subterfuges and harmonising hypotheses in the interpretation of the Markan accounts, did not exist for those who were provided with this *refugium ignorantiæ*.[1] St. Mark indeed knows as little of a development in our Lord's consciousness as Q; he also, like Q, places the revelation of the Divine Sonship (the Messiahship) at the beginning of our Lord's active ministry, and it is only because of the careless and naïve fashion in which one may say he has gathered together and heaped up his materials—in strange contrast with the energy with which he follows his main purpose and finds it vouched for in the most discrepant narratives—that we (against the will and intention of St. Mark) receive any hint of stages of development in the ministry of our Lord.

Q, a compilation of sayings originally written in Aramaic (*vide* Wellhausen, Nestle, and others),

[1] These show us, however, the relative faithfulness of their record.

belongs to the apostolic epoch. This is shown by its form and contents, nor can I discern any reasons for a contrary opinion; in particular, the destruction of Jerusalem is not here presupposed as having already occurred.[1] It is, moreover, more ancient than St. Mark. *The influence of "Paulinism" which is so strong in St. Mark is entirely wanting, and accordingly the main theme of St. Mark—that Jesus, His death and resurrection, form the content of His own gospel—is not to be found in Q.*[2] It is evident that Q was composed in Palestine—its Jewish and Palestinian horizon is quite obvious. St. Mark, however, wrote his gospel in Rome. No proof can be given of any literary relationship between the two works. This is an indication that we must not set Q too early; for if Q had been already long in circulation it is incomprehensible that St. Mark neither knew it nor used it, even though he wrote at a place far distant from Palestine.

Is Q of apostolic origin? I can make no new contribution towards settling this question. That Papias (like Eusebius) in the well-known passage (Euseb., "Hist. Eccl.," iii. 39) means *our* St. Matthew, is very probable; whether, however, the Presbyter meant this St. Matthew, is doubtful. Seeing that our St. Matthew cannot have been

[1] Moreover even in passages peculiar to St. Matthew sayings occur which must have taken form before the destruction of Jerusalem.

[2] There is surely no need for me to notice the theory that Q was intended as a complement to the Gospel of St. Mark, who had gathered together all the tradition within his reach.

composed by an Apostle, and that the tradition: Ματθαῖος Ἑβραΐδι διαλέκτῳ τὰ λόγια συνετάξατο, already dates from about A.D. 100, there is a strong balance of probability that Q is a work of St. Matthew; but more cannot be said. It is useless to discuss the historical and psychological question whether one of the Twelve could have composed such a compilation as Q; convincing reasons either for or against cannot be discovered. From the so-called charge to the Apostles we can only conclude that behind the written record there stands the memory of an apostolic listener. But whoever the author, or rather the redactor, of Q may have been, he was a man deserving of the highest respect. To his reverence and faithfulness, to his simple-minded common-sense, we owe this priceless compilation of the sayings of Jesus.

Our knowledge of the teaching and the history of our Lord, in their main features at least, thus depends upon two authorities independent of one another, yet composed at nearly the same time. Where they agree their testimony is strong, and they agree often and on important points.[1] On the rock of their united testimony the assault of destructive critical views, however necessary these are to easily self-satisfied research, will ever be shattered to pieces.

And yet again how different are these two sources! On the one hand St. Mark—wherein page by page the student is reduced to despair by the incon-

[1] Compare especially the historical background and the historical references in numerous sayings in Q.

sistencies, the discrepancies, and the incredibilities of the narrative—and yet without this gospel we should be deprived of every thread of consistent and concrete historical information concerning the life of Jesus; and on the other hand, this compilation of sayings, which alone affords us a really exact and profound conception of the teaching of Jesus, and is free from bias, apologetic or otherwise, and yet gives us no history. In St. Mark an almost complete inability to distinguish between what is primary or secondary, between what is trustworthy or questionable, an apologetic which grasps at all within its reach, to which everything is welcome and right—and yet at the same time a feeling for detail and for life, and even where this feeling is not present, the actual preservation of these traits; in Q, on the other hand, a many-sidedness in reference to that which is the most important, which quite compensates us for the want of "history."

Which is the more valuable? Eighteen centuries of Christianity have answered this question, and their answer is true. *The portrait of Jesus as given in the sayings of Q has remained in the foreground.*[1] The attempts which have been made to replace it by that of St. Mark have met with no success; they will lead ever and again into the abyss of confusion, they will come to nought through their own inconsistency. *The collection of sayings and St. Mark must remain in power, but the former takes precedence.* Above all, the tendency to exaggerate the apocalyptic and eschato-

[1] This is so even with the sketch of the personality of our Lord drawn by Wellhausen in his History of Israel.

logical element in our Lord's message, and to subordinate to this the purely religious and ethical elements, will ever find its refutation in Q. This source is the authority for that which formed the central theme of the message of our Lord—that is, the revelation of the knowledge of God, and the moral call to repent and to believe, to renounce the world and to gain heaven—this and nothing else.

We cannot tell how long this compilation remained in existence. Its traces in St. Clement of Rome and in writers after his time are not certain. It found its grave in the gospels of St. Matthew and St. Luke, and probably elsewhere in some apocryphal gospels. St. Mark alone could not have supplanted it; but the narrative type of gospel, which was created by the second evangelist and which answered to the needs of catechetical apologetics, no longer allowed the separate existence of a compilation of sayings. The final blow to the independent existence of Q was dealt when it was incorporated in the gospels of St. Luke and St. Matthew. In St. Luke it exists, split up and dispersed throughout the gospel in subservience to the historical narrative; in St. Matthew it was treated in more conservative spirit, though in some important passages it has suffered more from revision and shows clearer traces of the particular bias of the evangelist. In most skilful fashion—often only by means of an accent or by an arrangement of the context which seems quite insignificant—the first evangelist has made this compilation of discourses subservient to his own special interest in the Christian community and its organisation, while St. Luke, who has much more frequently altered the wording of his source, has nevertheless kept so closely to it in essential points that its original character is more clearly perceived in his reproduction.

APPENDIX TO CHAPTER II

Translation of Q

1.[1]

. . . . . .

(When John saw many [or: the multitudes] coming to baptism, he said to them): Ye offspring of vipers, who warned you to flee from the wrath to come? Bring forth therefore fruit worthy of repentance; and think not [begin not] to say within yourselves: We have Abraham for our father; for I say unto you that God is able of these stones to raise up children to Abraham. Already the axe is laid to the root of the trees; every tree therefore that bringeth not forth good fruit is hewn down and cast into the fire. I indeed baptize you with water unto repentance; but he that cometh after me is mightier than I, whose shoes I am not worthy to bear, he will baptize you with (the [Holy] Spirit and) with fire. Whose fan is in his hand, and he will thoroughly purge his threshing-floor and will gather

[1] The numbers are those of the Greek text on pp. 127–146. A line of dots preceding a passage shows that its original position in Q is uncertain. All that is otherwise uncertain is placed in brackets. In general, it must be remembered that in the case of quite short sayings, whose position in Q is doubtful, there is also a doubt whether they belong to Q at all. Such are found in 16, 19, 24, 26–28, 31, 32, 35, 36, 39–42, 44, 47–55.

his wheat into the barn, but the chaff he will burn up with fire unquenchable.

(The baptism of Jesus, together with the descent of the Spirit and the voice from heaven.)

2.

Jesus was led up by the Spirit into the wilderness to be tempted by the devil, and when he had fasted forty days and forty nights he afterwards hungered, and the tempter said to him: If thou art the Son of God, command that these stones become bread, and he answered: It is written, *Man shall not live by bread alone.* Then he taketh him with him to Jerusalem and set him on the pinnacle of the temple and saith to him: If thou art the Son of God, cast thyself down; for it is written, *He shall give his angels charge concerning thee, and in their hands they shall bear thee up lest haply thou dash thy foot against a stone.* Jesus said to him: Again it is written, *Thou shalt not tempt the Lord thy God.* Again he taketh him with him to an exceeding high mountain and sheweth him all the kingdoms of the world and the glory of them, and said to him: All these will I give thee if thou wilt worship me. And Jesus saith to him: It is written, *Thou shalt worship the Lord thy God and him only shalt thou serve.* And the devil leaveth him.

3, 4, 5, 6, 7, 8, 11, 12, 9, 27, 28, 31, 32, 35, 36, 39, 41, 47, 49, 51, 52.

(He taught his disciples in the presence of the multitude as follows):—

Blessed are the poor, for theirs is the kingdom of God;

Blessed are they that mourn, for they shall be comforted;

Blessed are they that hunger, for they shall be filled;

Blessed are ye, when they shall revile you and persecute you and say all manner of evil against you falsely; rejoice and be exceeding glad, for great is your reward in heaven; for so persecuted they the prophets which were before you.

Whosoever smiteth thee on the (thy right) cheek turn to him the other also, and if any man would go to law with thee and take away thy coat let him have thy cloke also.

Give to him that asketh thee, and from him that would borrow from thee turn not away.

I say unto you: Love your enemies and pray for your persecutors, that ye may become the sons of your Father, for he maketh his sun to rise upon the evil and the good (and sendeth rain on the just and the unjust). For if ye love those which love you, what reward have ye? Do not even the publicans the same? And if ye salute your brethren only, what do ye more than others? Do not even the Gentiles the same? Ye shall therefore be merciful as your Father is merciful.

All things whatsoever ye would that men should do unto you, even so do ye also unto them.

Judge not, that ye be not judged. For with what judgment ye judge, ye shall be judged; and with what measure ye mete, it shall be measured to you. But why beholdest thou the mote that is in thy brother's eye, but perceivest not the beam that is in thine own eye? Or how wilt thou say to thy brother: Let be, I will cast out the mote from thine eye, and the beam is in thine own eye? Thou hypocrite, cast out first the beam from thine own eye, and then shalt thou see clearly to cast out the mote from thy brother's eye.

The tree is known from the fruit. Do they gather grapes from thorns or figs from thistles? Even so every good tree bringeth forth excellent fruit, but the corrupt tree bringeth forth bad fruit. A good tree cannot bear bad fruit, neither can a corrupt tree bring forth excellent fruit.

(Not everyone that saith unto me: Lord, Lord! shall enter into the kingdom of God, but he that doeth the will of my Father.) Everyone therefore that heareth these my words and doeth them, I will shew you to whom he is like. He is like (or in place of the last twelve words: He shall be likened) to a man who built his house upon the rock. And the rain came down, and the floods arose, and the winds blew and beat upon that house, and it fell not; for it had been founded upon the rock. And everyone that heareth these my words and doeth them not, shall be likened to a man who built his house upon the sand. And the rain came down, and the floods arose, and the winds blew and smote upon that house, and it fell, and great was the fall thereof.

. . . . . .

If the blind lead the blind, both shall fall into the ditch.

. . . . . .

(Father, give us this day our bread for the coming day, and remit us our debts, as we also have remitted to our debtors, and lead us not into temptation.)

. . . . . .

Ask, and it shall be given you; seek, and ye shall find; knock, and it shall be opened to you. For everyone that asketh receiveth, and he that seeketh findeth, and to him that knocketh it shall be opened. Or what man is there of you, of whom his son shall ask bread, will he give him a stone? Or if he shall ask for a fish, will he give him a serpent? If then ye being evil know how to give good things (gifts) to your children, how much more will the Father from heaven give good things to those who ask him.

. . . . . .

Men do not light a lamp and place it under a bushel, but upon a lamp-stand, and it giveth light to all that are in the house.

. . . . . .

The light of the body is the (thine) eye; if then thine eye be single, thy whole body shall be full of light; but if thine eye be evil, thy whole body shall be darkened. If therefore the light which is in thee be darkness, how great will the darkness [*scil.* in the whole outlook of the soul] then be!

. . . .

Wherefore I say unto you: Be not anxious for your life, what ye shall eat; nor for your body, what ye shall put on. Is not the life more than meat and the body than raiment? Look at the ravens (or: the birds of the heaven), they sow not, neither reap nor gather into barns, and God feedeth them. Are ye not much better than they? Which of you by being anxious can add one cubit to his stature; and why are ye anxious about raiment? Consider the lilies, how they grow! They toil not, neither do they spin; but I say unto you, even Solomon in all his glory was not arrayed as one of these. If then in the field God so clothe the grass which is to-day, and to-morrow is cast into the oven, will he not much more you, O ye of little faith? Therefore be not anxious, saying: What shall we eat? or What shall we drink? or Wherewithal shall we be clothed? For after all these things do the nations (of the world) seek; for your Father knoweth that ye have need of all these things. But seek ye his kingdom, and all these things shall be added unto you.

. . . .

Lay not up for yourselves treasures upon earth, where moth and rust doth consume, and where thieves break through and steal: but lay up for yourselves treasures in heaven, where neither moth nor rust doth consume, and where thieves do not break through nor steal; for where thy (your) treasure is, there will thy (your) heart be also.

. . . . . .

Agree with thine adversary quickly, whilst thou art in the way with him; lest the adversary deliver thee to the judge and the judge to the officer, and thou be cast into prison. (Verily) I say unto thee, thou shalt by no means come out thence, till thou hast paid the last farthing.

. . . . . .

Enter in by the narrow gate; for wide (is the gate) and broad is the way that leadeth to destruction, and many there be that enter by it. Because narrow is the gate and straitened the way that leadeth to life, and few there be that find it.

. . . . . .

Ye are the salt (of the land); if however the salt have lost its savour, wherewith shall it be salted? It is thenceforth good for nothing but to be cast out and trodden under foot by men.

. . . . . .

No one can serve two masters, for either he will hate the one and love the other, or he will hold to the one and despise the other. Ye cannot serve God and mammon.

. . . . . .

(Verily I say unto you): Until heaven and earth

pass away, one iota or one tittle shall not pass away from the law.

. . . . . .

(I say unto you): Everyone who divorceth his wife maketh her an adulteress, and whosoever marrieth her that is divorced committeth adultery.

(After he had spoken these words), he entered into Capernaum, and a centurion came to him beseeching him and saying: Lord, my servant lieth in the house sick of the palsy, grievously tormented. He saith to him: I will come and heal him. But the centurion answered and said: Lord, I am not worthy that thou shouldest enter beneath my roof; but only say the word and my servant shall be healed. For I also am a man under authority, having soldiers under me, and I say to this one: Go, and he goeth; and to another: Come, and he cometh; and to my slave: Do this, and he doeth it. When Jesus heard he marvelled and said to those that followed: (Verily) I say unto you, Not even in Israel have I found such faith. (And Jesus said to the centurion: [Go thy way] as thou hast believed, be it done unto thee. And the servant was healed in that very hour.)

17, 18, 16, 20, 21, 22, 19, 34[a], 34[b], 38, 45, 46, 57, 10, 24.

(One said to him): I will follow thee whithersoever thou goest; and Jesus saith to him: Foxes have holes, and the birds of the heaven have nests;

but the Son of man hath not where to lay his head. Another said to him: Suffer me first to go away and bury my father; but he saith to him: Follow me, and let the dead bury their own dead.

He saith to them (or: to his disciples): The harvest is great but the labourers are few; pray therefore the Lord of the harvest that he send forth labourers into his harvest.

Go and preach, saying, that the kingdom of God is at hand.

(Carry no purse, no scrip, no shoes, and greet no one by the way). . . . When however ye enter into a house, salute it; and if the house is worthy, let your peace come upon it; but if it be not worthy, let your peace return to you again.

(Abide in the same house, and eat and drink what they give you); for the labourer is worthy of his meat.

(. . . Into whatsoever city ye enter and they receive you, eat that which is set before you and say to them: The kingdom of God is at hand. But into whatsoever city ye enter and they receive you not, go out into its streets and say: Even the dust of your city which cleaveth to our feet do we shake off and leave it to you). (Verily) I say unto you: It will be more tolerable for the land of Sodom and Gomorrha (or in place of the last six words: Sodom) in that day (or: in the day of judgment) than for that city.

. . . . . .

Behold I send you forth as sheep in the midst of wolves.

. . . . . .

Nothing is secret which shall not be revealed, and hidden which shall not be made known. What I say unto you in darkness speak forth in the light; and what ye hear in the ear publish upon the house-tops. And be not afraid of those that kill the body but cannot kill the soul; but rather be afraid of him who is able to destroy both soul and body in Gehenna. Are not two (five) sparrows sold for one farthing (two farthings)? And not one of them shall fall to the earth without God. But the very hairs of your head are all numbered. Be not (therefore) afraid, ye are of much more value than sparrows. Everyone therefore who shall confess me before men, him will the Son of man (or: I) also confess before the angels of God; but whosoever shall deny me before men, him will I also deny before the angels of God.

. . . . . .

. . . And whosoever shall speak a word against the Son of man, it shall be forgiven him; but whosoever shall speak (a word) against the Holy Spirit, it shall not be forgiven him.

. . . . . .

Think ye that I came to send peace on the earth?

I came not to send peace, but a sword. For I came to set a man at variance against his father, and the daughter against her mother, and the daughter-in-law against her mother-in-law. (And a man's foes are those of his own household.)

. . . . . .

(He that loveth father or mother more than me, is not worthy of me; and he that loveth son and daughter more than me, is not worthy of me.)

. . . . . .

Whosoever doth not take his cross and follow after me is not worthy of me.

. . . . . .

He that findeth his life shall lose it, and he that loseth his life shall find it.

. . . . . .

The disciple is not above his master, neither the servant above his lord. It is sufficient for the disciple that he become as his master, and the servant as his lord.

. . . . . .

(Whosoever receiveth you receiveth me, and whosoever receiveth me receiveth him that sent me.)

14, 50, 15.

But when John heard in the prison the works of the Christ, he sent by his disciples and said unto him: Art thou he that cometh, or do we look for another?

And he answered and said unto them: Go tell John what ye hear and see, the blind receive their sight, the lame walk, the lepers are cleansed, and the deaf hear, and the dead are raised up, and the poor have good tidings preached to them; and blessed is he whosoever shall find no cause of stumbling in me. And as these were on their way, he began to speak to the multitudes concerning John: What went ye out into the wilderness to behold? A reed shaken by the wind? But what went ye out to see? A man clothed in soft raiment? Behold they that wear soft raiment are in kings' houses! But why went ye out? To see a prophet? Yea, I say unto you, and more than a prophet! This is he of whom it is written: *Behold I send my angel before thy face, who shall prepare thy way before thee.* (Verily) I say unto you, there hath not risen among those born of women a greater than John (the Baptist); but he that is least in the kingdom of God is greater than he. . . .

The prophets and the law were until John; from then until now the kingdom of God suffereth violence, and the violent take it by force (or: From the days of John until now the kingdom of God, &c.; for all the prophets and the law prophesied until John). . . .

To what shall I liken this generation (and to what is it like)? It is like unto children sitting in the market-places, which cry unto their fellows, saying: We piped unto you, and ye danced not; we mourned unto you, and ye beat not the breast. For John came neither eating nor drinking, and they say: He hath a devil! The Son of man came eating and drinking, and they say, Behold a man gluttonous and a winebibber, a friend of publicans and sinners! And wisdom is justified of her children.

23.

Woe unto thee, Chorazin! woe unto thee, Bethsaida! For if the mighty works which were done in you had been done in Tyre and Sidon, they would long ago have repented in sackcloth and ashes. Yet (I say unto you) it will be more tolerable for Tyre and Sidon (in the day of judgment, or: in the judgment) than for you. And thou Capernaum shalt thou have been exalted to heaven? To hell thou shalt be cast down!

25.

At that time he said: I thank thee, Father, Lord of heaven and earth, that thou didst hide these things from the wise and prudent, and didst reveal them unto babes; yea [I thank thee] Father, for so it seemed good in thy sight. All [all knowledge] has been delivered to me by my Father, and no one hath known (the Son except the Father, neither hath any one known) the Father except the Son, and he to whomsoever the Son willeth to reveal him.

26.

. . . . . .

Blessed are your eyes, for they see, and (your) ears, for they hear; (for verily) I say unto you that many prophets (and kings) desired to see the things which ye see and have not seen them, and to hear the things which ye hear and have not heard them.

29.

(He healed) a dumb man possessed with a devil, (so that) the dumb spake and the multitudes (all) marvelled . . . every kingdom which is divided against itself cometh to desolation . . . and if I by Beelzebub cast out devils, by whom do your sons cast them out? therefore they shall be your judges. But if I by the Spirit of God cast out devils, then indeed is the kingdom of God come upon you. . . . He that is not with me is against me, and he that gathereth not with me scattereth. . . . Whenever the unclean spirit is gone out of a man he passeth through dry places seeking rest and findeth it not, (then) he saith: I will return unto mine house whence I came out; and when he is come he findeth it empty (and) swept and garnished. Then he goeth and taketh to him seven spirits more evil than himself, and they enter in and dwell there, and the last state of that man becometh worse than the first.

30.

(They said): We would see from thee a sign. But he said: An evil and adulterous generation seeketh after a sign, and a sign shall not be given to it except the sign of Jonah. For as Jonah became a sign to the Ninevites, so shall also the Son of man be to this generation. The men of Nineveh shall stand up in the judgment against this generation, and shall condemn it, because they repented at the preaching of Jonah, and behold here is more than Jonah. The queen of the south shall stand up in the judgment against this generation and shall condemn it, because she came from the ends of the earth to hear the wisdom of Solomon, and behold here is more than Solomon.

40.

. . . . . .

Unto what is the kingdom of God like? and to what shall I liken it? It is like unto a grain of mustard seed which a man took and sowed in his field, and it grew and becometh a tree, and the birds of the heaven nested in its branches.

(And again he said): To what shall I liken the kingdom of God? It is like unto leaven which a woman took and hid in three measures of meal until the whole was leavened.

44.

. . . . . .

He that exalteth himself shall be abased, and he that humbleth himself shall be exalted.

42.

. . . . . .

I say unto you: They shall come from the east and from the west, and shall sit at meat with Abraham and Isaac and Jacob in the kingdom of God;

but the sons of the kingdom shall be cast out; there shall be weeping and gnashing of teeth.

48.

. . . . . .

What think ye? If a man have an hundred sheep, and one of them has strayed, will he not leave the ninety and nine upon the mountains, and having set out doth he not seek that which is strayed? And if he happeneth to find it, (verily) I say unto you that he rejoiceth over it more than over the ninety and nine which had not strayed.

53.

. . . . . .

It is necessary that occasions of stumbling should come, yet Woe unto the man through whom the occasion of stumbling cometh.

54.

. . . . . .

If thy brother sinneth, rebuke him; if he hear thee, thou hast gained thy brother. . . . If my brother sinneth against me, how oft shall I forgive him? Until seven times? Jesus saith unto him: I say unto thee, not until seven times, but until seventy times seven.

55.

. . . . . .

If ye have faith so great as a grain of mustard seed, ye shall say to this mountain: Be removed from hence thither, and it shall be removed.

33, 43.

. . . They bind together heavy burdens and lay them upon men's shoulders, and they themselves will not touch them with a finger.

Woe unto you, Pharisees! for ye shut the kingdom of God before men; for ye yourselves enter not in, nor even do ye suffer them that are entering in to enter.

Woe unto you, Pharisees! for ye tithe mint, anise, and cummin, and neglect the weightier matters of the law, judgment and mercy.

. . . Now ye Pharisees, ye cleanse the outside of the cup and platter, but within they are full of extortion and excess.

Woe unto you, for ye are as tombs which appear not, and the men that walk over them know it not.

(Woe unto you, Pharisees! for ye are like unto tombs that have been whitened which outwardly indeed appear beautiful, but within are full of dead men's bones and all uncleanness.)

Woe unto you! For ye build the tombs of the prophets and say: If we had been in the days of our fathers we would not have been partakers with them in the blood of the prophets. So that ye bear witness against yourselves that ye are sons of those who slew the prophets (now fulfil the measure of your fathers)!

Wherefore also the Wisdom of God said: *I send to you prophets and wise men and scribes; some of them ye will slay and persecute; that there may come upon you all the blood shed upon the earth from the blood of*

Abel to the blood of Zacharias, whom ye slew between the temple and the altar. Verily I say unto you, All these things will come upon this generation. O Jerusalem! Jerusalem! which killeth the prophets and stoneth those that are sent to her! How often would I have gathered thy children together, even as a hen (gathereth) her chickens under her wings, and ye would not. Behold your house is left unto you desolate. (For) I say unto you: Ye shall not see me from henceforth until (it shall come when) ye say: Blessed is he that cometh in the name of the Lord.

56.

If then they say to you: Lo! he is in the desert! Go ye not forth. Lo! he is in the secret chambers! Believe it not. For as the lightning cometh forth from the east and is seen even unto the west, so shall be the coming of the Son of man. Wheresoever the carcase is, there will the eagles be gathered together.

As were the days of Noah, so shall be the coming of the Son of man. For as in the days before the flood they were eating and drinking, marrying and giving in marriage, until the day that Noah entered into the ark, and they knew not until the flood came and took them all away, so shall be the coming of the Son of man. There shall be two in the field, one is taken and one is left; two women shall be grinding at the mill, one is taken and one is left.

37.

But know this, that if the master of the house knew in what watch the thief would come, he would have watched and would not have suffered his house to have been broken through. (Wherefore be ye also ready, for at an hour that ye think not the Son of man cometh.) Who then is the faithful and wise servant whom his lord hath set over his household to give them their meat in due season? Blessed is that servant whom his lord when he cometh shall find so doing. Verily I say unto you, that he shall set him over all that he hath. But if that (evil) servant shall say in his heart: My lord tarrieth, and shall begin to smite his fellow servants, and shall eat and drink with the drunken, the lord of that servant shall come in a day when he expecteth not, and in an hour when he knoweth not, and shall cut him asunder and appoint his portion with the hypocrites.

58.

To him (to everyone) that hath it shall be given, and he shall have abundance; but from him that hath not, even that which he hath shall be taken away.

59.

Ye who follow me . . . shall sit upon twelve thrones, judging the twelve tribes of Israel.[1]

[1] Perhaps the parables of the Great Supper and the Talents stood in Q (*vide supra*, pp. 119 ff.).

EXCURSUS I

On the Sayings in St. Matt. xi. 25–27 (St. Luke x. 21, 22) and St. Matt. xi. 28, 29.

The peculiar contents of these sayings justifies us in subjecting their text, the most ancient history of their tradition, and their significance, to a minute examination. This is the more necessary in that in the last years it has been asserted with increasing confidence that these sayings are not genuine. This question cannot be brought nearer to its solution without the closest investigation. The exegesis of these passages, which had come to a standstill, has been set in motion again by the researches of Schmiedel and Wellhausen, which afford us most valuable hints.[1]

[1] *Cf.* Credner, "Beiträge z. Einl. i. d. bibl. Schriften," 1832, i. s. 248 ff.; Semisch, "Die apostolischen Denkwürdigkeiten des M. Justin," 1848, s. 364 ff.; Hilgenfeld, "Kritische Unters. über die Evv. Justins usw." 1850, s. 201 ff.; Volckmar, "Das Ev. Marcions 1852," s. 75 ff.; Westcott, "Canon of N. T.[4], "1875, p. 133 ff.; "Supernatural Religion[7]," i. p. 401 ff.; E. Abbot, "The Authorship of the Fourth Gospel," 1880, p. 91 ff.; Zahn, "Tatian," 1881, s. 148 f.; "Kanonsgesch." i. s. 555 f.; Bousset, "Evangelienzitate Justins d. M., 1891," s. 100 ff.; Resch, "Texte u. Unters.," Bd. 10, 2, 1895, s. 196 ff.; H. Holtzmann, "Lehrb. d. NTlichen Theol.," i. 1897, s. 272 ff.; H. Holtzmann, "Die Synoptiker," 3. Aufl., 1901, s. 238 ff.; Wellhausen, "Matth.," 1904; Schmiedel, "Das 4. Evangelium," 1906, s. 48 f.; the editions of St. Matthew and St. Luke by Blass. The verses are treated as a hymn by Brandt ("Ev. Geschichte," 1893, s. 562, 576 f.), Pfleiderer ("Urchristentum," 1902, i.[2] s. 435 f., 576, 667 ff.), Loisy, and others.

I

If we in the first place confine ourselves to ascertaining the text of the sayings *according to the Greek manuscripts*, there is scarcely any doubt as to the result we arrive at. The first saying runs as follows:—

St. Matthew.

Ἐξομολογοῦμαί σοι, πάτερ, κύριε τοῦ οὐρανοῦ καὶ τῆς γῆς, ὅτι ἔκρυψας ταῦτα ἀπὸ σοφῶν καὶ συνετῶν καὶ ἀπεκάλυψας αὐτὰ νηπίοις. ναί, ὁ πατήρ, ὅτι οὕτως εὐδοκία ἐγένετο ἔμπροσθέν σου.

πάντα μοι παρεδόθη ὑπὸ τοῦ πατρός [μου], καὶ οὐδεὶς ἐπιγινώσκει τὸν υἱὸν εἰ μὴ ὁ πατήρ, οὐδὲ τὸν πατέρα τις ἐπιγινώσκει εἰ μὴ ὁ υἱὸς καὶ ᾧ ἐὰν βούληται ὁ υἱὸς ἀποκαλύψαι.

μου om. ℵ.*

St. Luke.

Ἐξομολογοῦμαί σοι, πάτερ, κύριε τοῦ οὐρανοῦ καὶ τῆς γῆς, ὅτι ἀπέκρυψας ταῦτα ἀπὸ σοφῶν καὶ συνετῶν καὶ ἀπεκάλυψας αὐτὰ νηπίοις. ναί, ὁ πατήρ, ὅτι οὕτως ἐγένετο εὐδοκία ἔμπροσθέν σου.

πάντα μοι παρεδόθη ὑπὸ τοῦ πατρός [μου], καὶ οὐδεὶς γινώσκει τίς ἐστιν ὁ υἱὸς εἰ μὴ ὁ πατήρ, καὶ τίς ἐστιν ὁ πατὴρ εἰ μὴ ὁ υἱὸς καὶ ᾧ ἂν βούληται ὁ υἱὸς ἀποκαλύψαι.

πάτερ om. F^{w} — εὐδοκία ἐγένετο offerunt multi et boni testes — παρεδόθη μοι nonnulli Codd.; μοι παραδέδοται ΚΠ — ἀπὸ pro ὑπὸ D — μου om. D — τίς ἐστιν ὁ πατήρ . . . τίς ἐστιν ὁ υἱός U and one cursive.

We accordingly see that St. Matthew and St. Luke must have used the same source, namely Q, in a similar recension and translation.[1] The text in St. Matthew, in the two places where it differs from that of St. Luke, seems to be preferable, for it is the simpler (ἔκρυψας > ἀπέκρυψας, ἐπιγινώσκει τὸν πατέρα > γινώσκει τίς ἐστιν ὁ πατήρ).

Also the introduction to the saying shows a common source.

St. Matthew: Ἐν ἐκείνῳ τῷ καιρῷ ἀποκριθεὶς ὁ Ἰησοῦς εἶπεν·

St. Luke: Ἐν αὐτῇ τῇ ὥρᾳ ἠγαλλιάσατο τῷ πνεύματι τῷ ἁγίῳ καὶ εἶπεν·

Here also it is certain that St. Matthew is to be preferred; for (ἐν) αὐτῇ τῇ ὥρᾳ is a favourite expression with St. Luke (seven times), and is intended to be more exact than ἐν ἐκείνῳ τῷ καιρῷ, though it is true that the latter phrase is found again twice in St. Matthew. Likewise ἠγαλλιάσατο (ἀγαλλίασις) is of frequent occurrence in St. Luke (seven times in the gospel and the Acts, once in St. Matthew); lastly, the addition of "τῷ πνεύματι τῷ ἁγίῳ" is genuinely Lukan. The original therefore ran: "At this time Jesus answered and said." But the situation presupposed is different in St. Matthew and St. Luke. In the former the thanksgiving stands in contrast with the denunciation of Chorazin, Bethsaida, and Capernaum: Jesus had, after all, found souls sympathetic to His teaching, and for this He offers thanks to the Father. In St. Luke also the de-

[1] εὐδοκία ἐγένετο ἔμπροσθέν σου is a peculiarly obvious Hebraism; ἐξομολογοῦμαί σοι also is poor Greek.

nunciation of the Galilean cities comes indeed shortly before (x. 12–15); but in between, this evangelist inserts the record which the disciples returning from their mission give concerning their success, and connects with this the thanksgiving of our Lord.

St. Matthew connects the second saying with the first, so that we must suppose that he regarded it as the continuation of the first saying. It is wanting in St. Luke. According to the Greek manuscripts it runs as follows:—

Δεῦτε πρός με πάντες οἱ κοπιῶντες καὶ πεφορτισμένοι, κἀγὼ ἀναπαύσω ὑμᾶς. ἄρατε τὸν ζυγόν μου ἐφ' ὑμᾶς καὶ μάθετε [ἀπ' ἐμοῦ], ὅτι πραΰς εἰμι καὶ ταπεινὸς τῇ καρδίᾳ, καὶ εὑρήσετε ἀνάπαυσιν ταῖς ψυχαῖς ὑμῶν. ὁ γὰρ ζυγός μου χρηστὸς καὶ τὸ φορτίον μου ἐλαφρόν ἐστιν.

πεφορτισμ. ἐστέ D (Ital. Vulg.) — *ἀπ' ἐμοῦ* om. ℵ.*

Both sayings — the second in higher degree — have a poetical rhythm, and in their construction remind us of the poetical form of sayings in the Psalms and Prophets; but from this point of view they are not unique among the sayings of our Lord— indeed, not a few sayings have a similar form.

II

Is the form that has been arrived at above really the most ancient attainable form of the two sayings, so that we may at once proceed to exegesis? In the case of the second saying, and of the first half of the first saying, the question is to be answered in the affirmative—the second saying in the earliest times was much less often quoted than one might expect—but not in the case of the second half of the first saying; here we are rather led by indirect tradition (partly also by the Versions) to an older form of text, whether it be an older form of the text of St. Matthew and St. Luke or a form which is independent of them. We are here in the fortunate position of knowing the wording of the saying (the whole or some portion of it) as it was read by Marcion, by the Marcosians, by Justin, Tatian, Irenæus, Tertullian, Hippolytus, Clement of Alexandria, Origen, the Clementine Homilies, and by Eusebius. We have in addition the ancient versions.

We shall first consider the first half of the saying, and shall begin with Marcion. Here we have certain knowledge that we have before us in the main, not extra-canonical tradition, but the text of St. Luke; though it is true we also know that Marcion has altered many passages in accordance with his own peculiar tendency. Marcion read (according to Tert. iv. 25, supported in important points by Epiphanius): *εὐχαριστῶ* (*σοι* Epiph.) (*καὶ ἐξομολογοῦμαι*, Tert.), *κύριε τοῦ οὐρανοῦ, ὅτι ἅπερ ἦν κρυπτὰ σοφοῖς καὶ συνετοῖς, ἀπεκάλυψας νηπίοις. ναί, ὁ πατήρ, ὅτι οὕτως* ἐγένετο εὐδοκία ἔμπροσθέν σου [the last six words are not directly attested for Marcion, but follow from the ναὶ ὁ πατήρ which Epiphanius gives, and from the silence of both authorities as to alterations at this point]. Marcion's text differs from the canonical (1) in the addition of εὐχαριστῶ καί, (2) in the absence of πάτερ, (3) in the absence of καὶ τῆς γῆς, (4) in reading ἅπερ ἦν κρυπτά (hence καί and αὐτά must also have been wanting). Numbers (3) and (4) are alterations due to tendency; for the God of Marcion must not be "Lord of the earth," neither did He hide the true saving knowledge, but it lay hid of itself. On the other hand, (1) and (2) cannot be explained as due to the teaching of Marcion.

Of these four variants the first (εὐχαριστῶ, but without ἐξομολογοῦμαι) is found once in Epiph. Hær. 40, 7, and perhaps also in Tatian, but never elsewhere. In Tatian, however, the word is doubtful. Ephraem writes ("Evang. Concord.," p. 116, Mœsinger): "Gratias ago tibi, pater cœlestis—in Græco dicit: Gratias ago tibi, deus pater, domine cœli et terræ." In respect to the first word Ephraem therefore noticed no difference of text. The reading εὐχαριστῶ could easily have arisen, because ἐξομολογοῦμαι was not very intelligible—indeed because it seemed even objectionable. Εὐχαριστῶ was a word that naturally suggested itself and took its place, as in Epiphanius. *Cf.* Orig., "De. Orat.," 5: τὸ "ἐξομολογοῦμαι" ἴσον ἐστὶ τῷ "εὐχαριστῶ." The second variant (om. πάτερ) is also found in the canonical Lukan text in F[w] (*vide supra*); πάτερ is also wanting in Clem Hom. xviii. 15; the text there (Simon Magus speaks) is, however, a mixture of the canonical text and that of Marcion (*vide infra*), so that it cannot count as an independent witness. The omission in F^w is probably only accidental[1]—it is wonderful that in the MSS. *πάτερ* has not more frequently fallen out before *κύριε*, thus Marcion stands alone with his omission. We can scarcely assign any weight to it. The third variant (om. *τῆς γῆς*) is found also in Tatian, who besides omits *κύριε* (this very *κύριε*—but not *τῆς γῆς*—is also wanting in Clem. Hom. viii. 6, where St. Peter speaks). The absence of *τῆς γῆς* in Tatian is not accidental; he has substituted the usual expression "*πάτερ οὐράνιε*"—for this was his version—for the fuller but rarer phrase. There can be no connection here either with Marcion or with Clem. Hom. viii. 6, where the absence of *κύριε* is probably only a mistake. Thus Marcion's *κύριε τοῦ οὐρανοῦ* may be regarded as due to tendency, while Tatian's *πάτερ οὐράνιε* may be described as nothing more than a gloss.[2] The fourth variant is also found in Clem. Hom. xviii. 15; Simon Magus quotes *ἅπερ ἦν κρυπτὰ σοφοῖς, ἀπεκάλυψας αὐτὰ κτλ.*, *and in the context is therefore corrected by St. Peter.* Elsewhere in the Homilies Simon Magus adduces elements characteristic of Marcion; he here quotes according to the text of Marcion.

[1] It ought not to be asserted that *πάτερ* is wanting in "a" (Vercell.), since at this place a small gap (an undecipherable passage?) occurs in "a." [This gap occurs only in St. Luke; in St. Matthew, according to Belsheim, "a" reads "*pater*." Note by Translator.]

[2] It is possible that Tatian, whose system required a distinction to be made between God and a Demiurgus, changed *πάτερ, κύριε τ. οὐρ. κ. τ. γ.* into *πάτερ οὐράνιε*.

The other variants in the first half of the saying are as follows:—

ἐξομολογήσομαι: the Marcosians in Iren. i. 20, 3 (perhaps in accordance with Sirach li. 1; of no importance).[1]

domine pater: c.e.f.ff.[2] i. (of no importance, because the transposition was one that easily suggested itself).

deus pater domine: the reading which, according to Ephraem (*l.c.*), was offered by the Greek; but this is most improbable, seeing that none of the manuscripts that have come down to us present this reading. Yet in Clement of Alexandria ("Pæd." i. 6, 32) we read: *πάτερ, ὁ θεὸς τοῦ οὐρανοῦ καὶ τῆς γῆς*, but this is probably only a free quotation.[2]

οὐρανῶν καὶ γῆς: Epiph. *l.c.*, *τῆς γῆς καὶ τῶν οὐρανῶν*:[3] the Marcosians (in Epiph. the plural is probably an oversight, but scarcely so with the Marcosians).

ταῦτα: wanting among the Marcosians, but only in the Greek text (of no importance); L. reads *αὐτά*.

καὶ συνετῶν[4]: wanting in Syr. Sin. (but only in the text of St. Matthew), in "e" and in Clem. Hom.

[1] The Latin translation reads: "Confiteor."

[2] "*πάτερ κύριε*" was also understood as an Hendiaduoin; thus the heathen in "Macarius Magnus," iv. 7, writes: *ὅτι οὐρανοῦ καὶ γῆς πατήρ ἐστιν ὁ θεός, ὑπὸ τοῦ υἱοῦ ὡμολόγηται, "Πάτερ κύριε τοῦ οὐρανοῦ καὶ τῆς γῆς" λέγοντος.*

[3] So in the Latin text; the Greek has the usual order.

[4] 'Ἀπὸ συνετῶν καὶ σοφῶν: D. ἀπὸ σοφῶν καὶ δυνατῶν: 1* (both of no importance).

(*bis*); but in Clem. Hom. viii. 6 πρεσβυτέρων[1] stands in its place, and in both places in Clem. Hom. the word θηλάζουσιν occurs with νηπίοις, so that the text ran: σοφῶν πρεσβυτέρων . . . νηπίοις θηλάζουσιν. The omission of "καὶ συνετῶν" is explained from the circumstance that the following parallel clause has only one substantive; it is thus due to reflection. This omission is presupposed by the reading of the Clementine Homilies; it was felt that in σοφοί . . . νήπιοι the contrast was not striking enough, and therefore πρεσβύτεροι was (in a truly mechanical fashion) added to σοφοί, so as to make the contrast exact; then it was felt that a second word was required with νήπιοι, and so θηλάζοντες was chosen (from St. Matt. xxi. 16).[2] We therefore learn nothing here in regard to the original text. The formal incongruence only goes to prove that this original text really read σοφῶν καὶ συνετῶν . . . νηπίοις.

αὐτά: wanting in Tatian (of no importance).

οὐά, ὁ πατήρ μου: the Marcosians in Irenæus (οὐά is found again in the New Testament in St. Mark xv. 29); they also omit the following οὕτως, reading ὅτι ἔμπροσθέν σου εὐδοκία μοι [wanting in the Latin] ἐγένετο. In spite of these differences we may not assume a translation-variant in this verse, seeing that the Marcosians also had εὐδοκία. We cannot tell how

[1] Only one manuscript prefixes καί.

[2] It is noteworthy that the heathen in "Macarius Magnus" (iv. 9) quotes first in exact accordance with St. Matthew: "καὶ ἀπεκάλυψας αὐτὰ νηπίοις," but then continues: εἰ ἀπὸ τῶν σοφῶν κέκρυπται τὰ μυστήρια, νηπίοις δὲ καὶ θηλαζομένοις ἐκκέχυται.

these readings arose, but as they are quite isolated we can scarcely assign any weight to them.

γέγονεν (for *ἐγένετο*): only Epiph. Hær. 65, 6 (of no importance).

Result: *The first half of the first saying is transmitted by St. Matthew (and St. Luke) in its most ancient attainable form,* also the address: *πάτερ, κύριε τοῦ οὐρανοῦ καὶ τῆς γῆς*, is most probably more ancient than all other variants.

Again the introduction to the second half of the first saying presents a few variants. It is of importance that both Justin (Dial. 100) and Hippolytus (c. Noët. 6) give *παραδέδοται* for *παρεδόθη*.[1] This variant lies in a direction which we shall notice later on; *it aims at translating an historical action into the sphere of the timeless and transcendental.* For *ὑπὸ* (*τοῦ πατρός*) D (in St. Luke) reads *ἀπό*, Hippolytus *παρά* (this is unimportant). Again, while "*μου*" after *τοῦ πατρός* is wanting in only one of the uncials of St. Matthew and St. Luke (and besides in one cursive of St. Matthew), it is, on the other hand, wanting in quotations by Marcion, Justin, the Marcosians (Latin), Hilary, and Victorinus. In the versions it is also wanting in Syr.$^{\text{hier.}}$ of St. Matthew, and in a.c.l.Syr.$^{\text{sin.}}$ of St. Luke. Hence it follows with great probability that this word was originally wanting in St. Matthew and St. Luke, but was inserted in the text already at a very early date. Here again the motive of insertion may well have been similar to that of

[1] So also Codd. KΠ, the cursives 60, 254, p^{scr}, w^{scr}, and three Colbertine MSS. (all only in St. Luke).

the variant παραδέδοται, which however has not made its way into the MSS. that have come down to us.

In the remaining part of the saying two main streams of tradition may be distinguished, according as: (1) either the aorist ἔγνω or the present γινώσκει (ἐπιγινώσκει or οἶδεν) is used, and (2) either "to know the Father" or "to know the Son" stands first. Differences, moreover, occur in the last clause (καὶ ᾧ ἂν βούληται κτλ.).[1] Irenæus already noticed the first point. He asserts that the aorist ἔγνω was an heretical forgery, *vide* iv. 1: "*Nemo cognoscit filium nisi pater, neque patrem quis cognosit nisi filius, et cui voluerit filius revelare.* sic et Matthæus posuit et Lucas similiter et Marcus idem ipsum;[2] Johannes

[1] The remaining variants in this verse are not of much importance. Instead of καὶ οὐδεὶς . . . οὐδὲ . . . τις (St. Matthew, so also Iren. iv. 6, 1; Clem. Hom. xviii. 13 [*bis*], the disciple of Marcion in Adamant.), or καὶ οὐδεὶς . . . καὶ (St. Luke, and besides, *e.g.* the Marcosians in Irenæus, i. 20, 3; Marcion in Tertullian, Epiph.), we also find :—

οὔτε τις . . . οὔτ' αὖ τις (Euseb. "Hist. Eccl.," i. 2); and, moreover, in the first clause—

μηδεὶς (Clem., "Strom.," v. 84; Euseb., "De Eccl. Theol.," i. 12; Euseb., "Eclog.," i. 12); or

οὐδεὶς γάρ (*e.g.* "Clem., Strom.," vii. 109; Euseb., "De Eccl. Theol.," i. 15, 16); and in the second clause—

οὐδέ [without τις] (Justin [*ter*]; Marcion in Irenæus, iv. 6, 1; Irenæus [*bis*], Clem. Alex. [*semel*], Epiph. [*bis*].

ὡς οὐδὲ . . . τις (Clem. Hom. xvii. 4; xviii. 4, 20).

οὕτω καὶ οὐδεὶς (Euseb., "Demonstr.," iv. 3, 13),

μηδὲ . . . τις (Euseb., "De Eccl. Theol.," i. 12 [Marcellus]),

καὶ οὐδεὶς (Epiph. [*ter*]; Euseb., "Demonstr.," v. 1).

It is a peculiarity of Eusebius that he writes thrice: εἰ μὴ μόνος ὁ γεννήσας αὐτὸν πατήρ ("Hist. Eccl.," i. 2; "Demonstr." iv. 3, 13; "De Eccl. Theol.," i. 12). This looks like an amplification originating in a Syrian text. The Syrians loved such amplifications.

[2] Irenæus here makes a mistake; St. Mark has not the saying.

enim præterit locum hunc. hi autem qui peritiores apostolis volunt esse, sic describunt: *nemo cognovit patrem nisi filius, nec filium nisi pater et cui voluerit filius revelare*, et interpretantur, quasi a nullo cognitus sit verus deus ante domini nostri adventum, et eum deum qui a prophetis sit annunciatus, dicunt non esse patrem Christi."[1] Here Irenæus quite rightly feels that the sense of "cognovit" (ἔγνω) is different from that of "cognoscit" (γινώσκει), but his assertion that the reading ἔγνω is an heretical corruption is quite mistaken, as will shortly appear.

I shall first give a list of the passages in which ἔγνω is found, and "knowing the Father" stands first, then of the quotations with ἔγνω

[1] This passage is strangely misunderstood by the critics (even by Zahn, Tatian, s. 149; "Kanonsgesch.," i. s. 555 f.), as if the censure of Irenæus were directed against the precedence in order of the clause "to know the Father." This was to him a matter of complete indifference (he himself twice quotes in this order); he is only concerned with the difference of "cognoscit" and "cognovit." Again, this passage is usually referred to the Marcosians, because Irenæus in Book I. (20, 3) has quoted the verse in the version of the Marcosians. But in the context (*vide* iv. 1 ff.; iv. 6, 2; here he is quoting Justin's work against Marcion) he is dealing with the followers of Marcion. These heretics are doubtless in the forefront of his mind; though he may also be thinking of the Marcosians, who had in the main the same reading of this passage as Marcion. Moreover, the two quotations, i. 20, 3 and iv. 6, 1, vary somewhat from one another. Where Irenæus gives the Marcosian version of the saying (i. 20, 3), he writes: καὶ τὸν υἱὸν εἰ μὴ ὁ πατὴρ καὶ ᾧ ἂν ὁ υἱὸς ἀποκαλύψῃ (so also the Old Latin); in our passage he represents the heretics as reading: "*Nec* filium nisi pater, et cui *voluerit* filius revelare." This "nec" is also given by the disciple of Marcion in Adamantius.

and with "knowing the Son" at the beginning:[1] —

† ἔγνω τὸν πατέρα . . . τὸν υἱόν (without a verb): Justin, Apol., i. 63 [*bis*]; Marcosians in Iren., i. 20, 3; Marcion in Iren., iv. 6, 1.

ἔγνω τὸν πατέρα . . . ἔγνω τὸν υἱόν: Tatian;[2] Euseb., Demonstr., iv. 3, 13; Euseb., Demonstr., v. 1; Euseb., De Eccl. Theol., i. 12 (probably also Orig., De Princ., ii. 6, 1; "novit . . . novit").

ἔγνω τὸν πατέρα . . . γινώσκει τὸν υἱόν: the disciple of Marcion in Adamantius (p. 44, ed. van de Sande).

ἔγνω τὸν πατέρα . . . γνώῃ ποτὲ τὸν υἱόν: Euseb., Hist. Eccl., i. 2.

ἔγνω τὸν πατέρα . . . οἶδεν τὸν υἱόν: Clem. Hom., xvii. 4; xviii. 4, 13 [*bis*], 20.

[ἔγνω τὸν πατέρα . . . without the parallel clause (thus an imperfect quotation): Clem. Alex., Protrept., i. 10; Pædag., i. 5, 20 and i. 8;

[1] A dagger marks the passages in which only one verb is found; the passages in which the quotation is imperfect—*i.e.* where only one of the two clauses is given—are included within brackets. I have paid no attention to the difference between τὸν πατέρα and τίς ἐστιν ὁ πατήρ, because the more circumstantial phrase practically never occurs.

[2] The order is quite certain; it is not certain that Mœsinger's "novit" presupposes ἔγνω.—The "novit" which is found in a few Old Latin MSS. of St. Luke certainly = ἔγνω; for the great majority of these MSS. give (in St. Luke) "scit." Codex Veronensis (b) forms one of the minority, it reads here: "Nemo novit patrem nisi filius et que . . . bit [=novit] fili . . . nisi pater . . . voluerit, &c." (Perhaps for "que" we should read "qui[s]"—*vide* "q.") The reading ἔγνω is also attested by Cod. Vercell. (a)—for the reading here of this important codex *vide infra*—as well as by "q."

Strom., v. 84, vii. 58; Origen, Selecta in Ps. [T. 11, p. 393, Lomm.]; c. Cels., ii. 71, vii. 44; on St. John, p. (20), 49, 248, 301, 334, 474 f. (ed. Preuschen), &c.;[1] Concil. Antioch. c. Paulum Samos.; Euseb., Eclog., i. 12.; Tertull. adv. Marc., ii. 27 (*cognovit*); De Præscr., 21 (*novit*)].

† *ἔγνω τὸν υἱόν . . . τὸν πατέρα* (without a verb): Clem. Alex., Pædag., i. 9, 88; Strom., i. 178; Orig., c. Cels., vi. 17.

[*ἔγνω τὸν υἱόν . . .* without the parallel clause (thus an imperfect quotation): Orig. on St. John, p. 474].

οἶδε τὸν υἱόν . . . ἔγνω τὸν πατέρα: Epiph., Hær., 65, 6.

Now follow quotations without *ἔγνω*. Again we first give those in which "knowing the Father" comes at the beginning:—

† *γινώσκει τὸν πατέρα . . . τὸν υἱόν* (without a verb): Justin, Dial., 100.[2]

† *γινώσκει τίς ἐστιν ὁ πατήρ . . . τίς ὁ υἱός* (without a verb): Marcion [according to Tertull., iv. 25, but according to Iren. and Adamant. *ἔγνω*, *vide supra*], Cod. U of St. Luke.

[*γινώσκει τὸν πατέρα . . .* without the parallel clause (thus an imperfect quotation): Clem. Alex., Strom., vii. 109.]

[1] Ἔγνω is also found in other quotations in Origen and even in later Alexandrians (*e.g.* Alexander and Didymus).

[2] Justin here expressly says: *ἐν τῷ εὐαγγελίῳ γέγραπται εἰπών.*

† ἐπιγινώσκει τὸν πατέρα . . . τὸν υἱόν (without a verb): Iren., ii. 6, 1, iv. 6, 3; fragm. Syr., xv. (ed. Harvey).

[ἐπιγινώσκει τὸν πατέρα . . . without the parallel clause (thus an imperfect quotation): Clem. Alex., Dives, 8; Iren., iv. 6, 6].

οἶδε τὸν πατέρα . . . οἶδε τὸν υἱόν: Epiph., Hær., 69, 43; Ancor., 11.

† οἶδε τὸν πατέρα . . . τὸν υἱόν (without a verb): Epiph., Hær., 74, 4; 76, 1, Nr. 29; 76, 1, Nr. 32.

[οἶδε τὸν πατέρα . . . without the parallel clause (thus an imperfect quotation): Euseb., De Eccl. Theol., i. 16.[1]]

† γινώσκει τίς ἐστιν ὁ υἱός . . . τίς ὁ πατήρ (without a verb): St. Luke (with exception of the Codd. U, a, b).[2]

ἐπιγινώσκει τὸν υἱόν . . . ἐπιγινώσκει τὸν πατέρα: St. Matt. (so also Syr.$^{\text{sin.}}$; only one cursive reverses the order); Iren., iv. 6, 1.

† ἐπιγινώσκει τὸν υἱόν . . . τὸν πατέρα (without a verb): Iren., iv. 6, 7.

οἶδε τὸν υἱόν . . . οἶδε τὸν πατέρα: Epiph., Hær., 54, 4.

† οἶδε τὸν υἱόν . . . τὸν πατέρα (without a verb): Epiph., Hær., 64, 9; 76, 1, Nr. 7.

[1] Variations in Eusebius are also brought about by his use of the text of Marcellus.

[2] A peculiar variant occurs in Syr.$^{\text{sin.}}$ of St. Luke: "And who knoweth the Son save the Father, and who knoweth the Father save the Son?" *Cf.* the Latin codex "q": "Et quis novit patrem?" and perhaps also "h."

Codex Vercellensis (a) here stands quite by itself. *In the text of St. Luke (not in St. Matthew) it omits the "knowing the Son" altogether, and reads:* "Omnia mihi tradita sunt a patre, et nemo novit quis est pater nisi filius et cuicumque voluerit filius, revelavit."

Before we give our verdict on these readings, let us bring together the variants which occur in the concluding clause:—

1. *καὶ ᾧ ἂν βούληται ὁ υἱὸς ἀποκαλύψαι*: St. Luke, St. Matthew, Iren. iv. 6, 1, &c. &c. (Syr.[sin.] in St. Matthew does not read otherwise).

2. *καὶ ᾧ ἂν βούληται ἀποκάλυψαι αὐτὸς ἀποκαλύπτει* Syr.[hier.]; *cf.* "Et cuicumque voluerit filius revelavit" (a).

3. *καὶ ᾧ ἂν ὁ υἱὸς ἀποκαλύψῃ*: Marcion; the Marcosians; Clem. Alex. (*septies*); Origen (*sæpe*); Tert. De Præscr., 21 ("revelavit"); Euseb., Eclog., i. 12; Concil. Antioch.; Epiphan. (*nonnull. loc.*).

4. *καὶ ᾧ ἂν ἀποκαλύψῃ*: Epiph. [*sæpius*], both after "knowing the Father" and "knowing the Son."

5. *καὶ ᾧ ἂν αὐτὸς ἀποκαλύψῃ*: Nicetas (after "knowing the Son").

6. *καὶ ᾧ ἂν ὁ υἱὸς ἀποκαλύπτει*: Epiph., Hær., 74, 4.

7. *καὶ οἷς ἂν βούληται ὁ υἱὸς ἀποκαλύψαι*: Clem., Hom. [*quater*].[1]

8. *καὶ οἷς (ἂν) ὁ υἱὸς ἀποκαλύψῃ vel ἀποκαλύψῃ ὁ υἱός*: Justin [*ter*], Iren. [*ter*].

[1] The passage, Clem. Hom. xviii. 7: *καὶ οἷς* (not *ᾧ* as Blass gives it) *ἂν βούληται ὁ υἱὸς ἀποκαλύπτει*, ought not to be taken into consideration, because it is a free quotation.

A

1. A section of the Marcionites,[1] the Marcosians, Justin (in the "Apology"), (Tatian), the Alexandrians (Clement, Origen [both practically always], and still later writers), and Eusebius (practically always) agree in reading ἔγνω. Accordingly ἔγνω is the reading which has in its favour the most ancient testimony.

2. *The reading ἔγνω stood in St. Luke;*[2] for this is suggested by the reading in Marcion's gospel, and the hypothesis is supported by the "novit" of the very ancient Latin codices Vercellensis (a) and Veronensis (b) in St. Luke, while the remaining Old Latin codices (with the exception of "q") read "scit." The hypothesis finally receives very strong support in the other aorists—ἔκρυψας, ἀπεκάλυψας, ἐγένετο, παρεδόθη.[3]

[1] According to the testimony of Irenæus (and Adamantius). We may well believe that Tertullian read γινώσκει ("scit") in his exemplar of the gospel of Marcion; but there is no difficulty in supposing that this reading also found its way into exemplars of Marcion's gospel, although ἔγνω was welcome to them. *The same thing, therefore, happened with them as with Justin, who also gives both readings.* If, however, any one feels bound to take up the position that Tertullian alone presents the genuine and unique text of Marcion—who accordingly read γινώσκει—still the number of ancient witnesses for ἔγνω is great enough to compel us to decide that St. Luke wrote ἔγνω.

[2] This is also the opinion of Blass, Keim, Meyer, and Schmiedel.

[3] Weiss, on the contrary, asserts that ἔγνω arose from conformation with παρεδόθη. But why is it that this conformation takes place only in the text of St. Luke and not also in St. Matthew? That ἔγνω was supplanted by γινώσκει may however also be explained from the fact that the following clause: ᾧ ἂν ἀποκαλύψῃ, seemed to demand the present tense in the preceding verb.

3. We can, moreover, conjecture how it was that the reading γινώσκει arose in St. Luke, from the remarks of Irenæus in the passage quoted above; the present made its way from St. Matthew into St. Luke and established itself there as an anti-Marcionitic reading. It is already attested by Justin but in a later work (the Dialogue), and it predominates in ecclesiastical manuscripts of Irenæus. In the West ἔγνω disappeared at an earlier date than in the East.

4. The persistence of ἔγνω and its correct interpretation in the East is especially manifest in those quotations where this historic aorist was regarded as suitable when applied to the knowledge of the Father (on the part of the Son), and was accordingly preserved, while a present (in accordance with St. Matthew, *vide infra*) was inserted into the Lukan text as applied to the knowledge of the Son (on the part of the Father), as in Adamantius (γινώσκει) and in Clem. Hom. [five times] and Epiph. Hær., 65, 6 (οἶδεν).

5. In the text of St. Matthew the present, ἐπιγινώσκει, stood from the beginning (ἐπέγνω does not occur in any authority); it was also from the beginning repeated in the second clause, while the ἔγνω in St. Luke was not repeated. This formal difference between the two gospels explains those instances of mixed text wherein sometimes the ἔγνω is repeated (*vide* Eusebius), sometimes the ἐπιγινώσκει is not repeated (Irenæus), while the clauses are sometimes conjoined by καί, sometimes by οὐδέ.

6. The reading οἶδεν is found only in the

Clementine Homilies and in Epiphanius,[1] sometimes once, sometimes repeated in the two clauses; it was thus confined to Syria and need not therefore be considered. It is probably to be explained from the influence of the Johannine vocabulary.

B

The clause concerning "knowing the Father" stood first in Marcion (according to Iren., Tertull., and Adamant.), in the version of the Marcosians, in Justin, Tatian, Irenæus (but not always), the Clementine Homilies, Eusebius, in Codex U of St. Luke (and in Codex Veronensis), while the clause concerning "knowing the Son" stood first in the text of St. Matthew (with the exception of one cursive, which means nothing), in the remaining authorities for St. Luke, and in Clement of Alexandria. Irenæus, Origen, the later Alexandrians and Epiphanius, attest both arrangements of the clauses. The solution of the problem presented by these facts—seeing that Marcion had the Lukan text before him[2]—is that in St. Luke the clause concerning "knowing the Father" certainly stood first, and that the contrary was probably the case in St. Matthew. We cannot be quite certain about the passage in St. Matthew, only because we have no instance of quotation of the text of St. Matthew before Irenæus and

[1] The one place in Eusebius is an imperfect quotation, which has no weight.

[2] For this very reason it is not permissible to explain the precedence of this clause by the influence of oral tradition or of an apocryphal gospel.

Clement of Alexandria; the witness of Irenæus, however, is divided.

C

In regard to the concluding clause:—

1. It is certain that ὁ υἱός was repeated in it; for the omissions in Syr. hier., in Epiphanius (often) and Nicetas (who substitutes αὐτός), are of no account in the criticism of the text.

2. The short form ἀποκαλύψῃ (for βούληται ἀποκαλύψαι) has earlier attestation than the other, seeing that it occurs in Marcion, in the Marcosian version, Justin (thrice), Irenæus (as a rule), Clement of Alexandria, Origen (often), &c.

3. The form οἷς ἄν has excellent sponsors in Justin, Irenæus (except in one passage), and the Clementine Homilies, but Marcion and the Marcosians do not give it.

4. The indicative ἀποκαλύπτει (ἀπεκάλυψεν) in Syr. hier., Cod. Vercell. ("revelavit"; so also Tertull., "De Præscr.," 21, but this does not say much), and *once* in Epiph., is too weakly attested for us to follow this reading.

Result: We have now no means of determining which of the three forms[1]—ὧ ἂν ὁ υἱὸς ἀποκαλύψῃ—οἷς ἂν ὁ υἱὸς ἀποκαλύψῃ—ᾧ ἂν βούληται ὁ υἱὸς ἀποκαλύψαι—is the original, whether at first this clause had different forms in St. Matthew and St. Luke, and how these readings were distributed between the two evangelists. On the strength, however, of the testi-

[1] The reading οἷς ἂν βούληται ὁ υἱὸς ἀποκαλύψαι is only attested by the Clementines, and thus falls out of account.

mony of Marcion, it is probable that ᾧ ἂν ὁ υἱὸς ἀποκαλύψῃ stood in St. Luke, especially seeing that the Marcosians also give this reading, and that they also (*vide supra*) have followed the Lukan text.[1]

D

The result of our investigations up to this point is that in St. Luke the saying read as follows:—

πάντα μοι παρεδόθη ὑπὸ τοῦ πατρός, καὶ οὐδεὶς ἔγνω τίς ἐστιν ὁ πατὴρ εἰ μὴ ὁ υἱός, καὶ τίς ἐστιν ὁ υἱὸς εἰ μὴ ὁ πατὴρ καὶ ᾧ ἂν ὁ υἱὸς ἀποκαλύψῃ, but in St. Matthew: πάντα μοι παρεδόθη ὑπὸ τοῦ πατρός, καὶ οὐδεὶς ἐπιγινώσκει τὸν υἱὸν εἰ μὴ ὁ πατήρ, οὐδὲ τὸν πατέρα τις ἐπιγινώσκει εἰ μὴ ὁ υἱὸς [*vel:* τὸν πατέρα . . . ὁ υἱός . . . τὸν υἱὸν . . . ὁ πατήρ] καὶ ᾧ [οἷς] ἂν βούληται ὁ υἱὸς ἀποκαλύψαι [*vel:* ἂν ὁ υἱὸς ἀποκαλύψῃ].

But can we remain satisfied with this result? It is impossible, for the following reasons. (Let us at first consider the Lukan text):—

1. We do not at all expect to find the clause concerning "knowing the Son" in this connection (though of course it cannot be said to be a discrepancy); for this ascription of praise is concerned both at the beginning and the close with the *knowledge of God.*

2. The historic aorist "ἔγνω" suits excellently the

[1] It is possible to suppose that the original form read: ᾧ (οἷς) ἂν βούληται ὁ υἱὸς ἀποκαλύπτειν ἀποκαλύπτει, and that from this the two shorter forms were derived; but this cannot be proved.—Ἀποκαλύψῃ and βούληται ἀποκαλύψαι may, besides, be taken as translation-variants, if βούληται ἀποκαλύψαι is regarded as simply a periphrasis for the future.

Son's knowledge of the Father, *but it does not suit so well the Father's knowledge of the Son;* this has been noticed by thoughtful copyists, who have tried to overcome the difficulty in various ways (*vide supra*).

3. *The clause* καὶ ᾧ ἂν ὁ υἱὸς ἀποκαλύψῃ *only suits the clause* οὐδεὶς ἔγνω τίς ἐστιν ὁ πατὴρ εἰ μὴ ὁ υἱός, *but not the other clause with which it is connected above in St. Luke (the Son is God's interpreter and not His own). This also has been correctly seen by the copyists, who have accordingly overcome the difficulty by transposition*[1] (*or even by changing* υἱός *into* αὐτός, *which then refers to the Father*).

4. *In Cod. Vercell. of St. Luke we even now read* (vide supra) *the saying, without the clause concerning "knowledge of the Son."*[2]

In my opinion, we are simply forced to the conclusion that in St. Luke the words "καὶ τίς ἐστιν ὁ υἱὸς εἰ μὴ ὁ πατήρ" *were wanting.*[3]

If they were wanting in St. Luke, they were also wanting in Q;[4] this goes without saying. Then, however, it is a relatively insignificant question whether the first evangelist is to be regarded as responsible for their insertion, or whether originally

[1] But the transposition creates a new difficulty, seeing that "the knowing of the Son" now comes before "the knowing of the Father," which is very strange both in itself and in its context.

[2] The readings of this codex elsewhere are of great weight.

[3] On behalf of the originality of the words an appeal is made to the rhythmic structure of the saying, which it is said demands them. But even without these words a rhythm is present, and I do not see that with their addition the rhythm is a better one.

[4] This is also Wellhausen's opinion; but he does not enter closely into the history of the text.

they were also wanting in the first gospel.[1] On this point one cannot arrive at any definite decision. At all events the interpolation is very ancient; for all our authorities for St. Matthew and all our authorities, except one, for St. Luke have it. The most probable, because the simplest, hypothesis is that "St. Matthew" himself brought it into the text—the same evangelist who changed the historic aorist into the present and who wrote (xxviii. 18): "All power is given unto me in heaven and in earth." It is not quite certain what position he gave to the interpolation; it is, however, extremely probable that he gave it the first place; for this is in accordance with the testimony of the MSS., *and the history of the text is most simply explained on such an hypothesis.* If Greek Christians possessed from the beginning the two forms: οὐδεὶς ἔγνω τίς ἐστιν ὁ πατὴρ εἰ μὴ ὁ υἱός, and: οὐδεὶς ἐπιγινώσκει τὸν υἱὸν εἰ μὴ ὁ πατήρ, οὐδὲ τὸν πατέρα τις ἐπιγινώσκει εἰ μὴ ὁ υἱός—then *all* the mixed forms of text, together with their early appearance, are explained in the simplest way.[2] The interpolation into the Lukan text of the words "The Son no one save

[1] So far as the content is concerned, the clause shows itself as an interpolation in St. Matthew as clearly as in St. Luke; for if it is placed at the beginning it conflicts with the natural order (it is to the Son that the knowledge of the Father is delivered, and the knowledge of the Son ought not to stand before the knowledge of the Father); if it is placed at the end, then the concluding clause is out of harmony with it.

[2] We have therefore no need to have recourse also to the influence of a distinct oral tradition different from that of the gospels, or to an apocryphal gospel. Of course such an influence remains possible.

the Father," marks the first important step towards intermixture, which must have been taken almost at once, while the change of the aorist ἔγνω into the present marks the second step.[1]

The saying thus ran in Q as in St. Luke (or nearly as in St. Luke): ἐξομολογοῦμαί σοι, πάτερ, κύριε τοῦ οὐρανοῦ καὶ τῆς γῆς, ὅτι ἔκρυψας ταῦτα ἀπὸ σοφῶν καὶ συνετῶν καὶ ἀπεκάλυψας αὐτὰ νηπίοις· ναί, ὁ πατήρ, ὅτι οὕτως ἐγένετο εὐδοκία ἔμπροσθέν σου. πάντα μοι παρεδόθη ὑπὸ τοῦ πατρός, καὶ οὐδεὶς ἔγνω τὸν πατέρα [*vel*: τίς ἐστιν ὁ πατήρ] εἰ μὴ ὁ υἱὸς καὶ ᾧ ἂν ὁ υἱὸς ἀποκαλύψῃ.

III

The source gave no information concerning the situation in which this thanksgiving was spoken, for "ἐν ἐκείνῳ τῷ καιρῷ ἀποκριθεὶς ὁ Ἰησοῦς εἶπεν" says nothing. Nor may we draw any conclusion from the fact that in the source the thanksgiving

[1] In quotations of the passage torn from its context the Lukan form: τίς ἐστιν ὁ πατήρ (and τίς ἐστιν ὁ υἱός) almost everywhere disappears. No weight is, however, to be assigned to this circumstance.—That the original readings should have entirely disappeared in the Greek MSS. of St. Luke, and almost entirely in the Latin MSS., is unfortunately by no means exceptional. Compare, *e.g.*, how the true Lukan text has disappeared in the Lord's Prayer (*vide* "Sitzungsber. d. Preuss. Akad., 1904," s. 195 ff.), or how ὠνείδισας in St. Mark xv. 34 has been deleted from the whole tradition of the East (*id.* 1901, s. 261 ff.). The Lukan text has been far more thoroughly corrected from that of St. Matthew than our textual critics are inclined to admit. Our passage also bears witness to this fact. It is worthy of note that St. John i. 18 (θεὸν οὐδεὶς ἑώρακεν πώποτε· ὁ μονογενὴς υἱὸς ὁ ὢν εἰς τὸν κόλπον τοῦ πατρός, ἐκεῖνος ἐξηγήσατο) has had as good as no influence upon the textual history of our saying.

followed after (or soon after) the condemnation of the Galilean cities, seeing that the passages are in a contrary sense.[1] We have thus to deal with an isolated saying *which has, however, been torn from a definite context, as is shown by the "ταῦτα" at the beginning.* This fact of itself speaks against the hypothesis that our thanksgiving is a "Christian hymn"; in such an independent composition this retrospective "ταῦτα" would have been avoided.

The first half of the first saying presents no occasion for objection. Our Lord offers thanksgiving to the Father openly—are we perhaps to say that this is inconsistent with St. Matt. vi. 6? He addresses Him as "Father" (*not* "My Father") and as Lord of heaven and earth—so great is the Divine act for which praise is given! the context plainly shows that the thanksgiving is for something connected with our Lord's teaching—*i.e.* His revelation of the knowledge of God (not with miracles, &c.); for it is only in regard to teaching that men are called σοφοί and νήπιοι.[2] This distinction, and the statement that the νήπιοι show themselves receptive,[3] is

[1] St. Luke, very suitably so far as the thought is concerned, places the thanksgiving directly after the return of the disciples from their missionary journey, but it is quite improbable that this order rests upon tradition, because this evangelist also gives the condemnation of the cities just beforehand.

[2] Whether we are to lay any stress upon the absence of the article before σοφοί and νήπιοι is questionable. The absence can be interpreted as a limitation (not all the wise and not all the simple); its force can, however, also be rendered by the paraphrase: "from such people as are wise"—"to such people as are simple."

[3] The significance of νήπιοι ("Peta'im," as in Ps. xix. 8, cxvi. 6) is different from that of the word with St. Paul. In St. Paul the νήπιοι are always Christians who are still undeveloped like children.

quite in accordance with other sayings of our Lord, and is therefore not peculiar. He, however, praises the Father, not only for the revelation vouchsafed to the *νήπιοι*, but also because the Father has hidden this knowledge from the wise and prudent. There is a harsh note here which already sounded intolerable to Marcion, but it is also heard in other sayings and is an indication of genuineness. Moreover, we must here notice the aorists: not what God always does, but what He had done on the present occasion—in the success of the ministry of Jesus—was the subject of the thanksgiving. Hence some instance of success of this kind, notorious to all, which has not however been transmitted in history, must have preceded the thanksgiving. The *ναί* takes up the *ἐξομολογοῦμαι*, and the clause *ὅτι οὕτως εὐδοκία ἐγένετο ἔμπροσθέν σου* takes up the thought of the preceding clause.[1] The overpowering glory of the experience in the soul most naturally constrained the tongue to such repetition in the thanksgiving.[2]

The first half of the saying dominates and determines the second half. In the first half our Lord gives thanks for that which had happened (the revelation of the knowledge of God), in the second half He gives clear expression to the fact that this revelation had been vouchsafed *through Himself;* for it was just the success of *His own* ministry that incited

[1] *Cf.* St. Matt. xviii. 14: *οὕτως (οὐκ) ἔστιν θέλημα ἔμπροσθεν τοῦ πατρὸς ὑμῶν.* Εὐδοκία reminds us of the *εὐδόκησα* at the Baptism.

[2] Also the vocative *πάτερ* is taken up by *ὁ πατήρ*, but is this a simple repetition? May not *ὁ πατήρ* here signify, "Thou who art the Father."—The word *οὕτως* can only refer backwards, and has nothing to do with the introduction of what follows.

Him to offer praise. Thus what follows necessarily connects with what goes before. The πάντα is exactly determined by what goes before and by what follows, as well as by the verb παρεδόθη. It cannot mean "all things" but only the whole doctrine (the doctrine is "paradosis"), the complete revelation of the knowledge of God.[1] It has been "delivered" to Him by the Father, and indeed first to Him the Son—He has now learnt to know the Father; before Him no one knew the Father[2]—then through Him to those who

[1] We have no choice but either to give πάντα an entirely unlimited significance (the government of the world, the Messianic power and authority), or to refer it to the knowledge (doctrine) as do Grotius, Hofmann, Holtzmann, Schmiedel, Joh. Weiss, Wellhausen, and others. The latter alternative is, however, alone possible, seeing that the passage proceeds at once to speak, and to speak exclusively, of the knowledge of God, and seeing that the preceding ἀποκάλυψις is unequivocally determined, by the contrast between σοφοί and νήπιοι to which it refers, as a revelation of a knowledge. The objection that παραδιδόναι can only be used of *human* transmission of teaching, and that the word therefore cannot have this sense here (Pfleiderer), is perverse. In St. Matt. xxviii. 18, we do not read "παρεδόθη," but "ἐδόθη" μοι πᾶσα ἐξουσία ἐν οὐρανῷ καὶ ἐπὶ γῆς.

[2] The καὶ (οὐδεὶς ἔγνω) after παρεδόθη (ὑπὸ τοῦ πατρός) is not quite clear; it is easiest to take it as explicative or rather consecutive. "The knowledge of the Father is included in the delivery of the complete doctrine," or "The knowledge of the Father follows upon this delivery." Weiss, on the contrary, supposes that the clause introduced by καί gives the essential ground for the πάντα μοι παρεδόθη. So indeed we are compelled to interpret, if with Weiss we accept the words, "No man knoweth the Son save the Father," and regard their position at the beginning as correct; for this clause can be regarded neither as an explanation of nor as giving the result of πάντα μοι παρεδόθη. But of course we are forced simply to read into this clause the idea that it gives the ground of what goes before, for no hint of this is given in the passage itself. The words indeed fall quite out of the context. If one

were receptive, of whom it is therefore now true, just as of the Son, that: πάντα αὐτοῖς παρεδόθη.

In this train of thought, when it is compared with the utterances of our Lord, which are certainly genuine, there are two elements which might be regarded as strange: first, the abstract distinction that is drawn in the terms "the Father" and "the Son," then the assertion that "No man has known the Father save the Son." The same distinction is also found (according to Wellhausen) in St. Mark xiii. 32 (οὐδὲ οἱ ἄγγελοι οὐδὲ ὁ υἱός, εἰ μὴ ὁ πατήρ),[1] and that in a saying which denies our Lord's knowledge of the future, and thus assuredly belongs to the most ancient tradition. However, as to the οὐδείς, it ought not to be pressed nor taken as Marcion interprets it, as if it implied a rejection of the prophets of the Old Testament. It says no more than is said in St. Luke x. 24: πολλοὶ προφῆται καὶ βασιλεῖς ἠθέλησαν ἰδεῖν ἃ ὑμεῖς βλέπετε καὶ οὐκ εἶδαν, or in the words concerning the Baptist and the least in the Kingdom of God. On the other hand, importance is to be assigned to the aorist ἔγνω (in distinction from the present). Nothing is said of a relationship of the Son to the Father that is ever abiding—to say nothing

takes one's stand on the correct text, we should at first expect the passage to run in the following form: "All has been delivered to Me by the Father, and I alone have learned to know Him, and he to whomsoever I will to reveal Him." But it is quite intelligible that "the Son" should have taken the place of "I," seeing that this "I" showed itself as "Son" in the very fact of this complete and primary knowledge.

[1] *Cf.* also St. Luke xxii. 29: κἀγὼ διατίθεμαι ὑμῖν καθὼς διέθετό μοι ὁ πατήρ μου τὴν βασιλείαν, ἵνα ἔσθητε καὶ πίνητε ἐπὶ τῆς τραπέζης μου ἐν τῇ βασιλείᾳ μου, of which the "antiquity" is unmistakable.

of timeless; on the contrary, this ἔγνω also stands within the sphere of the ἐξομολογοῦμαι κτλ. at the beginning: our Lord offers thanksgiving to the Father because He has delivered to Him all knowledge, because He the Son is the first to learn to know the Father, because He the Father has revealed this knowledge to the νήπιοι, and because it will continue to be revealed only through Him the Son.[1] The passage throughout deals with circumstances of actual historic fact.

If the saying belongs to the best and most ancient tradition, it can have been spoken by our Lord only during the later period of His ministry, and it further presupposes that during this period our Lord upon other occasions called Himself "the Son." This conclusion will necessarily be disputed by those who suppose themselves bound not to allow our Lord any other self-designation than that of a Teacher, of a Prophet, and—at the close of His ministry—of the *future* Messiah. But the transition from the designations of Teacher and Prophet to that of the future Messiah demands, both in the self-consciousness of Jesus and also in outward expression, some middle term, and it is difficult to see why tradition must be supposed to be in error when it presents us here with the designation "the Son." If this could mean absolutely nothing else than "*I am* the present Messiah," then it would be unintelligible; but the concrete situation in which our Lord found Himself limited the sphere of significance of the expression both for Himself and for His hearers. At the pre-

[1] Note how the two halves of the saying are brought into correspondence by ἀπεκάλυψας and ἀποκαλύψῃ.

sent He is the Chosen One, the Beloved One, thus the Son, and therefore in the future—that is, soon—He will come in the clouds of heaven and will receive the office of Messiah, whose function is essentially active. If criticism can produce no valid objections against the tradition that our Lord towards the end of His ministry called Himself the Son of Man (in the sense of Daniel), so, in my opinion, there is still less ground for hesitation in accepting the genuineness of the tradition that our Lord called Himself "the Son," because it is absolutely impossible to imagine how He could have arrived at the conviction that He was the future Messiah without first knowing Himself as standing in an unique relationship to God. What, however, our Lord in this passage says of Himself as the Son, goes beyond what is expressed in other sayings, not in the thought itself, but only in its pregnant form.[1]

[1] In conclusion, I would with all reserve also bring forward an historical witness to the antiquity, even to the genuineness of this saying. I do not share the confidence with which lately countless conceptions and words of St. Paul are traced back to utterances of our Lord; but whenever I read 1 Cor. i. 19, 21 (*γέγραπται γάρ· ἀπολῶ τὴν σοφίαν τῶν σοφῶν, καὶ τὴν σύνεσιν τῶν συνετῶν ἀθετήσω . . . ἐπεὶ γὰρ ἐν τῇ σοφίᾳ τοῦ θεοῦ οὐκ ἔγνω ὁ κόσμος διὰ σοφίας τὸν θεόν, εὐδόκησεν ὁ θεὸς διὰ τῆς μωρίας τοῦ κηρύγματος σῶσαι τοὺς πιστεύοντας*), I am ever again struck by the coincidence here both in thought and vocabulary with our saying, though all of course has passed through the crucible of the Pauline mind. Nevertheless, impressions are deceptive, and are in this instance far from attaining to the dignity of a proof. Pfleiderer, "Das Urchristentum," i.[2] s. 435 f., thinks that it is very probable that the saying is dependent upon St. Paul. But *νήπιοι* is not Pauline (*vide supra*), and "the specifically Pauline thought that the real knowledge of Christ and of God is hidden from the natural man and is only revealed to human perception by the Spirit of God," is simply read by Pfleiderer into our text, which is concerned with a contrast of quite a different nature.

The original version of the saying (in Q) may be defended on good grounds; but the canonical version in both gospels is "Johannine" in character and indefensible. By the interpolation of the clause, "no man knoweth the Son save the Father" before the clause concerning "knowledge of the Father," and by the change of the aorist into the present, the whole complexion of the saying is altered[1]—so seriously altered that even the significance of the ταῦτα and the πάντα in the clause "πάντα μοι παρεδόθη" tends to become a matter of doubt.[2] A formal likeness of Father and Son, who are distinguished only by the different names, and a relationship of Father and Son which never had a beginning, but remains ever the same, now come to expression. Of course we are not absolutely obliged thus to interpret the canonical saying,[3] yet we cannot by any method of interpretation make it much less metaphysical.[4] If the first

[1] Note also that by the interpolation the rhythmic structure of the saying is emphasised. This is not unimportant in reference to the question whether, and in what measure, the rhythms in the sayings of Jesus are original.

[2] In logical consequence an attempt was now made also to change παρεδόθη into παραδέδοται (*vide supra*, Justin and Hippolytus), but this correction is no longer found in the manuscripts.

[3] We can also interpret the present ἐπιγινώσκει in St. Matthew, as if it were determined by the preceding παρεδόθη, and therefore as if it were not to be understood as timeless but as describing the result of an historical action.

[4] Zahn ("Matth.," s. 441) expounds the passage as follows: "The Son is thus not only the agent of revelation, who imparts the knowledge of God to those who are receptive, but He is also Himself a mystery, which was at first hidden from man and which needed a revealing. The Son belongs to the objects (ταῦτα) which are now opened to knowledge. The knowledge of the Son as the only Son of God, in the full sense of the word, is inseparably

evangelist himself wrote the passage as we read it, then —even with the most cautious interpretation of the passage—his own Christology approached very nearly to that of the Johannine writings in one of the most important points, and it can therefore be only due to his relatively faithful reproduction of his sources that this characteristic does not more frequently appear in his gospel.

IV

The second saying, which in St. Matthew follows immediately after the first, has come down to us only

connected with the knowledge of God as the Father of Jesus and of those who become sons because they belong to Jesus. It is, however, significant that the knowledge of the Son is mentioned first. This is the new fact, that which distinguishes the present revelation from all which preceded it—the fact of a Man whom to know is the way to attain to the knowledge of God. For this very reason the knowledge of God, which is now attainable, is a new thing. We moderns would say: With the personality of Jesus a new religion, Christianity, came into existence. While, concerning the knowledge of the Father, it is expressly said that the Son alone imparts it, a corresponding statement in regard to the knowledge of the Son is wanting. It is, however, obvious that this knowledge can only be imparted by Him, of whom it is said that He alone possesses such knowledge—namely, the Father. The Father reveals the Son as the Son reveals the Father [!]. As, however, the knowledge of the Father and the knowledge of the Son are only two sides of the same mystery which is now revealed, *it follows that the Father and the Son in fellowship with one another are both subject and object of the Revelation*" [the italics are mine]. This is quite enough to help us to a definite decision concerning the historical character of the saying as given in St. Matthew. It is noteworthy that Zahn's exegesis justifies the placing of the clause concerning "knowing the Son" at the beginning, while this place was really given to it because it was felt to be absolutely necessary not to separate the clause, "and to whomsoever the Son will reveal Him," from the clause concerning "the knowledge of the Father."

in the Gospel of St. Matthew. Scarcely any variants are found in the versions and quotations: (1) In verse 28 πάντες is wanting in Tatian; (2) in the same author, "et qui habetis graves afflictiones" (or "onera gravia") was probably interpolated before καὶ πεφορτισμένοι;[1] (3) in verse 29 Ephraem quotes: ὅτι ἥσυχός εἰμι, πραῢς καὶ ἐπιεικὴς καὶ ταπεινὸς τῇ καρδίᾳ. The omission of πάντες is alone worthy of consideration; this omission also occurs in Syr.$^{cur.}$ and Syr.$^{sin.}$ 'Απ' ἐμοῦ in verse 29 is, so far as I know, never wanting in the Versions and in quotations; it is not therefore permissible to delete it on the sole authority of א (pr. man.).

This saying—whose Aramaic origin is unmistakable—is from the point of view of rhythm still better constructed than the former saying, and is dominated by the conceptions φορτίον and ἀνάπαυσις. It runs as follows:—

Δεῦτε πρός με (πάντες) οἱ κοπιῶντες καὶ πεφορτισμένοι,
κἀγὼ ἀναπαύσω ὑμᾶς·
Ἄρατε τὸν ζυγόν μου ἐφ' ὑμᾶς
καὶ μάθετε ἀπ' ἐμοῦ, ὅτι πραῢς εἰμι καὶ ταπεινὸς τῇ καρδίᾳ,
καὶ εὑρήσετε ἀνάπαυσιν ταῖς ψυχαῖς ὑμῶν·
Ὁ γὰρ ζυγός μου χρηστός,
καὶ τὸ φορτίον μου ἐλαφρόν (ἐστιν).

[1] The variants in Pistis Sophia and Agathangelus are of no account, seeing that they are mere paraphrases. In Pseudocyprian adv. Jud. 7, the saying reads: "Venite ad me omnes qui *sub onera laboratis*, et ego vos reficiam . . . est enim iugum meum placidum et onus [the African version read 'sarcina,' *vide* Tertullian and Cyprian] *levissimum*."

It is addressed, not to the circle of disciples, but to those standing outside; yet it has in view, not the νήπιοι (still less sinners), but those who were suffering under the burden of the heavy yoke of ordinances.[1] It should therefore be compared with St. Matt. xxiii. 4. The form of this saying is similar to that of the preceding saying. As there the first thought is for the revelation itself, and then this revelation is described as being brought about by the Son, so here there is first a general proclamation of the "rest," and then it is said that this rest is attained through the acceptance of *His* yoke. The conception ἀνάπαυσις reminds us of the Beatitudes and of the conclusion of a saying which is handed down in the gospel of the Hebrews (βασιλεύσας) ἐπαναπαύσεται,[2] the second half is founded upon Jer. vi. 16.[3] The outward form reminds us of the saying in St. Mark vi. 31: δεῦτε . . . ἀναπαύσεσθε, and the situation brings to mind the passage which immediately follows in St. Mark (verse 34): εἶδεν πολὺν ὄχλον, καὶ ἐσπλαγχνίσθη ἐπ' αὐτούς, ὅτι ἦσαν ὡς πρόβατα μὴ ἔχοντα ποιμένα. Also the

[1] Perhaps this interpretation is too definite: οἱ κοπιῶντες signifies in general "those who are wearied"; but from the combination of πεφορτισμένοι and μάθετε ἀπ' ἐμοῦ, it can with probability be deduced that our Lord had in His eye those who stood under the burden of Pharisaic teachers and of Pharisaic legal observance.

[2] *Vide* "Sitzungsber. 1904," s. 175 ff.; ζητεῖν ἀνάπαυσιν, St. Matt. xii. 43.

[3] The whole saying is full of reminiscences of the Old Testament, *cf.* above all Isa. lv. 1 (also xiv. 3, xxviii. 12); Jer. xxxi. 25; Isa. xlii. 2. Note that Jer. vi. 16 is given in an independent translation; for ἀνάπαυσις is not found in the LXX version of the passage where ἁγνισμός is read. This is important in connection with the question of the origin of the saying.

commandments of Jesus—for with these the saying is concerned—are a yoke,[1] like all commandments that deal with doctrine and life, but compared with the burdens which were imposed by the scribes, they are a "gentle"[2] yoke and a light[3] burden. The "καί" before "μάθετε" *may* be taken as consecutive, and the ὅτι should not be taken as casual; we translate therefore: "Thus will ye learn of Me,[4] that I am meek and lowly."[5] In these words our Lord assigns to His personality a significance both in relation to the character of His commandments and also indirectly in relation to their appropriation; in this point, therefore, there exists a distinct connection in thought with the former saying.

It was just this connection in thought and inward relationship that moved "St. Matthew" to place the one saying directly after the other; but this can scarcely have been their original relative positions, for the situation presupposed in each of the

[1] In Didache 6, the doctrine (the Commandments) of Jesus are called "ὁ ζυγὸς τοῦ κυρίου." *Cf.* also Acts xv. 10: *νῦν οὖν τί πειράζετε τὸν θεόν, ἐπιθεῖναι ζυγὸν ἐπὶ τὸν τράχηλον τῶν μαθητῶν, ὃν οὔτε οἱ πατέρες ἡμῶν οὔτε ἡμεῖς ἰσχύσαμεν βαστάσαι.* With the Rabbinic writers, "yoke" is a technical term for commandments.

[2] Χρηστός is found again in the gospels only in St. Luke v. 39, vi. 35; in the latter passage it is used of God, so also in Rom. ii. 4 and 1 Pet. ii. 3 (from the Psalms). Χρηστότης is likewise often used of God. Both the Latin versions and Syr.^{sin}. translate χρηστός in our passage by "suavis."

[3] Ἐλαφρός is only found again in the New Testament in 2 Cor. iv. 17.

[4] Μανθάνειν ἀπό τινος also in St. Mark xiii. 28 (St. Matt. xxiv. 32); Gal. iii. 2; Col. i. 7; Heb. v. 8.

[5] ταπεινός; only here in St. Matthew.

two sayings is different;[1] the first saying is concerned with the knowledge of God and its revelation, the second with directions for the conduct of life; besides this, the first saying is a thanksgiving, the second is the cry of a missionary preacher.[2] Moreover, it is not certain that the second saying is derived from Q, seeing that it is wanting in St. Luke. If its inward relationship to the first saying be brought forward as an argument in favour of its belonging to Q, it must not be forgotten that the first saying is unique in Q and does not represent a type of sayings in that source. In favour of its belonging to Q one might appeal to the fact that while the beginning of the first saying seems to be fashioned after Sirach li. 1 (*ἐξομολογήσομαί σοι, κύριε βασιλεῦ*), so also the second saying has parallels in Sirach li. (verse 23: *ἐγγίσατε πρός με*, verse 26: *τὸν τραχηλον ὑμῶν ὑπόθετε ὑπὸ ζυγόν*, verse 27: *καὶ εὗρον ἐμαυτῷ πολλὴν ἀνάπαυσιν*). But these parallels are too general to be of much weight. Hence the question, from what source the first evangelist derived this saying, must remain open.

Are we, however, compelled to assume that this saying was derived from secondary tradition? I see no convincing reasons for such a supposition; certainly not in the form of the saying, for it is mere perversity to assert that the most ancient tradition

[1] It is much more probable that the continuation of the saying is more original in St. Luke (x. 23, 24)—St. Matthew has this continuation in xiii. 16, 17—but this also does not admit of proof.

[2] Δεῦτε occurs often in St. Matthew; it is not, however, peculiar to this gospel among the writings of the New Testament.

could not have represented Jesus as speaking in this way, or that Jesus could not have so spoken; nor in its general content, for it cannot be doubted that our Lord regarded those who were plagued with the Pharisaic ordinances as heavy laden, and that He promised rest to such persons (the word "souls" ought not to be pressed).[1] Neither, finally, can such reasons be deduced from the specific content of the saying—namely, that a man after accepting His yoke would learn of Him that He was meek and lowly; for though this peculiar form of self-assertion is unique there is no want of self-assertion elsewhere, even in tradition which is quite trustworthy. Here it is probably Messianic,[2] and

[1] There was no need to say wherein the rest consisted; and the question whether it belonged to this world or to the coming Kingdom is not to the point here.—If it is certain that our Lord devoted Himself to the relief of the sick and diseased, then these *κοπιῶντες* are covered by the saying.

[2] Isa. xlii. 2 and allied passages probably stand in the background. It is most noteworthy that there is here absolutely no reference to the cross and the death. This could scarcely have been wanting in a Christian hymn of later times. Jesus simply says that meekness and lowliness are to be learned from Him, and that the meek and lowly will find rest—nothing else. The saying that men must take up their cross and follow Him is at all events later than our saying. Moreover, the seeming discrepancy with those commandments in which great emphasis is laid upon keeping the Law, and with those sayings in which it is said that one *must* through much tribulation enter into the Kingdom of God, is rather a sign of genuineness than of the contrary. I know of no proof that the primitive community felt the yoke of Jesus to be easy and His burden to be light—with the exception of 1 John v. 3 (*αἱ ἐντολαὶ αὐτοῦ βαρεῖαι οὐκ εἰσίν*), a passage which perhaps looks backward to our saying. The solution of the discrepancy in the mind of our Lord lies in the thought that by His example, from which men are to learn, the commandments become light.

moreover finds noteworthy support in 2 Cor. x. 1. St. Paul writes there: Παρακαλῶ ὑμᾶς διὰ τῆς πραΰτητος καὶ ἐπιεικείας τοῦ Χριστοῦ. Hence by means of the preaching of the Apostle the πραΰτης καὶ ἐπιείκεια of Christ had become to the Corinthians something that was not only well known and constantly spoken about, but also something that partook even of the nature of a set formula. If then the πραΰτης καὶ ἐπιείκεια Χριστοῦ had thus become quite a technical term, it is not too much to suppose that St. Paul was acquainted with our saying. The contrary hypothesis that 2 Cor. x. 1 was the source of the saying would be indeed adventurous. However, here also the evidence adduced is not sufficient for a proof of dependence.

Of the two sayings the first, which is derived from Q, belongs to the best authority which we possess concerning our Lord, nor can any valid objections be alleged against its content when once it is restored to its original form. The second saying may come from Q, but it can also come from another source; it is also most probably not the continuation of the first saying. No proof can be given that it belongs to secondary tradition.

In neither case is the verbal accuracy of the tradition of course guaranteed; but it is decisive for the recognition of the relative genuineness of the sayings that in the first saying the whole emphasis is laid upon the knowledge of God and its revelation, in the second upon the yoke of Jesus in the sense of *commandments;* that, further, in the first saying the primary condition of the knowledge of God is simplicity, while in the second saying the primary condition of the "ἀνάπαυσις" is meekness and lowliness; that, moreover, in both sayings the (Pharisaic) "perfect ones" form the contrast and everything is strictly confined within the Jewish horizon; and, finally, that in the first saying Jesus is represented as the revealer of the knowledge of God, while in the second He is represented as the instructor and pattern of the quietistic virtues without a single reference to the Cross and Passion.[1] If by the word "Gospel" one understands what St. Paul and St. Mark understood by this word, then these sayings are not "gospel sayings" and have nothing in common with the specific conceptions of Paulinism. We have only the choice between assigning them to the creation of a later prophet of the primitive Jewish-Christian community who—strangely enough—omits all reference to the Crucifixion, or assigning them to our Lord Himself. Given the two alternatives, there seems to me no doubt about which to choose.

EXCURSUS II

Concerning the Voice from Heaven at the Baptism (St. Luke iii. 22)

Even in St. Matthew and St. Luke the Baptism of our Lord by St. John presented a certain difficulty

[1] This negative element is in itself a proof that these sayings belong to Q, or at least are nearly allied to that source, for in Q also there is no reference to the Cross and Passion.

(*vide* J. Bornemann, "Die Taufe Christi durch Johannes," Leipzig, 1896), and the fourth evangelist by the method of his description of the event has almost got rid of the Baptism itself. Also from the fact that (1) the Baptism was not included among the articles of the ancient Roman Symbol, and that (2) reference was made to the event much more rarely than from its importance we should have expected—we see that in later times the inconvenience of the tradition was still felt. In this connection the behaviour, for example, of the African writers is instructive: in spite of the multitude of quotations from the New Testament found in Tertullian, Cyprian, and the more ancient African writers, it is impossible to ascertain the words of the voice from heaven as read by either of these writers, because it is never quoted by any of them (nor by Novatian).[1]

But by far the most inconvenient version of the tradition must have been that which gave the voice from heaven (after Ps. ii.) in the form: υἱός μου εἶ σύ· σήμερον γεγέννηκά σε—for, unless sophistical reasonings were called to aid, it excluded the miraculous Conception.

This version of the voice from heaven is nowhere found in the MSS. of St. Matthew; but in St. Luke it is attested by D and the Old Latin codices Vercell., Veron., Colbert. Paris., Corbei. (ff.[2]), Rhedig. Vratisl.[2] In agreement with these authorities we find, in the West, Justin (twice), "Acta Petri et Pauli," 29;

[1] Neither is it quoted by the Apostolic Fathers and the Clementine Homilies.

[2] According to Epiphanius both versions stood in the Gospel of the Ebionites.

Lactant., Juvenc., Hilary (five times), the translator of Origen ("Hom. in Ezech." 17, 3),[1] the author of the pseudo-Augustinian "Quæst. Vet. et Nov. Test.," Tychon., Faustus in Augustine, and Augustine.[2] After the beginning of the fifth century the reading vanishes completely; the Vulgate gave it its death-blow.

In the East, omitting Justin, who ought also to be reckoned among Eastern authorities, it is *not* attested by Tatian[3] and Irenæus, but is given by Clem. Alex.,[4] the "Didascalia Apost." (therefore also by the "Apost. Constit."), and by Methodius.

With our present knowledge of textual criticism we are accordingly safe in deciding that the most ancient exemplars of St. Luke's gospel, which were current in the West, *agreed* in reading the version of Psalm ii., while in the East this reading was found only in a few exemplars.

[1] Was this also the reading of Origen himself? We may not appeal with certainty to "Comm. in Joh." p. 37 (ed. Preuschen). Also Hom. 27 in "Luc." speaks to the contrary.

[2] Augustine writes ("De Consensu Evv.," ii. 14, 31): "Illud vero quod *nonnulli* codices habent secundum Lucam, hoc illa voce sonuisse, quod in psalmo scriptum est: 'Filius meus es tu; ego hodie genui te,' *quanquam in antiquioribus codicibus Græcis non inveniri perhibeatur* [the Greek codices are *ipso facto* the more ancient for Augustine], tamen si aliquibus fide dignis exemplaribus confirmari possit, quid aliud quam utrumque intellegendum est quolibet verborum ordine de cœlo sonuisse?"

[3] This of course proves nothing, as Tatian's Diatessaron is a gospel harmony; but Syr.$^{sin.}$ of St. Luke does not give the version according to Psalm ii., nor does the Peshitto.

[4] It is remarkable that in "Pæd." i. 6, 25, he gives the two versions one after another, just as in the Gospel of the Ebionites according to Epiphanius.—It is uncertain whether the reading is attested in the Epistle to Diognetus, chap. xi.; the version of Celsus in Origen, "Contra Celsum," i. 41, is also uncertain.

If we now ask what St. Luke wrote himself; here also, after what we have now learned, there can be no doubt about our decision. We know that conformation of the texts of (St. Mark and) St. Luke to the text of St. Matthew not only began very early *but that it was most actively carried on at the time which lies before our manuscripts, indeed before the time of the quotations made by the Fathers;* and that the predecessors of the most ancient Western manuscripts did not suffer therefrom so much as those of the East. It therefore follows that we must insert the voice from heaven, according to the version of Psalm ii., into the text of St. Luke.[1]

If, however, St. Luke wrote thus, we cannot possibly suppose that he intentionally, and upon his own authority, altered the tradition which lay before him in St. Mark (σὺ εἶ ὁ υἱός μου ὁ ἀγαπητός, ἐν σοὶ εὐδόκησα); for he could not but have found the version according to Psalm ii. inconvenient, after what he had narrated in chapters i. and ii. He thus accepted this reading and substituted it for the reading of the Markan account, because it was presented by a tradition which he regarded as more credible than, or at least as credible as the tradition contained in St. Mark.

[1] Recourse to an apocryphal gospel or to the hypothesis of a variant translation in oral tradition is not to be commended here, seeing that in critical problems of this kind one must try to confine oneself to known quantities, so far as these exist, and to make the best of them. Here, as a matter of fact, they are quite sufficient for the solution of the problem. The hypothesis of a *later* intrusion of the reading into the Lukan text is improbable, because of its content, and has no analogy in its favour after the Canon of Four Gospels had once been formed.

Seeing, however, that St. Luke directly before and directly afterwards follows the source Q, and that it therefore is *a priori* very probable that an account of the Baptism of our Lord stood in Q, it is also not less probable that the version of the voice from heaven in St. Luke (according to Psalm ii.) is derived from Q, and that St. Luke substituted this version for that of St. Mark because he regarded it as more trustworthy.[1]

From this it follows (1) that St. Luke valued the source Q at a higher rate than, or at least at as high a rate as he valued St. Mark; (2) that the story of the Baptism together with the voice from heaven is not an invention of St. Mark, but goes back to a legend which lies behind St. Mark and Q; (3) *that this legend had its more original form in Q*, for the voice from heaven in the version of St. Mark (which is followed by St. Matthew) is clearly seen to be an attenuated form when compared with the version of Q (St. Luke).[2]

[1] It is possible that the narrative of the appearance of a light at the Baptism, of which the earliest witness is given in Tatian, also originally stood in St. Luke, and thus also in Q; but the evidence is not so strong as in the case of the voice from heaven, seeing that St. Mark and St. Matthew give nothing which corresponds and that the narrative is wanting in D.

[2] The *σήμερον* is decisive even though the Markan account may contain it implicitly. On the other hand, it seems to me scarcely worthy of attention that in Q the Son is spoken of as being "begotten" (as in the first chapters of St. Matthew and St. Luke, there in realistic fashion, but in Q metaphorically), while St. Mark does not give this conception at all. Perhaps the version of the voice from heaven, according to Psalm ii., has an ancient witness in Heb. i. 5 f.; for this passage perhaps refers to what occurred at the Baptism—yet this is not certain.

INDEX TO THE RECONSTRUCTED TEXT OF Q